CAMBRIDGE LIBRARY COLLECTION

Books of enduring scholarly value

Travel and Exploration

The history of travel writing dates back to the Bible, Caesar, the Vikings and the Crusaders, and its many themes include war, trade, science and recreation. Explorers from Columbus to Cook charted lands not previously visited by Western travellers, and were followed by merchants, missionaries, and colonists, who wrote accounts of their experiences. The development of steam power in the nineteenth century provided opportunities for increasing numbers of 'ordinary' people to travel further, more economically, and more safely, and resulted in great enthusiasm for travel writing among the reading public. Works included in this series range from first-hand descriptions of previously unrecorded places, to literary accounts of the strange habits of foreigners, to examples of the burgeoning numbers of guidebooks produced to satisfy the needs of a new kind of traveller - the tourist.

Narratives of Voyages Towards the North-West

The publications of the Hakluyt Society (founded in 1846) made available edited (and sometimes translated) early accounts of exploration. The first series, which ran from 1847 to 1899, consists of 100 books containing published or previously unpublished works by authors from Christopher Columbus to Sir Francis Drake, and covering voyages to the New World, to China and Japan, to Russia and to Africa and India. Volume 5, published in 1849 and edited by Thomas Rundall, contains a collection of accounts relating to the search for the 'North-West Passage' – the hoped-for route to the Far East and India through the scattered islands and freezing seas to the north of Canada. Narratives of attempts by famous explorers such as Cabot, Frobisher, Hudson and Baffin, as well as lesser known figures, are accompanied by an editorial introduction and conclusion, and by explanatory notes.

Cambridge University Press has long been a pioneer in the reissuing of out-of-print titles from its own backlist, producing digital reprints of books that are still sought after by scholars and students but could not be reprinted economically using traditional technology. The Cambridge Library Collection extends this activity to a wider range of books which are still of importance to researchers and professionals, either for the source material they contain, or as landmarks in the history of their academic discipline.

Drawing from the world-renowned collections in the Cambridge University Library, and guided by the advice of experts in each subject area, Cambridge University Press is using state-of-the-art scanning machines in its own Printing House to capture the content of each book selected for inclusion. The files are processed to give a consistently clear, crisp image, and the books finished to the high quality standard for which the Press is recognised around the world. The latest print-on-demand technology ensures that the books will remain available indefinitely, and that orders for single or multiple copies can quickly be supplied.

The Cambridge Library Collection will bring back to life books of enduring scholarly value (including out-of-copyright works originally issued by other publishers) across a wide range of disciplines in the humanities and social sciences and in science and technology.

Narratives of Voyages Towards the North-West

In Search of a Passage to Cathay and India, 1496 to 1631

Edited by Thomas Rundall

CAMBRIDGE UNIVERSITY PRESS

Cambridge, New York, Melbourne, Madrid, Cape Town, Singapore,
São Paolo, Delhi, Dubai, Tokyo

Published in the United States of America by Cambridge University Press, New York

www.cambridge.org
Information on this title: www.cambridge.org/9781108008020

This edition first published 1849
This digitally printed version 2010

ISBN 978-1-108-00802-0 Paperback

This book reproduces the text of the original edition. The content and language reflect
the beliefs, practices and terminology of their time, and have not been updated.

Cambridge University Press wishes to make clear that the book, unless originally published
by Cambridge, is not being republished by, in association or collaboration with, or
with the endorsement or approval of, the original publisher or its successors in title.

WORKS ISSUED BY

The Hakluyt Society.

———————×———————

VOYAGES TOWARDS THE
NORTH-WEST,

1496-1631.

M.DCCC.XLIX

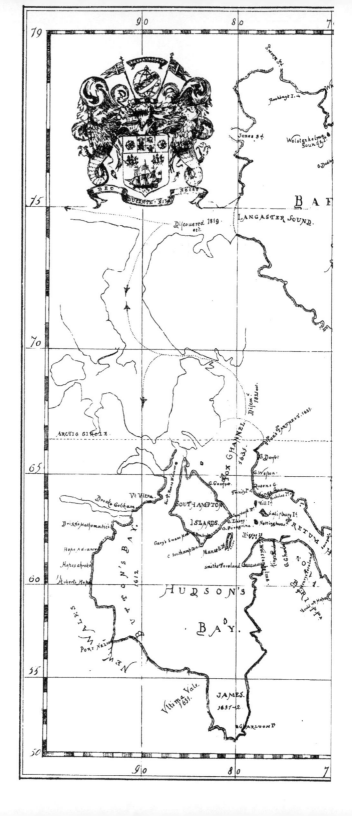

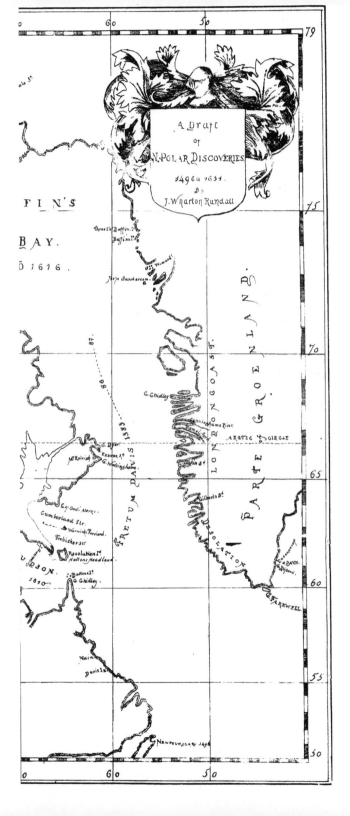

A Draft
of
N. POLAR DISCOVERIES
1496 a 1631.
By
J. Wharton Rundall.

FIN'S

BAY.

D 1676.

Three I's Baffin.
Baffins I's.

Isle Sanderson.

Womans

G. Chidley

Cunninghams River.
Hames Sd.

G. Dyer.
Exuma Sd.
Mt Raleigh.
G. Walsinghams.

Cay God's Mercy.

Cumberland Str.
Warwick Forriand.
Trobisher Str.
Resolution I.
Hattons Headland.

Buttons I.
G. Chidley.

U DSON
1610

Nain
Davis I.

Newfoundland 1496

LONDON COAST.

FARTE EI GROENLAND.

ARCTIC CIRCLE.

DISOLATION.

FRETUM DAVIS 1585.

Gilberts Sd.

DAVIS
Gisford.

C. FAREWELL.

79

75

70

65

60

55

50

0 60 50

0 60 50

NARRATIVES OF VOYAGES

TOWARDS

THE NORTH-WEST,

IN SEARCH OF

A PASSAGE TO CATHAY AND INDIA.

1496 TO 1631.

WITH

SELECTIONS FROM THE EARLY RECORDS OF THE HONOURABLE
THE EAST INDIA COMPANY AND FROM MSS.
IN THE BRITISH MUSEUM.

BY

THOMAS RUNDALL, ESQ.

LONDON:

PRINTED FOR THE HAKLUYT SOCIETY.

M.DCCC.XLIX.

RICHARDS, 100, ST. MARTIN'S LANE.

THE HAKLUYT SOCIETY.

TABLE OF CONTENTS.

Introduction:

A.D.   P.

Of the claims of SIR HUGH WILLOUGHBY to be considered
a discoverer   i

Of the probability of an Englishman named WILLIAM ADAMS
having made a voyage to Spitzbergen, A.D. 1595 xii

Narratives:

1496	SEBASTIAN CABOTA; from *Hakluyt*	4

SIR MARTIN FROBISHER:

1576	1st voyage	7
1577	2nd „	15
1578	3rd „	19
1581	4th „ projected	32

From *Best: Hakluyt;* and *Mss. Brit. Mus.*

MASTER JOHN DAVIS:

1585	1st voyage	35
1586	2nd „	41
1587	3rd „	45

From *Hakluyt.*

A.D.   P.

CAPTAIN GEORGE WAYMOUTH:

1601 Preliminary Proceedings   51
      Of the Outfit:
          I.   Instruments of Navigation   59
          II. Provisions   ...   .   —
          III. Apparel ...   .   —
          IV. Muster-roll and wages ...   . (0
          V.   Miscellaneous   ...   .   —
      Captain Waymouth: his entertaynm$_t$ 61
          From the *Ms. Records of the East India Company.*
1602 Voyage; from *Purchas*   64
      Proceedings subsequent to the voyage; from *E. I. Mss.*   ... 69

1606 MASTER JOHN KNIGHT; from *Purchas* 71

1610 MASTER HENRY HUDSON ; from *Purchas*   76

1612 SIR THOMAS BUTTON:
      Instructions for the voyage, given by Henry Prince of Wales,
          from a rare *fac-simile* of the original document[1] 82
      Voyage ; from *North-west Foxe*   86

  „   JAMES HALL; from *Purchas*   91

1614 CAPTAIN GIBBONS; from *North-west Foxe*   94

      BYLOT and BAFFIN:
1615 Chart of the Track within Resolution Island, from an auto-
          graph draft by Baffin (*Mss. Brit. Mus.*)   97
      Prefatory remarks   ...   . —
          I.   Letter from Baffin to Sir Thomas Smith, and others ;
               from the writer's autograph (*Mss. Brit. Mus.*)   ... 98
          II. The Breefe Iournall of pertyculer courses, latytudes,
               longitudes, windes, leagues run, and varyation of the
               compas ; from the navigator's autograph(*Mss. Brit. Mus*) 101
          III. A Tru Relation of such thinges as happened during the
               voyage of 1615; from Baffin's autograph (*Mss. Brit. Mus.*) 106

[1] The *Grenville Library*, vol. i, p. 319 (see Cat.), contains a copy " bound up in blue morocco, with a letter from Mr. Hanrott", at whose expense the fac-simile was made. This letter was referred to in the expectation of finding some account of the original document ; but it proved to be a note of no interest, or value, whatever.

A.D.   P.

"The forme of the harboure we weare in", on the W. side of
Resolution Island, 1 June 1615; from a sketch by Baffin
(*Mss. Brit. Mus.*) 112

1616 Observations on charges made against Baffin in connexion with
his discoveries in Baffin's Bay 131

Voyage; from *Purchas* 135

Letter addressed by Baffin to Sir John Wolstenholme; from
Purchas 144

1619 CAPTAIN HAWKRIDGE; from *North-west Foxe* and *E. I. Mss.* 150

1631 CAPTAIN LUKE FOX; from *North-west Foxe* 152

" CAPTAIN JAMES; from a Collection of Voyages and Travels
by *Harris* 186

CONCLUSION 224

Appendix: Supplementary Notes:

Note A. SHIPPING:

Ships, officers, etc. 229
Discipline 230
Stores 232
Armament 233
From *Hakluyt* and *E. I. Mss.*

—— *B.* DUTCH VOYAGE, from *Purchas* 236

—— *C.* WAYMOUTH'S EXPEDITION:

Muster-roll, etc. of officers and crews 238
Autographs of officers and mariners ... ... ——
From *E. I. Mss.*

—— *D.* PRICES:

I. Particulars of the apparel supplied to Waymouth's
Expedition 239
II. Particulars of charges of setting forth three ships to
Bantam, etc., A.D. 1606 240
III. Sundries 244
IV. Table of prices of provisions from 1621 to 1638 ... 245
From *E. I. Mss.*

NOTE   P.

E. BUTTON'S EXPEDITION:

Answers, in writing, to certain demands made by the General 245

From *North-west Foxe.*

F. FIRST EAST INDIA SUBSCRIPTION LIST ... 250

From *E. I. Mss.*

G. VARIATION OF THE COMPASS:

I. Of the manner to observe the Variation of the Compasse, etc., By Thomas Harriott, (*Mss. Brit. Mus.*) ... —

II. Letter from Master Rudston to Master Harriott (*Mss. Brit. Mus.*) 255

III. Examples of the Variation of the Compass: Parry's Expedition of 1819 256

IV. Tables of the Magnetic Declination and Dip at London from 1550 to 1844 257

H. DRAFT OF NORTH-POLAR DISCOVERIES from 1496 to 1631; etc. 258

Errata, etc.

Page 39, line 3 from bottom, for *hugh*, read *huge.*

— 46, — 5 — top, — *were*, — *was.*

— 135, — 4 — — — 1606 — 1616.

— 175, — 17 — — — *Aurora* — *Auriga.*

— 176, — 7 — — — *wherein* — *whereon.*

— 232, APPENDIX. To the "Victualling extraordinarie", *add* (total for the three ships): Proines, French or damaske, 010 C.; Rasonns of the sonne 7 C.½; Currants 10 C.; Ginjer ¼ C.; Nutmeggs 000-12li.; Poulder Sugar 002 C.; Pepp' 0-12li.; Sope 001 C.½; Synamon; Cloves; Mace; and Lemon water.

— 244, Note 1, for *Stroud*, read *Strond.*

INTRODUCTION.

Before entering on the narratives of the voyages undertaken for the discovery of the North-west passage, some observations will be offered on two points connected with the general subject of North-polar researches, viz.: I. The claims of Sir Hugh Willoughby to be considered a discoverer; and, II. The probability of an Englishman, named William Adams, having made a voyage to Spitzbergen, A.D. 1595.

I. *Of the Claims of Sir Hugh Willoughby to be considered a Discoverer.*

By injudicious advocacy on one hand, and by careless oversight, or wilful neglect, on the other hand, the reputation of Sir Hugh Willoughby is at present left to the mercy of conjecture. One authority has laboured to prove him to be entitled to the merit of a particular discovery. Another authority peremptorily denies the validity of the grounds on which the claim is made on his behalf. Neither takes any pains to ascertain whether he is entitled to distinction for any other service than the one particularized.

It is Purchas who claims the merit of a particular discovery for Sir Hugh Willoughby. Purchas states, that in his progress towards the North-east, the navi-

b

gator was driven to the height of 72°, where he fell in with an island which is designated WILLOUGHBY LAND, lying in a particular direction, and at a specified distance from a place named SEYNAM. *"From thence"*, it is said, he proceeded in a certain direction, saw certain lands, and finally cast anchor in a certain locality: which is described, and to which the following remark is applied; *"And this is the land which is now called* GREENLAND, *or King James his New Land, and is known to the Hollanders by the name of* SPITZBERGEN". In continuation it is observed: *" Sir Hugh Willoughby returned into Lapland, where he and his company were frozen to death in the haven called* ARZINA NEER KEGOR". From the construction of this narrative, the reader is induced to apply the phrase "from thence" to Seynam: to infer that the course subsequently alluded to, was that followed between Seynam and Willoughby Land, only given with more detail; and to view the observation *" And this is the land"*, etc., as being introduced merely for the sake of defining the discovery attributed to Sir Hugh Willoughby, more precisely than by the previous simple designation of Willoughby Land.

Conforming to this view, Mr. Joseph Moxon, " Hydrographer to the King's Most Excellent Majesty", author of some scientific treatises, and a Fellow of the Royal Society, places, in a " Polar Draft" constructed by him in 1676, Willoughby Land in the position, or nearly so, of Edge's Land, otherwise called Staads Vorland, at the south-eastern extremity of Spitzbergen. The constructor of a map in Harris's Collection of Voyages and Travels, 1748, adopts, however, another view. He places Willoughby Land mid-way between Lapland and Nova Zemla.

So far the history of the matter merely exhibits a difference of opinion in regard to the locality of a discovery, acknowledged to have been made by Sir Hugh Willoughby. Subsequently, the case presents another aspect: suggesting doubts of the fact, if not denying the fact, of that navigator having made any discovery.

In opposition to the claim set up by Purchas on behalf of Sir Hugh Willoughby, a modern author of considerable celebrity, and in connexion with such subjects esteemed an authority, declares : " *The brief journal* of Sir Hugh Willoughby by no means sanctions such a supposition, that this ill-fated commander was ever within many degrees of Spitzbergen", adding, " the discovery of this land is certainly due to the Dutch".[1] With this summary decision the subject is dismissed, leaving only one inference to be drawn: that Sir Hugh Willoughby's reputation has been dependent on a misrepresentation, and must sink with the fallacious ground on which it has hitherto rested.

Such, however, is not the case; and that such is not the case, may be demonstrated by rejecting all authority but that of the " brief journal" to which the above appeal is made.

The first step to be taken in this investigation, is to

[1] *A Chronological History of Voyages into the Arctic Regions,* etc. By *John Barrow,* F.R.S. (pp. 159.) London, 1818.

ascertain with precision, or with as much precision as
possible, the course actually followed by Sir Hugh
Willoughby when he sailed from Seynam: which is in
70°, on the coast of Norway. From this place, the
navigator started on the 2nd of August, A.D. 1553;
and he took a course which brought him, on the 14th
of the same month, in sight of land. To reach Spitzbergen from Seynam, the course lies either N. by W.
¾ N., or N. by E. ½ N., or in some direction between
those two points. Sir Hugh proceeded neither N. by
W. ¾ N., nor N. by E. ½ N., nor in any intermediate
direction. He took a course nearly at right-angles
with the track to Spitzbergen; and when he sighted
land, it was " *in 72°, one hundred and sixty leagues
E. by N. of Seynam*": far away, to the south-east-
ward, from Spitzbergen. Either by tracing on a chart
the course taken by Sir Hugh,[1] by taking the bearing

---

[1] *Analysis of Sir Hugh Willoughby's Track.* (*Hakluyt*, vol. i,
pp. 261, 263.) *August 2, off Seynam.* Trying to make the harbour: driven by a storm out to sea: sailed N. by E.: storm encreasing, sails taken in: lying adrift....3, at daylight, The Con-
fidence, one of the expedition, seen to leeward: " spread an
hullocke of our foresail, and bare roome with her"....4. Storm
abated: sail made: course, N.E. by N., towards Wardhouse: made
50 leagues....5. [No account.]....6. S.E. by S.: 48 leagues....7.
[No account.]...8. Wind strong from N.N.W.: "shook sails and
lay adrift"....9. Wind S.S.E.: course, N.E.: 25 leagues....10.
Wind N.E.: course, S.E.: 48 leagues....11. Wind S.: soundings
in 40 fathoms, fair sand....12. Wind S. by E.: "we lay with
our sails E. and E. by N.": 30 leagues....13. [No account.]....14.
Land 72°, 160 *leagues from Seynam, E. by N.*: unable to reach
the shore in a boat, " the land so very shoal, and very much ice,
also". [Distance sailed, accounted for, 201 leagues.]

from Seynam of the new land he sighted, or by com-
bining the two means of forming a judgment, it will
be found, that the land-fall made on the 14th of August was on the COAST OF NOVA ZEMLA, somewhere,
it may be assumed, between the promontories named
in the Admiralty Chart of the North-polar seas, *North*
and *South Gousinoi Nos.* It is to this discovery
that the designation of WILLOUGHBY LAND may be
correctly applied; and, it may be hoped, will be so
applied.

Ignorant, however, as the countrymen of Sir Hugh
Willoughby have hitherto been on the subject, the
Dutch, at an early period, seem to have been well informed.   During the year 1596, William Barents, a
navigator of that nation, was engaged in a voyage to
seek Cathaia and India by a northern passage. Having
proceeded for some distance easterly, from Bear, or
Cherry Island, an observation was taken in latitude
73° N.; and the chronicler of the voyage, Gerart de
Veer, remarks: " *Then were we of opinion that we*
were by Willoughby Land . . . . and not farre from
Nova Zemla".[1]   Strong in his preconceived notion,
Purchas, in a marginal note, derisively terms this
opinion " *map-conceited*".   Probably he would have
applied the same epithet to the opinion of a subsequent author of the same nation, who, referring to

---

[1] This occurred on the 13th of July in the year above named.
Barents proceeded northerly, but his progress was greatly impeded
by a vast accumulation of ice; and he did not fall in with the coast
of Nova Zemla, actually, till the 17th: about *Lomsby*, to the southward of *Admiral's Island.—Purchas*, vol. iii, p. 486.

Sir Hugh Willoughby, observes: "Il y a grande ap-
parence qu'il aborda à la NOUVELLE ZEMBLE".[1] Perhaps, also, he would not have exempted from sarcasm
a modern writer who takes the same view.[2]

After sighting land on the 14th of August, Sir
Hugh Willoughby "plyed northerly" for three days;
then, on the 18th, "bare roome S.S.E. 70 leagues";
and, after taking various courses, fell in with land on
the following days, viz.: the 23rd and 28th of August; the 1st, 8th, and 11th of September. On the
18th of the latter month, the expedition was off a
coast which lay N.W. by W. and S.E. by E., along
which they cruized for some days, and eventually returned and entered into a haven that had been before
examined.[3]

---

[1] *Recueil des Voyages au Nord.* (Disc. Prelim. p. xx.) Amster-
dam, 1715.

[2] *Dr. Hamel,* in his *Tradescant,* p. 27. Petersburgh, 1847.

[3] *Further Analysis of Sir Hugh Willoughby's Track. August* 15,
16, 17. Plying northerly....18.—Wind N.E.: "bare roome S.S.E.
70 leagues....19, 20. [No account.]...21. Sounded in 10 fathoms,
shoaling to 7 : no land in sight: " bare roome into the sea all night",
N.W. by W....22. Soundings 20 fathoms: course W.S.W. until,
23. *Low Land discovered,* apparently uninhabitable : " westward
along the land, which lyeth W.S.W. and E.N.E.: wind strong
from the W.": haled into the sea N. by E. 30 leagues : wind
N.E., sailed W.N.W.: wind N.W.: "lay with our sails W.S.W.
about 14 leagues"....28. *Descried land:* worked into 4 fathoms,
water still shoaling, and dry sands ahead. " Haled out again N.E.
along the land until we came to the point thereof": " that land
turning westward, we ran along 16 leagues N.W.": a fair bay :
landed, uninhabited, but tokens of being visited : thence all along
the coast westward.... *September* 4. *Lost sight of land,* " by rea-

Being safely moored, they "sent out three men
S.S.W., to search if they could find people, which
went three dayes journey, but could find none. After
that they sent out three W. four dayes journey, which
also returned without finding any people. Then they
sent out three men S.E. three dayes journey, which
in like sorte returned without finding any people, or
any similitude of habitation". These are the concluding words of Sir Hugh Willoughby's journal; and
this document was eventually recovered through the
agency of some Russian fishermen, who discovered
two of the ships, which formed part of the expedition,
in " *the haven of Arzina, neer Kegor, in Lapland*".
In this desolate place perished miserably, through cold
and starvation, it may be apprehended, the ill-fated
commander, with no less than seventy of his equally
hapless associates.[1]

son of contrary winds"....8. *Land seen again:* within two days,
lost sight of. Running W. by S. 30 leagues, *land again seen:*
" bare in with it till night": being "a lee shore, gat into the sea".
...12. *Haled to shoreward again:* anchored in 30 fathoms....13.
Along the coast, which lay N.W. by W. and S.E. by E....14.
Came to anchor, within two leagues of the shore, in 60 fathoms:
went on shore, and found two or three good harbours, land
rocky and high, inhabitants none....15, 16. Running along the
shore....17. Wind contrary: tack towards the harbour visited
before....18. *Came to anchor,* 6 fathoms, in former haven (*Arzina*).

[1] *Hakluyt,* vol. i, p. 263. *Milton,* " A Brief History of Muscovia", adds: " Whereof the English Agent at Mosco having notice, sent and recovered the ships with the dead bodies, and most
of the goods, and sent them for England; but *the ships being un-
staunch,* as is supposed, by their two years' wintring in Lapland,
sunk by the way with their dead, and them also that brought them."
Prose Works, p. 577.

Yet, what is not a little singular, it is to this spot, that Purchas applies the remark: "*And this is that land which is now called Greenland . . . and is known to the Hollanders by the name of Spitzbergen*". It is also no less singular, that, without any authority that can be traced, certainly not with the authority of Sir Hugh Willoughby's journal, Purchas represents Sir Hugh as sailing from the spot above described, to the spot where he encountered his melancholy fate.

That Sir Hugh Willoughby did not discover Spitzbergen during his progress from Seynam to Nova Zemla is evident. The question is, did he make the discovery while "wandering on those desolate seas" between Nova Zemla and Arzina?

On leaving the coast of Nova Zemla, it is stated, that Sir Hugh "plyed northerly" for three days. The solution of the question depends on the sense to be attached to the term *plyed*. If by that term the navigator intended to state that he *went* northerly for three days, there is every reason to believe that he did fall in with Spitzbergen: in fact, he could not, between Nova Zemla and Arzina, have fallen in with any other land than Spitzbergen. Of this opinion, was the author of the *Recueil des Voyages au Nord*. After stating the great probability of Sir Hugh having touched at Nova Zemla, he adds: " Et au GROENLAND, d'où le froid et les glaces l'aiant chassé, il descendit plus au midi jusqu'à l'ARZINA, où CE GRAND HOMME et ses compagnons furent trouvés morts de froid dans leur vaisseau". But if the term "*plyed*" is to be taken in its strictly technical sense, as a nautical phrase, it must be understood, that for three days he was striving unsuccessfully to make way against a head-wind, which would prevent him from making much, if any, progress toward the northward. Then indeed must specious advocacy, personal predilection, and national feeling yield to candour. It must be confessed that the discovery of Spitzbergen by him, is rendered essentially apocryphal.[1]

If such be the case, the fame of Sir Hugh Willoughby is only affected in regard to a proceeding which has been erroneously assigned to him. He cannot be deprived of the credit of having been the first Englishman by whom the coast of Nova Zemla was visited; while the subsequent part of his voyage remains to be reviewed.

[1] A manuscript copy of the journal (in the British Museum), about the time of Elizabeth, has been consulted to ascertain whether the term *plyed* is used, or not; but without success, the passage in which the word should occur being rendered illegible by fire. *Falconer's* definition (*Mar. Dict.*) of the word is: "to make a progress against the wind", and gives "*convoyer*" [? *convier*] as the corresponding term in French. *Milton*, describing the opposition of the Britons to the landing of the Romans, states it was rendered ineffectual by "Cæsar causing all his boats and shallops to be filled with soldiers, commanded to *ply up and down* continually, with relief when they saw need". (*Hist. of England*, bk. ii.) *Steven Burrough*, in his voyage to Russia in 1556, observes: "July 28. Saturday at north-north-west sunne the wind came to east-north-east, and then we weied, and *plied* towards the northwards". (*Hakluyt*, vol. i, p. 310.) In the following pages, all passages are cited where the word occurs. The reader will thus be enabled to judge for himself of the meaning attached to it by the elder mariners, and how far it agrees with the modern interpretation.

After plying northerly for three days, it is said, Sir Hugh Willoughby " bare roome S.S.E. 70 leagues". In other words, he shaped a fair course towards Muscovia. From the 23rd of August, the day on which he first saw land after quitting Nova Zemla, to the 8th of September, when he arrived in Lapland, he was exploring an unknown coast, which could have been no other than the northern shore of Russia, if the claim to Spitzbergen be abandoned. The north of Russia was new ground; and Sir Hugh Willoughby is entitled to the merit of an achievement, which has been pronounced by one whose judgment is indisputable, and whose commendation is an honour, to be " *almost heroic*".[1]

It is not uninteresting to trace the different degrees in which the simple record of Sir Hugh Willoughby's services, contained in his " brief journal", have affected the fame of the gallant, but ill-fated man. Either through misrepresentation, the result of injudicious zeal, or by misapprehension, he was invested, in the first instance, with an honour to which he had but a doubtful title, though his right was not disputed for the space of two centuries, and more. Next, on the authority of the same simple record, the right was

---

[1] "*The discovery of Russia by the northern ocean,* made first of any nation that we know, by Englishmen, *might have seemed an enterprize almost heroic ;* if any higher end than excessive love of gain and traffic had animated the design." (*Milton. A brief History of Muscovia. Works,* 1834, p. 577.) But the gallant men who perilled their lives in the adventure must not be included with the promoters, as being influenced by sordid motives.

questioned; and in disputing the right, his fame altogether was placed in jeopardy. Now, from the same
source, after a lapse of three centuries from the period
when he encountered his lamentable fate, an attempt
is made, earnest in purpose and honest in intention,
to demonstrate, on grounds hitherto unsuspected by
his countrymen, that he merits no uneminent station
among those who have a claim to honourable notice
in the annals of their country. An attempt has been
made to shew, that the renown to which Sir Hugh
Willoughby has a claim, is neither dependent for support on misrepresentation, or misapprehension, nor
liable to be shaken by detraction or error. No less
intrepid in action, than ardent in temperament, he
boldly pursued untried paths and perilous ways.[1] He
sought and found new regions; and the merit of the
action is not the less, because his discoveries are ill-

---

[1] A cotemporary gives the following account of Sir Hugh Willoughby's selection for the command of the expedition: " Nowe
prouision being made and carrid aboord, with armour and munition
of all sorts, sufficient Captaines and Gouernours of so great an
enterprise were yet wanting: to which office and place, although
many men offered them selues, yet *one Sir Hugh Willoughby*, a
most valiant gentleman, and well borne, uery ernestly requested to
haue that care and charge comitted to him: of whom before all
others, both by reason of his goodly personage (for he was of a tall
stature) as also for his singular skill in the seruices of war, the
company of *the Marchants* [of Muscovia] made greatest accompt;
so that at the last they concluded and *made choyce of him for the
Generall of this voyage,* and *appointed to him the Admirall,* with
authoritie and command ouer all the rest." (*Clement Adams. Hakluyt,* vol. i, p. 270.) An explanation of the terms Generall and
Admirall will be found in the *Appendix.*

defined, or because their localities are difficult to be
established. Bodily, he fell a sacrifice to his adventurous spirit; and his reputation was left to the uncertain mercy of the robustious elements. To chance,
and the kindly care of semi-barbarians, posterity are
indebted for all they know of the proceedings of the
hapless Sir Hugh. Had he survived to return home,
all obscurity would doubtlessly have been cleared up;
and neither cavil nor dispute would have affronted his
memory.

II.

*The probability of an Englishman named Wm. Adams,
having made a voyage to Spitzbergen, A.D. 1595.*

The author of the *Arctic Voyages* having sum-
marily dismissed the claim of Sir Hugh Willoughby,
or rather the claim preferred on his behalf, and having
declared the " discovery of Spitzbergen to be certainly
due to the Dutch", proceeds to observe: " It might
not have been suspected, from De Veer's account of
Barent's three voyages, that the extraordinary man",
William Adams, " whose name stands at the head of
this section, was one of the Englishmen employed
on one or more of those voyages"; adding: " It is
very probable, however, that the fact is so, and that,
in the year 1596, he accompanied Cornelis Ryp to
Spitzbergen".

In support of this opinion, the author states, there
can be no doubt of his having lived in Holland, and
of his having been in the practice of piloting Dutch

vessels, although Adams does not allude to the circumstance in the brief account he gives of himself
in two letters he addressed to his wife from Japan:
he adverts to an ill-fated expedition that was sent by
the Dutch round Cape Horn in 1598, under the command of " Simon de Cordes"; and he notices the fact
of one of the vessels, having an English pilot on board,
being driven by stress of weather on the coast of
Japan: he cites a passage from the *Decadas* of Diogo
de Couta, which is to the effect, that the pilot in question averred to the Jesuits at Meaco, the capital of the
empire, that he had been employed on various services
of importance by the Prince of Orange, particularly
in 1593-94 and 95, in the discovery of a " route above
Biarmia and Finmarchia" to Japan, China, and the
Moluccas; and that on the last occasion he reached
" eighty-two degrees north": finally, it is decided, this
personage was William Adams, and that it could be
no other than " himself" who gave the narrative to
the Portuguese Jesuits at the court of Japan; " for his
good friend Timothy Shelton of London, who, he tells
us, was pilot of the Admiral, was lost in that ship;
and Thomas Adams, his brother, was slain in battle".

On this statement some observations may be made.
They follow:

It is true that Adams wrote two letters from Japan;
but he addressed only one of them to his wife. The
letter addressed by Adams to his wife is short, and
does not contain any allusion to his career before he
arrived in Japan. The other letter[1] was intended to

[1] Two copies of this communication are preserved among the

interest in his behalf any influential personage into whose hands it might fall; and is a lengthy piece of autobiography, from his youth upwards. From this document it is ascertained that Adams " was bound prentis to Master Nicholas Diggines of Limehouse", when he was of the age of twelve years; and that he continued in the service of Master Diggines till he was twenty-four years old. It further appears, that Adams next served as " master and pilot in her maiesties shipps" for a certain period, but for how long is not stated; and then he was engaged with the " Worshipful Barbarie Companie" for eleven or twelve years. This statement, so far, is certainly brief; but it appears too specific to justify the supposition, that, for any part of the period, he had either resided in Holland, or been engaged in piloting Dutch ships: while he had evidently an English reputation that rendered him independent of Dutch patronage. The supposition that has been advanced of the employment of Adams in Holland is rendered still less probable, if that be necessary, by what follows. Adams states that he continued in the service of the Barbary Company " untill the Indian trafficke from Holland began"; he says, " being desirous of making a little experience of the knowledge God had given him", he took service with the Dutch; and was made " Pilot maior" of the fleet under the command of Sir Jacques

records of the East India Company: probably transmitted by their agents abroad. When Adams wrote, there was continual intercourse between Japan and Bantam, and other places where the Company had established *Factories*. Both letters are printed in *Purchas*.

Mahu.[1] This representation appears to fix with precision the period when Adams became first connected
with the Dutch.[2]

Throughout his autobiography, it is evident, that
Adams is solicitous to display his character in the
most favourable light. The fact of his having made
a voyage to Spitzbergen would, undoubtedly, have
added to his reputation; and it can scarcely be imagined he would have been so careless of his fame, or
so regardless of his interests, as to have omitted all
notice of the action, had he been actually engaged
in it.

Of the fact, that Adams was neither ignorant of,
nor insensible to the renown likely to ensue from experience in the navigation of the North-polar seas,
there is abundant evidence. In a letter reporting
the arrival of Captain Saris at the Court of Japan,
whither he had been deputed by " The Worshipfull
Fellowship of the Marchants of London trading into
the East Indies", to obtain for them the privilege of
trading with that empire, there are some singularly
interesting and curious passages on the subject.[3] After
having stated the result of the interview which Cap-

[1] This voyage is of an interesting character; and a summary will
be found in the *Appendix*.

[2] First Dutch Voyage to India, A.D. 1595. *Harris's Collection
of Voyages and Travels*, vol. i, p. 926. Lond. fol. 1744.

[3] This letter was addressed to the Governor of the Company of
Merchants, etc., and is dated [?] December 1613. (*E. I. Mss.*)
At this period Adams had not had any intercourse with his countrymen for nearly fifteen years, which will account in a degree for
the peculiar idiom of the letter.

tain Saris had with the Emperor, and some subsequent proceeds, Adams proceeds to say: " The Emperor hauing much talk wth me of his (Captain Saris) couming, I told him to settell a factory in his land, at wch he seemed verry glad.[1] And hauing had mvch speech heer and thear he asked me yf pt of his coomming was not for discouer [y] to farther ptes to the nor͡wstward or nor͡wards. I told him our countri still douth not ceess to spend mvch monny in discoueri thearof. He asked me whear [? *whether*] thear wear nott a way, and whether it wass not very short or neer. I told him we douted not but thear is a way, and that veery neeir; at wch tym called for a mape of the wholl world and so sawe that it wass verry neeir. Hauing speechis wth me, whether we had no knolledg of a land lying

---

[1] " Captain Saris upon his arrival in Japan, which was in June 1613, repaired forthwith to the Court of the Emperor Ongoschiosama, who then resided in Surunga, and was admitted to an audience of that monarch on the 8th of September, of whom he obtained ample privileges, very honorable to the British Nation . . . . and exceedingly advantageous to the East India Company, one of which, and certainly not the least considerable, was, that they should have leave to set out upon discovery of the country of Iedso (Yesso) or any other part in or about the Empire of Japan, a privilege which the Portuguese, even at the time of their highest interest with the Japanese, were not able to procure on any terms whatever. *The good success Captain Saris met with in his negotiations at the Imperial Court was owing, in a great measure, to the assistance of one William Adams, a Kentish man*" . . . . (Scheuchzer: translator and editor of Kæmpfer's Hist. of Japan, Introduction, p. xliv.) Adams, on account of his extraordinary merits, was deservedly a great favorite with Ogosho Sama, and possessed almost unlimited influence at the Imperial Court.

hard by his countri, on the north pt of his land, called Zedzoo and Mattesmay.[1] I told him I did neuer see it pvt into anny mape or gllobe. I told him it myght bee that the worshipfull Company would send soum ship or other to discouer. He told me that in the yeir of our Lord 1611, a ship wass seen of theis cost, on the est syde, in latitude of 38° or thearabout, whether that weear any of our countri ship. I told him I thought it not. He told me agayn it could be no ship of the Spayniards going for Novo Spania: for this ship wass seen in Apprill, wch tym no ship goeth not from the Manillieus [Manillas]. He asked me yf I did deesir to go that waye. I told him, yf the wourshipfull Coompanie should dessire svch a thing, I would willingly ymploy my self in svch an honorabell accion. He told me, yf I did go, he would geue [give] me his letter of frindship to the land of Zedzoo, wheear his svbjects hav frindship, hauing a stronge towne and a castell: thorough wch menes haue 30 dayes jovrney frindship wth thoos pepell; wch peopell be, as I do

---

[1] For some time it was doubtful whether *Yesso* did not form a part of *Nipon*, the principal of the Japanese islands; or, if an island, whether *Mattesmaye* did not lye between the two. *Yesso* has been proved to be an island, of which *Mattesmaye* is one of the principal towns. *Broughton*, in 1795, visited *Yesso*, and coasted the east side. He visited the island again in 1797, and sailed through *The Straights of Sangar*, which divide *Nipon* from *Yesso*. He was the first and only European by whom the navigation was, or has since been, effected. The western and northern sides have been explored by *Krusenstern* and others. *Golownin*, a Russian, was detained a prisoner on Yesso for nearly three years; but although a captive, saw a good deal of the country.

gather, Tartares joyning to the *Cam*, or borders of Cattay. Now in my sympel judgment, yf the norŵest passag be euer discouered, it wilbe discouered by this way of Jappan; and so thuss, wth diuers other speechis most frindli evsed [used], I toouk [took] my leaue of him". After some irrelative matter, Adams resumes the subject in the following terms, viz.: "Conserning this discouerie to the norŵard. Yf it stand wth your wourshipps liking, in my judgment neuer hath bin better menes to discouer. My ressons. First, this kingdoum of Japan wth whoum we have frindship: the emperador hath pmyssed his assistance to geu [give] his letter of frindship to the countri of Zedzoo and Matesmaye, whear his subiects are ressident. Secondly: languiges, that can speak the Corea and Tartar langwage for Japan langedge, not to be reckined. For shipping: yf your wourship send not, yet may you hau bylded, or cass to be bylder, such shipes or piñces [pinnaces] necessary for svch a discouery, wth lesse charges. Things are heer good cheep, as tymber, plank, irroun, hemp, and carpenters: only tarre heere is none; rosen annouf, but verry deer. Thess thinges I hau experienc[e] of, becass I hau byllt 2 shipes in this contri for the emperor: the on[e] of them sold to the Spaynards [bein of burden¹ 170 tunnes], and the other I sayld in my sellf vppon dyuers voyages vppon this cost. So that neuertheless by my pfession I am no shippwright, yet I hop to mak svch shipping as shalbe necessary for anny svch discouery. Now men to sayll

¹ Introduced from a second letter from Adams, without address, preserved among the *E. I. Mss.*

wth only excepted, the peopell are not acquainted wth our maner. Therefor yf your wourships have anny svch pirposs, send me good mariners[1] to sayll wth; and yf you send but 15 or 20, or leess, it is no matter, for the people of this land are very stoutt seéa men, and in what way I shall go in, I can hau so manny as I will. Now for vytelling. Heir is in this land annouf and svch plenty, and so good cheep, as is in Jngland, as thoss who hau bin heer can satisfi your wourship therin. So that I say agayn, the wantes be cordesh [ropes], pouldaues [canvas], and tarr, pitch, or rossen, and compasses, rounninglasses [hour-glasses], a payr of globes for demonstracion, and soum cardes [charts] or mapes contayninge the wholl world. Thees things yf your wourship do furnish me wth, you shal find me not neglegent in svch an honorabell serues [service], by God's grace. Thus much I hau thought good to wrytt to your wourship, being soumwhat longe in making the pticullers apparent of this discouree: *wch discouree I do trust in Allmightie God should be on[e] of the most famost that euer hath bin.*"[2]

But it is alleged by De Couto, that he had been informed by certain Jesuits, that a certain English pilot had averred to them, that he had been up to 82° N.

---

[1] Men acquainted with the *science of navigation*.

[2] The second letter, to which reference has already been made (N. p. xviii), concludes thus: "*I do not dought, by God's grace, thear wilbe greate thinges found out, wch to this tym hath not bin heeard of, and for my p't, shal think my self a most happie man to be imployed in svch an honorabell axcion*".

The claimant on behalf of William Adams alleges, as before noticed, it could have been no other than Adams "himself" who made this statement; "because Timothy Shelton", correctly *Shotten*, "his friend, and Thomas Adams, his brother, were dead". In this representation a material fact is omitted. The captain of the ship on which Adams served, was one of the persons who arrived in Japan, and he remained in the empire for five years. His office might have been misapprehended; and his nation might have been concealed. It is notorious the Dutch never scrupled, when occasion served, to assume the English name. In this case, the Dutch captain had good cause for adopting the expedient: to secure his personal safety.[1]

It remains only to be observed : that, in order to make the voyage attributed to Adams correspond with that accomplished by Cornelis Ryp, it has been deemed necessary to alter the date communicated by the Jesuits. According to De Couto,[2] the fathers alleged that the pilot asserted he went up to 82° N. *in* 1595 : which the advocate for Adams declares was "*probably* 1596".

Without deciding whether the voyage attributed to Adams were performed by him, or not, it cannot be considered that sufficient evidence has been adduced to prove the fact.

[1] See Adams's narrative in *Purchas.*

[2] See a brief narrative of this celebrated writer in the Introduction to *Kæmpfer's Hist. of Japan,* by *Scheuchzer,* p. xxx.

NARRATIVES OF VOYAGES

TOWARDS

THE NORTH-WEST.

Narratives of Voyages,

etc.

A PERIOD of about three centuries and a half has elapsed since the project of seeking a passage to the eastern hemisphere, by way of the North-west, was first entertained. HENRY VII, then reigning in England, earnestly desired to promote maritime enterprise on the part of his subjects; and, under the influence of that feeling, had sought, but failed, to secure the services of CHRISTOVAL COLON, whose fame, as CHRISTOPHER COLUMBUS, is universal, and will endure for all time. After the failure of the overture made to Columbus, a Venetian, by name JOHN CABOTA, accompanied by his three sons, LEWIS, SEBASTIAN, and SANCIUS, visited this realm; and the high reputation enjoyed by the father, for skill in navigation, and intrepidity as a seaman, caused him to be deemed a welcome visitor, and gained for him a cordial reception. This talented foreigner may be considered to have introduced a new era in the annals of English navigation, and to have originated the idea of an enterprise invested with no ordinary interest: in the prosecution of which, the energies of men of no ordinary character have been enlisted; and for the accomplishment of which, anxiety of no ordinary description is experienced.

Further than this, the accounts of John Cabota are vague and discrepant. He is represented to have made one attempt, or more than one attempt, to explore the North-polar seas; but the record of his proceedings is imperfect; and nothing authentic can be collected, except the simple fact of his having been engaged in the enterprise. Such being the case, the voyage undertaken by his son Sebastian, who proved himself worthy of the name he inherited, will be brought under notice.

§ I.

Voyage of Sebastian Cabota.

THIS voyager states, that he arrived in the city of London while he was very young, though "having, neverthelesse, some knowledge of the letters of humanitie, and of the sphere." From his account it further appears : his father died "in that time when newes were brought, that Don Christopher Colonus Genuese had discovered the coasts of India." [1] This event, it is added, caused "great talke in all the courte of Henry VII; insomuch that all men, with great admiration, affirmed it to be a thing more diuine than humane, to sail by the west into the east, where spices growe, by a way that was never knowen before." Stimulated by the fame of this noble achievement, and hoping to rival in renown the successful Genoese, the young Cabota resolved to attempt some enterprise of note. "Understanding, by reason of the sphere", that if he should sail by the Northwest, he might be enabled to reach India by a shorter route than Columbus had pursued, Cabota determined to make the attempt, and "caused the king to be advertised" of his "devise". Without hesitation Henry VII acceded to the suggestion, and placed at the command of the adventurer two caravels, furnished with all things appertaining to the voyage, and manned with sufficient crews.

---

[1] Columbus sailed on his first voyage of discovery, the 3rd of August, A.D. 1492. He arrived, on his return, at Lisbon on the 4th of March 1493. His second voyage was commenced the 25th of October, in the latter year.—*Gomara, Hist. Gen.* quoted by *Hakluyt*, vol. iv, p. 416.

A.D.
1496. } As well as he remembers, Cabota sailed early in the summer of 1496. He did not accomplish what he anticipated. What he did effect may be thus succinctly stated. On the 24th of June, about five o'clock in the morning, a "mainland" was discovered, and in front of it an island. To the former was given the name of PRIMA VISTA, because it was the first land that had been seen since the departure of the expedition from England; and the latter was called ST. JOHN, because, "as it is thought, it was discovered upon the day of John the Baptist." What is termed the "mainland", may be considered as having been NEWFOUNDLAND; and the island in front corresponds with that which retains the name by which it was originally called.

After making this discovery, Cabota continued to coast along the land, in the hope of finding an opening; but, being disappointed, he retraced his way on reaching, according to his own account, lat. 56° N.; or, according to Gomara, 60° N.[1] Pursuing a southerly course, still anxiously looking out for a passage to the Indies, he reached "that part of the firme lande now called FLORIDA"; and from thence, his supplies failing, directed his course to England. On his arrival he found great tumults among the people, and preparations in progress for war against the Scots; "by reason whereof there was no more consideration had to this voyage".[2]

Of Cabota it has justly been observed: "By his knowledge and experience, his zeal and penetration, he not only was the means of extending the foreign commerce of England, but of keeping alive that spirit of enterprise, which, even in his life-time, was crowned with success, and which ultimately led to the most happy results for the nation that had so wisely and honourably enrolled this deserving foreigner in the list of her citizens".[3] These results were not, however, immediate. Shortly after the voyage which has been the

[1] Hakluyt, vol. iv, p. 416.   [2] Ibid. vol. iii, pp. 25-32.
[3] Arctic Voyages, p. 36.

subject of notice, Cabota quitted England; whether in dis-
gust at his views not being seconded, or "by the command
of His Catholic Majesty of Castile", is not certain; and he
did not return till the year 1548, during the reign of the
eighth Harry. In the following reign he was created, by
patent, "Pilot Maior of England", with a pension, for life, of
500 marks, or £166 : 13 : 4 per annum;[1] and he was subsequently invested with the office of "Gouernour of the Mys-
terie and Companie of the Marchant Aduenturers for the
Discovery of New Trades", better known by the shorter
title of the "Muscovia Company". This digression, which
might be deemed impertinent but for the subject, will not
be materially lengthened by the following incident in the
career of this "man, for the knowledge of sea-affairs much
renowned", recorded by *Steven Burrough* in the relation of his
voyage to Russia, undertaken in the year 1556. He says:
"The 27th of April, being Monday, the right worshipfull
Sebastian Cabota came aboord our pinnesse at Grauesende,
accompanied with diuers gentlemen and gentlewomen; and
after they had viewed our pinnesse, and tasted of such cheere
as we could make them aboord, they went on shore, giving
to our mariners right liberall rewards; and *the good olde
gentleman*, Master Cabota, gave to the poore most liberall
almes, wishing them to pray for the good fortune and prosperous successe of the Serchthrift, our pinnesse. And then,
at the signe of the Christopher, he and his friends banket-
ted, and made mee, and them that were in the company,
great cheere; and for very joy that he had, to see the toward-
nes of our intended discouery, he entred into the dance him
selfe, amongst the rest of the young and lusty company;
which being ended, he and his friends departed most gently,
comending vs to the gouernance of Almighty God."[2]

[1] The patent is dated the 6th of February, 1st and 2nd of Philip and
Mary.—*Hakluyt*, vol. i, p. 304.
[2] Hakluyt, vol. i, p. 306.

§ II.

The Three Voyages of Martin Frobisher.

EXCEPT an abortive attempt, of which the particulars are not known, made by the DOMINUS VOBISCUM and another vessel, in 1527, "no more consideration was had for the voyage" for eighty years after the failure of Sebastian Cabota. The project was revived by SIR MARTIN FROBISHER, a man of no eminent lineage, but endowed with superior mental qualifications. It appears that, at an early age, he was sent from his native place to a school in London, and placed under the care of " *Sir John Yorke,* knight, his kinseman ; who, perceiving him to be of great spirit and bould courage, and naturall hardnes of body, sent him to the hote cuntrye of *Guinea*", on board a ship forming part of a fleet fitted out by several merchants of London.[1] As he advanced in years, he is represented to have been "thorowly furnished of the knowledge of the sphere, and all other skilles appertayning to the arte of navigation".[2] By incessant and long study of the subject; by "sundry sure reasons and secret intelligence ", the nature of which, however, is not communicated, Frobisher wrought himself to a conviction of being able to accomplish the notable design he contemplated. His fortune was not commensurate with his desire : "he lacked altogether meanes and abilitie to performe the same"; and for fifteen years he conferred earnestly, but fruitlessly, with his private friends, and with merchants, on the project. The former proved lukewarm ; and the latter, he soon perceived, were not wont to regard " vertue, without sure, certaine, and present gaines". Eventually he repaired to the court ; and there, it is said, he found many honourable

---

[1] Fragment of a notice by Michael Lok.—MSS. Brit. Mus. *Cotton ; Otho,* E. 8-47.

[2] Hakluyt, vol. iii, p. 85.

minds able and willing to favour his views : particularly
AMBROSE DUDLEY, EARL OF WARWICK.

Such, at least, is the information communicated by Hakluyt; but a very large share in promoting the success of the
undertaking, is claimed by an individual named MICHAEL
LOK. He asserts, that the parties principally engaged in the
adventure, were, with himself, *Mr. George Barn*, Sheriff of
London ; *William Towerson*, who was afterwards engaged in
the East India trade ; and *Steven Burrough*, whose name
has already occurred, and who had sailed as master, under
Chancelor, in Willoughby's ill-fated· expedition. Burrough
appears, however, to have confined his assistance to advice,
which he freely bestowed; but whether it was deemed more
valuable than a money contribution would have been considered, is not apparent. If the statement of Lok be correct,
the supplies for the voyage were obtained mainly through
his means and credit. The total cost of the adventure, he
represents to have amounted to £2,400 ; and he complains
that the subscribers supplied no more than £1,600, leaving
him responsible for the residue of £800.

From this narrative it further appears, that the views of
Lok and his associates were for some time thwarted, by opposition on the part of the Muscovia Company. Although this
association had been incorporated for the special purpose of
promoting "New Trades", they would neither engage to enter
on the undertaking on their own account, nor permit others
to engage in it. At length the difficulty was overcome. An
appeal was made to the Lord Treasurer; and, in obedience
to a mandate issued by that functionary, the Muscovia Company, in February 1574, granted a license, under their common seal, for the project to be proceeded with.

In strong contrast with the proceedings of the Muscovia
Company, was the conduct of DR. JOHN DEE, who is introduced by Lok, for the first time, in connexion with this
matter. Dr. John Dee entertained serious doubts respect-

ing the practicability of the intended voyage; and he was invited to investigate the matter. At an interview, at which Frobisher, Barn, Towerson, and Borough, were also present, held on the 20th of May 1576, Lok took pains, fully and plainly, to expound his reasons, in opposition to the adverse opinion entertained by the Doctor. He laid before him "his bokes and authors, his cardes and his instruments"; together with all the notes he had made in writing regarding the undertaking, which he had been collecting during many years, and forming, he states, a bulky volume. Posterity might have been instructed had he carried out the intention he entertained, of giving publicity to his researches.

The Doctor acknowledged the cogency of the arguments maintained by Lok; and, when the crews were assembled on board the vessels, and while they were completing their arrangements, the learned man joined them, and "took greate paines to instruct the masters and mariners in the rules of geometry, cosmography, the use of instruments in their voyage, and for casualties happening at sea, which did them service; whereby", Lok truly observes, "he deserveth just cõmendãcon".[1]

These conflicting statements being concluded, the narrative of the voyage will be proceeded with.

1ST VOYAGE, A.D. 1576. } The expedition consisted of two barks and a pinnace, victualled and found for twelve months. The barks, the GABRIEL and the MICHAEL, were "*between twenty and twenty-five tunne a-piece*": the pinnace measured *ten tons*, with a "close deck"; and the crews amounted, in the aggregate, to thirty-five hands. MARTIN

---

[1] *Paper by Michael Lok; Cotton MSS. (Brit Mus.) Otho, E.* 8, 42, 43, 45. Amongst this collection of documents is (78) a rough draft of instructions, framed in connexion with a voyage in search of the North-east passage to China and India, which concludes with the words, "p. me John Dee".

FROBISHER was nominated "captain and pylot"; CHRISTO-
PHER HALL, master of the GABRIEL; and OWEN GRYFFYN, to
the same post on the MICHAEL.[1]

Seemingly uninfluenced by the superstitious feeling which
not unfrequently, in the present day, influences seamen,
Frobisher and his companions started on a *Friday*. They
weighed, from Deptford, on the noon of the 7th of June;
but proceeded no further, that day, than "Greenwhich",[2]
where Elizabeth and her court then lay.

Three-and-twenty years before, at the same spot, the ill-
fated expedition, proceeding under SIR HUGH WILLOUGHBY,
in search of a North-east passage to India, had exhibited "a
triumph (in a sort) for the gratification of good King Edward;
but he being then sick, beheld not the sight. Presently"
(that is, on Willoughby's expedition coming to an anchor,)
"the courtiers came running out; the privy council at the
windows, and the rest on the towers and battlements of the
palace. The mariners, all apparalled in watchet (or sky-
colored cloth), discharged their ordnance according to the
order of war, insomuch that the hills sounded therewith, the
valleys and the waters giving an echo; while the mariners
and the beholders shouted in such sort, that the skie rang
again with the noyse thereof."[3] This example was imitated
by the people under Frobisher, to the best of their means;
and the Queen's Majesty, standing at an open window, not
only greeted her faithful and adventurous subjects with the
waving of her hand, but sent a gentleman on board, "to make
known her good liking of their doings, and thanking them
for it, willing the captaine to visit the court the next day, to
take his leave of her". Furthermore, during the evening of

---

[1] Some details have been added from Lok's paper, ut suprà.

[2] By the long-shore people, and the working population generally, the
pronunciation of Greenwich according to the old orthography, is still preserved.

[3] Hakluyt, *Narrative of Clement Adams.*

the same day, one of the Queen's secretaries was despatched with a message, giving them charge to be obedient to their captain and governors, and wishing them " happie successe".

Except a leak, sprung by one of the ships off the Shetlands, which was speedily repaired, nothing material occurred during the voyage, till the 11th of July, when land was discovered in lat. 61° N. The land, observed to the W.N.W. distant sixteen leagues, rose like " pinacles of steeples, and all covered with snow ", and was supposed to be FRIESLAND, a land occasionally spoken of, yet never identified.[1] Attempts were made to land; but "the great store of yce ", and the heavy mists which covered the coast, prevented the intention from being carried into effect. A severe tempest was also experienced ; during which, the pinnace, with all hands on board (four in number), foundered; and the people of the MICHAEL, " mistrusting the matter, privily conveyed themselves away". This vessel reached England in safety. Frobisher, now left to himself, altered his course, and stood to the S.W.; and, seventeen days afterwards, other land, judged to be LABRADOR, was sighted in lat. 62° 2′ N.

On the 13th of July an incident occurred, which is not noticed in the printed accounts of the voyage, but which is too creditable to Frobisher to be suppressed. On the day above named, the GABRIEL was in the utmost danger of foundering, and the crew ran great hazard of perishing with their vessel. From this melancholy fate they were saved by the promptness, energy, and judgment of their commander. On the day above named, the manuscript states : " In the rage of an extreme storme, the vessell was cast flat on her syde ; and, being open in the waste,[2] was fylled with water, so as

---

[1] " This island, whose position has so greatly puzzled geographers, could not be the Frisland of Zeno ; but, being in 61° of latitude, was evidently the southern part of Greenland".—*Arctic Voyages*, p. 82.

[2] It is elsewhere stated, that the GABRIEL laboured under the additional disadvantage of being low in the water.

she lay still for sunk, and would neither weare nor steare with
any helpe of the helme ; and could neuer have rysen agayn,
but by the merveilous work of God's great mercy to help
them all. In this distres, when all the men in the ship had
lost their courage, and did despayr of life, the captayn, *like
him selfe*, with valiant courage, stood vp, and passed alongst
the ship's side, in the chayn wales [channels], lying on her
flat syde, and caught holde on the weather leche of the fore-
saile; but in the weather-coyling [going about] of the ship,
the fore-yarde brake". To ease her, the mizen-mast was cut
away; but she still rolled heavily, so that the water "yssued
from both sydes, though, withall, without any thing fleeting
over". As soon as practicable, the poor storm-buffeted bark
was "put before the sea"; and all hands were set to work to
repair damages.[1]

In lat. 62° 30' "north from Newfoundland", high land
was fallen in with on the 31st of July, to which the name of
QUEEN ELIZABETH'S CAPE was given ; and, sailing from Queen
Elizabeth's Cape, more northerly, another foreland was descried, in lat. 63° 8' N., which formed the southern point of
" a great gut, bay, or passage, divided, as it were, by two
maine landes or continents, asunder".[2] Frobisher's desire was
to have crossed this passage ; but, being baffled by ice, currents, and winds, he determined to enter it. This was effected
on the 11th of August ; and the passage received the name
of FROBISHER'S STRAIT, though it has since been known as
LUMLEY'S INLET. Up these straits, Frobisher sailed sixty
leagues. Ten leagues from the entrance, they found an island,
to which the name of GABRIEL was given; then PRIOR'S SOUND;
and a mile further on, PRIOR'S BAY. From the former, the
land bore S.E. ; and good anchorage was found, with a sandy

---

[1] From a paper without signature, but in Lok's handwriting.—*MSS.*
ut suprà, 48.

[2] The entrance to these straits was more particularly observed during
the second voyage.

bottom.   Next, THOMAS WILLIAMS' ISLAND ; and ten leagues
beyond, BURCHER'S ISLAND, were discovered.

On the extreme point to which he navigated, Frobisher
landed, and fell in with a " salvage " people, greatly resembling Tartars in appearance. They used canoes, made of seal
skins, with a keel of wood within the skin ; and in shape, in
some respects, resembling the shallops of Spain. A boat, containing five hands, was here lost ; but whether the people
deserted, or were captured by the natives, is not clear. However, in retaliation of the real or supposed injury, one of the
aborigines was taken by stratagem : " whereupon, when he
found himself in captivity, for very choler and disdaine, he
bit his tongue in twaine within his mouth ; notwithstanding,
he died not thereof, but lived untill he came to England, and
then died of cold which he had taken at sea."

Arriving, on his return, at the mouth of the straits, Frobisher anchored for a few days ; and, on the 26th of August,
weighed for England.   Harwich was made on the 2nd of
October.

At home, the adventurer " was highly commended, of all
men, for his great and notable attempt; but specially famous
for the great hope he brought of the passage to Cataya ".
Yet, but for an accidental circumstance that occurred some
time subsequent to the completion of the voyage, it is not
improbable the matter would have died away.   This incident
is thus alluded to by Hakluyt.   The crews of the vessels, it
seems, had brought home divers articles as memorials of the
regions they had been exploring ; and among these memen-
toes were some pieces of stone "much like sea cole in colour".
By chance, one of these pieces came into the hands of the
wife of one of the adventurers : by another chance she threw
it into the fire ; and, when it became heated, for some
reason which is not explained, quenched it with vinegar :
" whereon it glistened with a bright marquesset of golde ;
and, the matter being called in some question, it was brought

to certain goldfyners in London, to make assay thereof; who gave out that it held golde, and that very richly for the quantity". Michael Lok gives a different version of the story. He says, that some of the stone was publicly given to him on board one of Frobisher's ships, after the return of the expedition. A piece of the stone he had thus acquired, he further states, he carried, in the first instance, to Mr. William Sayer, Master of the Tower. Another portion he afterwards, by direction of that officer, supplied to "one Wheeler, a gold fyner"; and some was also handed over to one Nedham. Sayer and Wheeler reported, "it was but a marquesite stone"; and Nedham declared "he could fynde no mettall therein". But Lok seems to have satisfied himself that the stone *would* yield gold; so he applied to a certain *John Baptista Agnello*, who, on three different occasions, exhibited gold to Lok, which the "gold fyner" declared he had extracted from as many different specimens. Hereon, Lok expresses himself as having been very much astonished; and with real or affected incredulity, inquired of Agnello: How it was he should have succeeded in the experiment, when other skilful men had failed? To this inquiry the wily adept replied: "*Bisogna sapere adulare la natura*". Lok's statement, of which the commencement is wanting, concludes thus: "The xviij of Januarie he sent me, by his mayde, this littel scrap of paper, written 'No. 1, herinclosed'; and therein inclosed the grayne of golde, which afterwards I delivered to your Majesty. 1577".[1]

There are no means of deciding which of these two versions is correct; but the fact is certain, that a second expedition was determined on: less, however, for the purposes of discovery, than to gratify cupidity; and many, in the true spirit of greedy speculation, seem to have been not unwilling to ensure gain at the expense of their neighbours. £4,400 were required to fit out the expedition. Subscriptions to that

---

[1] MSS. ut suprà.

amount were promised, but only £3,000 were paid; and Lok, who acted as treasurer on this and the first and third voyages, was left to meet the balance, of £1,400, in the best way he could.[1]   At least, such is his statement.

2ND VOYAGE, A.D. 1577.   The second expedition under Frobisher, consisted of the following vessels, viz., the AID, a royal ship, of between one hundred and eighty and two hundred tons, having one hundred persons on board : that is, thirty gentlemen and soldiers, the rest " sufficient and talle sailers"; the GABRIEL, eighteen persons, viz., six soldiers and twelve mariners; the MICHAEL, sixteen persons, viz., five soldiers and eleven seamen.[2]

The ships sailed from Blackwall on Whitsunday, the 26th of May, 1577. They arrived at the *Orkney islands* on the 7th of the following month ; and the manners of the inhabitants are described in the following not very flattering terms :

[1] MSS. ut suprà.

[2] The particulars are as follow :

Aboord the AYDE was	*Generall* of the whole company for her Maiesty	Martin Frobisher.
	His Lieutenant . . .	George Best.
	His Ensigne	Richard Philpot.
	Corporall of the shott .	Francis Forder.
	The rest of the Gentlemen	Henry Carew. Edmund Stafford. John Lee. M. Harnie. Mathew Kinersly. Abraham Lins. Robert Kinersly. Francis Brakenbury. William Armshow.
	The Maister	Christopher Hall.
	The Mate	Charles Jackman.
	The Pylot	Andrew Dier.
	The Maister gunner . .	Richard Cox.
Aboord the GABRIEL was	*Captaine*	Edward Fenton.
	One Gentleman . . .	William Tanfield.
	The Maister	William Smyth.
Aboord the MICHAEL was	*Captaine*	Gilbert Yorke.
	One Gentleman . . .	Thomas Chamberlaine.
	The Maister	James Beare.

"Their houses are builded of Pibble stone, without chimneis, the fire being made in the middest thereof. The good-man, wife, children, and other of their family, eate and sleepe on the one side of the house, and the cattell on the other. Very beastly and rudely in respect of civilitie. They are destitute of wood; their fires are turffes and cowshards. . . . . . Their houses are but poore without, and sluttish ynough within; and the people, in nature, thereunto agreeable. They have great want of leather, and desire our old shoes and apparrell, and old ropes (before money), for victuals; and yet they are not ignorant of the value of our coine".

The 4th of July, in lat. 60° 30′ N. they again fell in with the land denominated FRIESLAND. On this occasion Frobisher had with him "a card" of the coast, made by the two Venetians, Nicolaus and Antonius Zeni.[1] He compared the card with the coast, and found them "very agreeable".

July the 16th the expedition arrived off the mouth of FROBISHER'S STRAITS. No mention is made, in this voyage, of the foreland described in the first voyage as being in lat. 63° 8′ N. The QUEEN'S CAPE, lat. 62° 30′, is represented to form the southernmost point of the entrance, and a piked island to form the northernmost point. This island, in lat. 62° 50′ N., was called by the name of HALL, after one of the masters, who was present when the stone, supposed to be gold ore, was found last year.

Although Frobisher continued in the straits till the 23rd of August, he made little progress in exploring them. The utmost extent of his navigation was thirty leagues. His commission, it seems, "directed him, in this voyage, onely for the searching of the ore, and to deferre the further discovery of the passage untill another time".

The period which was included between the 16th of July and the 23rd of August, was spent in traversing the country

[1] A narrative of their voyage is to be found in *Hakluyt*, vol. iii.

for gold : in collecting what appeared to contain the precious
metal ; and in combating with the aborigines. In one of the
skirmishes two females were captured. One was aged : the
other was a young mother, with an infant. The elder of the
twain, with little observance of courtesy styled the " old
wretch", was suspected by many of the sailors to be either a
devil or a witch ; and her buskins were pulled off, to ascertain whether she had cloven feet or not. Proving to be only
of an " oughly hew " (it may be presumed, ill-featured), she
was dismissed. The child of the younger captive had been
wounded by a chance shot from a caliver, and the surgeon
applied salves. Thereon was exhibited, what is termed in a
marginal note, "a pretty kind of surgery, which nature teach-
eth". Not understanding the intentions of the surgeon, the
mother "plucked those salves away ; and, by continuall lick-
ing with her owne tongue, not much vnlike vnto a dogge,
healed up the child's arme". This captive is not represented
to have been of " oughly hew ". She was detained.

For the reason before stated, little was effected during this
voyage, for the extension of discovery ; but the following
places were named in addition to those visited in the former
voyage. On the south side of the straits, MOUNT WARWICK
and JACKMAN'S SOUND ; on the north side, BEARE'S SOUND,
LEICESTER'S ISLAND, and the COUNTESS of WARWICK'S SOUND
and ISLAND.

On the way home, if the narrator may be credited, occurred one of those singular coincidences which afford food for
the distempered imaginations of the superstitious. " The
30th of August, with the force of the wind, and a surge of
the sea, the master of the Gabriel, and the boatswain, were
stricken both over boord ; and hardly was the boatswain
recovered, hauing hold on a rope hanging over boord in the
sea ; and yet the bark was laced fore and after, with ropes a
breast high within boorde. This master was called William
Smith, being but a yong man, and a very sufficient mariner ;

D

who, being all the morning before exceeding pleasant, told his captaine he dreamed that he was cast over boord ; and that the boatswain had him by the hand, and could not saue him. And so, immediately vpon the end of his tale, his dreame came right euilly to passe ; and indeed, the boatswain, in like sort, held him by one hand, hauing hold on rope with the other, vntill his force fayled, and the master was drowned."

The 1st of September, a violent storm arose, and the ships were in great danger. " Lying a hull ", in order not to outstrip her consorts, a precaution which proved futile, the Aid was most grievously buffeted by the waves.   Threatened, momentarily, to be overtaken and overwhelmed by the tremendous sea that was running, they were constrained, at length, "with a hoist of their sail, to try it out, and ease the rolling of the ship".   The following day proved calm ; and search being made to ascertain what damage had been sustained, it was found that the rudder was "reft in twain, and almost ready to fall away".   Though somewhat dismayed, the stout mariners did not allow their energies to be damped by this discovery.   Advantage was at once taken of the weather : "they flung[1] half-a-dozen couple of the best men overboard, who, taking great pains, vnder water, driuing plank, and binding with ropes, did well mend and strengthen the matter "; though the most part returned more than half dead out of the water.

The Voyage terminated by the arrival of the AID at Milford Haven on the 23rd of September ; by the arrival of the GABRIEL at Bristol about the same time ; and by the MICHAEL getting safe to some place in the north.[2]

On the return of the expedition, the subject was submitted to " special commissioners, chosen for this purpose : gentlemen of great judgment, art, and skill ; to look thorowly into the cause, for the true triall and due examination thereof, and

---

[1] ? *slung*.

[2] Narratives by Masters Dionise Settle and Best.—*Hakluyt*, vol. iii, pp. 56-65 ; 88-104.

for the full handling of all matters thereunto appertayning".
The evidence on which the decision of these gentlemen was
founded, is not recorded; and it is uncertain whether their
art did not exceed the judgment and skill they were presumed to possess.   However this may be, the commission
decided, "that the matter of the gold ore had appearance,
and made show, of great riches and profit; and the hope of
the passage to Cataya, by this voyage, was greatly increased".
The Queen's Majesty adopted the opinion of the commissioners, or, the commissioners had anticipated the opinion of
the Queen's Majesty; and a new expedition was ordered to
be set forth.   The object of this expedition was to colonize
the newly-discovered territory, which Elizabeth herself named
"Meta incognita".   Before their departure, the general and
all the captains appeared at court, to take their leave of the
Queen; at whose hands, on that occasion, they received great
encouragement and gracious countenance.   Frobisher was
especially noticed.   Besides " other good gifts, and greater
promises, a faire chaine of golde " was bestowed on him :
which seems rather a superfluous gift, when it is considered
on what an expedition he was bound, and what riches, it was
imagined, he would obtain.

3RD VOYAGE, }   The third expedition, consisting of fifteen
  A.D. 1578. }   sail of ships,[1] assembled at Harwich on the
27th of May 1578; and sailed on the 30th of the same month.

---

[1] The names of the vessels, and of their commanders, were as follow, viz.:

1. In the AYDE, *being Admirall, was the Generall*	Frobisher.
2. In the THOMAS ALLEN, *Vice-Admirall* .	Yorke.
3. In the JUDITH, *Lieutenant-Generall* . .	Fenton
4. In the *Anne Francis*	Best
5. In the *Hopewell*	Carew.
6. In the *Beare*	Filpot.
7. In the *Thomas of Ipswich* . . .	Tanfield.
8. In the *Emmanuel of Exeter* . . .	}Captaine{ Courtney.
9. In the *Francis of Foy*	Moyles.
10. In the *Moone*	Vpcot.
11. In the *Emmanuel of Bridgewater* . .	Newton.
12. In the *Salomon of Weymouth* . . .	Randal.
13. In the *Barke Dennis*	Kendal.
14. In the *Gabriel*	Haruey.
15. In the *Michael*	Kinnersly.

The 20th of June, WEST FRIESLAND was fallen in with : taken formal possession of for the English crown; and re-named WEST ENGLAND. Leaving this part, a high cliff, the last in sight, was, on account of "a certaine similitude, called CHARING CROSSE". Ten days afterwards, "the Salamander, being under both her corses and bonets, happened to strike a great whale with her full stemme, with such a blow, that the ship stoode still, and stirred neither forward or back-ward. The whale thereat made a great and ugly noyse, and cast up his body and taile, and so went under water". Some days after, a carcase was fallen in with, supposed to be that of the whale which had been struck by the Salamander.

As in the case of the first and second voyages performed by Frobisher, there are two narratives of the third voyage. The two accounts differ materially. According to the repre-sentation of THOMAS ELLIS, one of the narrators, the general and the majority of the fleet were knocking about in the straits for a considerable period. According to the other narrator, MASTER BEST (the general's lieutenant), they, for some time, "mistooke the place", Frobisher being the first to perceive the error : "yet he perswaded the fleete always that they were in the right course and knowen straights": dissembling his opinion to induce the people not to abandon the enterprise. The fleet, however, congregated by degrees ; and towards the middle of August they were all safely an-chored in the Countess of Warwick's Sound, with the excep-tion of two vessels : the bark Dennis, which had foundered ; and the Thomas of Ipswich, which had furtively sailed for England.

The period intervening between the 2nd of July, when the expedition was supposed to be off the mouth of Frobisher's straits, and the middle of August, when the fleet assembled in the Countess of Warwick's Sound, proved an interval of fearful peril, which was only equalled by the courage, perse-verance, and steady endurance of the people.

The first misadventure was the loss of the bark Dennis, of a hundred tons. This vessel "received such a blow from a rock of yce, that she sunk down therewith in sight of the whole fleet"; but her crew were saved by the ready succour given by the boats of the other ships. Presently following this fearful catastrophe, which was viewed by the fleet as an ill-omen, a "sudden terrible tempest" arose from south-east, the wind blowing from the main sea. Weathering the tempest, the ships became encompassed on every side by ice, "having left much behind them, thorow which they had passed, and finding more before them, thorow which they could not passe"; while the pressure of the ice, occasioned by the force of the wind, prevented them from putting back. In this hazardous situation, different men resorted to different means to secure their safety. "Some of the ships, where they could find a place more cleare of yce, and get a little berth of sea roome, did take in their sayles, and there lay adrift; other some fastened and moored anker upon a great island of yce; and againe, some were so fast shut up, and compassed in amongst an infinite number of great countreys and islands of yce, that they were faine to submit themselves and their ships to the mercy of the unmerciful ice, and strengthened the sides of their ships with junk of cables, beds, masts, planks, and such like, which being hanged overboord, on the sides of their ships, might better defend them from the outrageous sway and strokes of the said yce".

This state of imminent peril was well calculated to test the skill of the captains and the temper of the people. Neither of the parties were found wanting. Full and impressive testimony is borne to this fact by an eye-witness, a participator in the dire struggle for life against death in a most appalling form. Captain Best, in his narrative of the voyage, states : "But as in greatest distresse, men of best valor are best to be discerned, so is it greatly worthy commendation and noting, with what invincible minde every captaine encouraged

his company, and with what incredible labour the painefull
mariners and poore miners (unacquainted with such extremities), to the everlasting renowne of our nation, did overcome
the brunt of these so great and extreme dangers ; for some
even without boord, upon the yce, and some within boord,
upon the sides of their ships, having poles, pikes, pieces of
timber, and ores, in their hands, stood almost day and night
without any rest, bearing off the force, and breaking the
sway of the yce, with such incredible paine and perill, that
it was wonderfull to beholde".[1] But for the extraordinary
and unceasing exertions of the crews, it is represented that
the ships would have " been stricken through and through
their sides ", notwithstanding the provision that had been
made against such a casualty, and which did actually happen
to one of the ships separated from the fleet. In corrobora-
tion of this representation, it is related, that "plankes of
timber of more than three inches thick, and other things of
great force and bignesse, by the surging of the sea and billowe, with the yce, were shivered and cut in sunder at the
sides of the ships; so that it would seeme more than credible
to be reported of ".   And in further illustration of the dan-

[1] On the 6th of August 1818 (lat. 75° 50'.30" N.; long. 64° 47'.00" W.;
var. 90° 32'.00" W.), the *Isabella*, commanded by *Captain John Ross*, and
the *Alexander*, commanded by *Lieutenant William Edward Parry*, were
placed in circumstances of peril remarkably similar to those encountered
by the fleet under *Sir Martin Frobisher ;* and the similarity of the conduct of the officers and crews, at both periods, is no less remarkable. The
commander of the modern expedition, *Sir John Ross*, with a just and
generous spirit, such as characterized his predecessor *Master Captain Best,*
bears emphatic testimony to the zeal and activity of all hands under the
severest fatigues, and to their patience and fortitude under the most trying circumstances. The result also of the indomitable perseverance and
courage displayed on both occasions was the same. Like the gallant men
of the sixteenth, they of the nineteenth century " did overcome the brunt
of these so great and extreme dangers": adding another to the numerous
instances in which the British mariner has contributed " to the everlasting renowne of our nation".—See *Ross's Voyage to Baffin's Bay*, pp. 75-
79 (Lond. 1819).

gerous position of the vessels, an appeal is made to "substantiall witnesses, who can faithfully and plainly prove that the ships, even of the greatest burdens, with the meeting of contrary waves of the sea, were heaved up betweene islands of yce, a foot wel-neere, out of the sea above their water-marke, having their knees and timbers within boord, both bowed and broken therewith". The precarious situation in which the vessels were placed, justifies the writer's concluding remark, that "he that held himself in best securitie, had (God knoweth) but onely bare hope remayning for his best safetie". By the next day, however, four ships had succeeded in extricating themselves from the ice, and were riding in comparatively clear water. They rejoiced fervently at their own release; but were in sorrow and fear for the safety of their fellows; "and devoutly kneeling about their main mast, they gave unto God humble thanks, not only for themselves, but besought Him likewise highly for their friendes deliverance". The hour was nearer at hand than the anxious people contemplated. "Even whilest amiddest these extremities, this gallant fleete and valiant men were altogether overlaboured and forewatched, with the long and fearefull continuance of the foresayd dangers, it pleased God, with His eyes of mercy, to looke downe from heaven, to send them help in good time; giving them, the next day, a more favorable winde, at the west-north-west, which did not only disperse and drive forth the yce before, but also gave them liberty of more scope and sea-roome; and they were, by night of the same day following, perceived of the other four ships, where (to their greatest comfort) they enjoyed the fellowship one of another". Then ensued a scene which is thus graphically described : " Some in mending the sides of their ships, some in setting up their top masts and mending their sayles and tacklings; againe, some complayning of their false stemme borne away, some in stopping their leakes, some in recounting their dangers past, spent no small time and labour ".

Some days after the fleet had escaped from the perilous
scenes which have been described, they came into a locality,
the whereabouts of which they were unable to determine;
but in which a tremendous current from the north-east was
encountered.   According to Master Best's representation,
" truely it was wonderfull to heare and see the rushing and
noise that the tides did make in that place; with so violent
a force, that the ships, lying a hull, were turned sometimes
round about, even in a moment, after the manner of a whirl-
pool ; and *the noyse of the streame no lesse to be heard afarre
off, than the waterfall of London Bridge*".[1]

With the above incident, the adventures of the fleet, in
the aggregate, may be considered to have terminated; but
the people of individual ships had their particular trials and
sufferings. Those of the JUDITH and the captain of the ANNE
FRANCIS are worthy of being cited.

The JUDITH was commanded by CAPTAIN FENTON, the lieutenant-general of the fleet.   She parted company from the
ships about the first day of July ; and the captain reported,
on rejoining the fleet, that, "from that day to the 26th of the
same month, they never saw any one day or houre wherein
they were not troubled with continuall danger and feare of
death ; and were twentie dayes, almost together, fast among
the yce.   They had their ship stricken through and through
on both sides, their false stemme borne quite away, and could
goe from their ship, in some places, upon the yce very many
miles; and might easily have passed from one iland of yce to
another, even to the shore ; and if God had not wonderfully
provided for them and their necessitie, and time had not
made them more cunning and wise to seeke strange reme-
dies for strange kindes of dangers, it had bene impossible
for them ever to have escaped : for among other devices,
wheresoever they found any iland of yce of greater bignesse

---

[1] See Davis, 3rd Voyage, 29th and 31st of July, 1587.

then the rest, they commonly coveted to recover the same, and thereof to make a bulwarke for their defence; whereon having mored anker, they rod under the lee thereof for a time, being thereby guarded from the danger of the lesser driving yce. But when they must foregoe this new-found fort, by meanes of other yce, which at length would undermine and compasse them round about; and when that, by heaving of the billowe, they were therewith like to be brused in peces, they used to make the ship fast to the most firme and broad pece of yce they could find, and binding her nose fast thereunto, would fill all their sayles; whereon, the wind, having great power, would force forward the ship, so the ship bearing before her the yce; and so one yce, driving forward another, should at length get scope and sea roome. Having, by this meanes, at length put their enemies to flight, they occupyed the cleare space for a prettie season, among sundry mountaines and Alpes of yce". One, it is stated, was found, by measure, to be sixty-five fathoms above water, and, "for a kind of similitude, was called Solomon's porch"; and it was conjectured by some, that these islands, on account of the enormous weight which was to be supported above, must be eight times their height under water.

During his wanderings in company with the Moon, CAP-TAIN BEST, of the ANNE FRANCIS, discovered "a great blacke island, where was found such plenty of black ore of the same sort which was brought into England this last yeere, that, if the goodnesse might answere the great plentie thereof, it was thought it might reasonably suffice all the *golde-gluttons* of the worlde". From this circumstance the island was named BEST's BLESSING. In entering the bay in which the island was situated, the Anne Francis, notwithstanding the precaution had been taken of sending a boat before to sound, struck on a sunken rock, and heeled over so much, that it was necessary to "undersette" her with the mainyard, to

E

prevent a total capsize. The Moon came in safely, and was of great service to the distressed ship.

Aboard the Anne Francis were some materials for the construction of a pinnace; but "they wanted two especiall and most necessarie things, that is, certaine principal tymbers that are called 'knees', which are the chiefest strength of any boate; and also nayles". Nevertheless, it was determined that, while the sailors were "romaging" their ships, and the miners engaged in collecting ore, the carpenters should do their best in setting up the boat. By good chance there was a smith amongst the company, though unfurnished with the necessary tools to make the coveted article of nails. However ingenuity triumphed over this difficulty. "They were faine, of a gunne chamber, to make an anvil to worke upon, and to use a pickaxe instead of a sledge, to beate withall; and also to occupy two small bellowes, instead of one payre of greater smith's bellowes. And for lacke of small yron for the easier making of the nayles, they were forced to breake their tongs, grydiron, and fireshovell, in pieces". This work commenced on the 10th of August. On the 18th, the "pinnesse, with much adoe, being set together, the said Captaine Best determined to depart up the straights" (at the entrance of which they were lying), "as before was pretended: some of his companie greatly persuading him to the contrary, and specially the carpenter that set the same together; who sayde, that he would not adventure himselfe therein for five hundreth pounds, for that the boate hung together but onely by the strength of the nayles, and lacked some of her principal knees and tymbers". But the captain was resolute. He expressed his determination to enter on the undertaking, and appealed to the crew to join with him. His appeal was not in vain. "The master's mate of the Anne Francis, called JOHN GRAY, manfully and honestly offering himself unto his captaine in this adventure and service, gave cause to others of his mariners to follow the

attempt". Master Captain Best, the promoter and chronicler
of the enterprise, displays a noble spirit in the unostenta-
tious manner in which he states his own share in the service,
in his hearty commendation of his gallant and willing asso-
ciate, and in recording for the information of posterity the
name of *manful and honest John Gray.*

On the 19th, Captain Best, accompanied by CAPTAIN UPCOT
of the MOON, a worthy compeer, and eighteen hands, embarked in the "small pinnisse", in prosecution of the hazardous voyage that was in contemplation. "Having onely the
helpe of man's labour with ores", and encountering much
difficulty and danger in forcing their way through ice, they
accomplished, by the 22nd of August, between forty and
fifty leagues; and entered, as they imagined, the Countess
of Warwick's Sound; but the identity of the place is not
clear. Wherever they were, however, a variety of circumstances concurred to involve them in sore perplexity. On
landing, the adventurers found great stones set up, as it
seemed, by the natives for marks. They also found crosses
of stone, as if Christian people had been there. Re-embark-
ing, and pulling along the shore, they noticed the smoke of
a fire under a hill's side: "whereof they diversely deemed".
Human figures then appeared in the distance; but too far
off to be distinguished. Drawing nearer, the people ashore
wafted, or seemed to waft, a flag: but the natives were wont
to do the same when they saw a strange boat. Anon, the
perplexed mariners perceived certain tents; and they made
the ensign to be "of mingled colours, black and white, after
the English fashion". This discovery rather increased than
diminished their amazement. No ship was to be seen: no
harbourage was known of in the vicinity. Besides, it was
not the practice of the English to visit those parts. Apprehension ensued. It was feared that, by storms, some ship
had been driven up: or, in some dense fog, had missed the
way; that the people had been wrecked and spoiled by the

natives; by whom, it was conjectured, might be "used the sundry-coloured flagge for a policie to bring others within their danger". The resolution of the party was immediately taken. "They determined to recover the same ensigne, if it were so, from the base people, or els to lose their lives, and all together". But, "in the ende, they discerned them to be their countreymen; and then they deemed them to have lost their ships, and so to be gathered together for their better strength". On the other hand, "the companie ashoare feared that the captaine, having lost his ship, came to seeke forth the fleete for his reliefe in his poor pinnesse. So that their extremities caused eche parte to suspect the worst". Under these circumstances, Captain Best took the precautions which prudence dictated. On nearing the shore, he "commanded his boate carefully to be kepte aflote, lest, in their necessitie, they might winne the same from him, and seeke first to save themselves; for every man, in that case, is next himself". But no strife, he observes, followed the meeting of the two parties. On the contrary, unbounded delight predominated. "They haled one another according to the manner of the sea, and demanded, *What cheer?* and either party answered the other, that *all was well*: whereupon there was a sudden and ioyfull outshoote, with great flinging up of caps, and a brave voly of shotte, to welcome one another. And truly," it is observed, "it was a most strange case to see how ioyfull and gladde every partie was to see themselves meete in safetie againe, after so strange and incredible dangers: "yet, to be short", the narrator devoutly remarks, "as their dangers were great, so their God was greater".

Having proceeded so far in company with the "poore pinnisse", the reader will probably take an interest in her fate. She foundered at sea, under the following circumstances. Arrangements having been made for the departure of the fleet to England, a terrific storm occurred on the eve of their

sailing, by which all the ships but three were driven from
their moorings; and, with one exception, all the vessels that
got to sea, took the opportunity of making the best of their
way home.   The vessels left behind, were the Gabriel, the
Michael, and the Busse of Bridgewater. The following morning the Gabriel departed with the general, the tempest yet
raging, in search of the fleet.   The Busse of Bridgewater,
hampered among rocks and ice, was unable to move.   The
Michael was well afloat.   Most of the company of the Anne
Francis were ashore, and the commander had landed to take
them off; but his intention was frustrated by the storm.
He was thus left "in hard election of two evils : eyther to
abide his fortune with the Busse of Bridgwater, which was
doubtfull of ever setting forth; or else to be towed, in his
small pinnisse, at the sterne of the Michael, thorow the raging seas; for the barke was not able to receive, or relieve,
halfe his companie".   This undertaking was not a little perilous in itself; but Captain Best had to encounter the additional risk of missing his vessel, tempest-tossed on the waste
of waters.   He made his election : that was, "to commit
himself, with all his companie, unto that fortune of God and
sea; and was dangerously towed at the sterne of the barke
for many myles, untill they espyed, at length, the Anne
Francis under sayle, hard under their lee; which was no
small comfort to them", as may be readily supposed.   The
crew of the pinnace were indebted for their preservation to
the praiseworthy conduct of the officer in charge of the vessel
they were seeking; and his commander bestows his commendation on him in the following terms: "The honest care
had by the master of the Anne Francis of his captaine, and
the good regard he had of duetie towardes his generall, suffered him not to depart; and he honestly abode to hazard
a dangerous roade all night long, notwithstanding all the
stormy weather, when all the fleete besides departed".   Most
narrow was the escape experienced by the adventurous crew

embarked in the frail craft : for, "the pinnesse came no sooner aboord the ship, and the men entred, but she presently shivered and fell in pieces, and sunke at the ship's sterne, with all the poore men's furniture. .... But (as God would) the men were all saved".

The date on which the majority of the fleet were blown to sea, was the 31st of August. After a tempestuous passage, in which many of the ships "were dangerously distressed, and severed allmost all asunder", the whole arrived safe at home, in different ports, and at different times : the last on the 1st of October 1578.[1]

In point of discoveries, this voyage, like the former, proved a decided failure. The only new places seen, were HATTON's HEADLAND and BEST's BLESSING, in close vicinity. Both these places were first visited by Captain Best; who also expresses his conviction of there being no such continent as that called "Meta Incognita". He alleges, that what was deemed to be a continent, was, really, an aggregation of "broken lands and islands, which being very many in number, do seem to make an archipelagus". A passenger on board the Busse of Bridgewater, however, reported on his arrival in England, that, to the south-east of Friesland, in lat. 57° 30′ N., a large island had been fallen in with, and coasted for three days. It was represented to contain fine champaign country; to be fertile and well wooded.[2]

[1] Narratives by *Thomas Ellis* and *Captain Best.—Hakluyt,* vol. iii, pp. 65-70 ; 104-129.

[2] A report of *Thomas Wiars* . . . "concerning the discoverie of a great island in their way homeward, the 12th of September 1578."—*Hakluyt,* vol. iii, p. 70. "On this authority", *Barrow* observes, "the island was laid down on our charts ; but it was never afterwards seen, and certainly does not exist ; though a bank has recently been sounded upon, which has revived the idea of the Friesland of Zeno, and the Busse of Bridgewater having been swallowed up by an earthquake".—*Arctic Voyages,* 1818, p. 94.

Ross (Voyage of 1818, p. 25 : Lond. 1819) remarks : " At noon [May 16th] we found ourselves exactly in the latitude of the *sunken land of Busse,* as it is laid down in some charts, 57° 28′ N. ; and being desirous

With regard to its main object, the discovery of gold-ore, this voyage also proved abortive ; and a character who has appeared with prominence during the course of the action, is introduced at its close, under very pitiable circumstances.

In a distressingly desponding letter, dated the 16th of November [——], and addressed from " *The Fleete pryson in London* " to some person unknown, MICHAEL LOK represents himself, with a family of fifteen children, to be involved in irremediable ruin ; and his ruin he attributes to breaches of faith, in various particulars, on the part of Sir Martin Frobisher : a man, he observes, whose interests he had zealously been striving to promote for a space of about six years. Lok specifically charges Frobisher with having failed to perform an engagement he contracted, to bring home, on the third voyage, five hundred tons of " a rich red ore ", a sample of which, procured the voyage before, had " yeelded 120lb. a tonn " [? of metal].   From remarks which follow, it may be inferred, though the fact is not distinctly stated, that Lok had entered into bonds for sums of money raised to forward the adventure, in the expectation of being provided with means to meet the claims ; and those means failing him, through the non-performance of Frobisher's engagement, he

of determining whether such a bank really existed in long. 29° 45′ [W.], we altered our course, being then in 28° 20′, to N. W., for the purpose of ascertaining the fact. We made all sail a-head, kept a good look-out, with the lead constantly going ; and at sun-set, being near the spot, shortened sail, and hove to, in order to sound ; but found no bottom in one hundred and eighty fathoms.   This we repeated every four miles, with no better success ; and . . . . being then thirty miles past the spot marked out for this sunken land, we made all sail, but kept the lead constantly going ". It is added, " the existence of this bank has long been doubted by the masters of Greenlandmen ; and certainly it is not to be found where laid down in the charts.   Various stories respecting it were related by people on board ; but it appeared, on comparing their testimonies, that no soundings had actually been found.   I am more inclined to imagine, that when the ships have been struck in this quarter by heavy seas, the shocks have erroneously been attributed to the sunken land of Busse."

was subjected to actions at law, followed by incarceration, from which he despaired of being released. Of the wretched condition to which Lok was reduced, no reasonable doubt can be entertained; but of the causes of his misery there are no means of forming a correct opinion; and there is nothing besides the representations of the unhappy man, to indicate that Frobisher contributed, in any degree, to his sufferings.[1]

PROJECTED FOURTH VOYAGE UNDER FROBISHER.

A.D. 1581. Included among the manuscript documents in the British Museum, connected with the North-west passage, already cited, are various notes and memoranda connected with a voyage of discovery intended to be made in some direction which is not specified ; but, from certain circumstances, it may be inferred they relate to a projected fourth voyage towards the North-west under the command of Sir Martin Frobisher. The circumstances are: the arrangement of the papers, combined with the interest taken in the project by Frobisher ; by his former Lieutenant-General, Fenton ; and by other parties, who, it may reasonably be presumed, were engaged in promoting the preceding undertakings, in which those navigators were employed. Positive evidence of the fact is nevertheless wanting, and the researches of some future inquirer may prove the opinion now expressed to be erroneous. Yet, lest information should be omitted by rejecting the supposition, the substance of the documents is communicated.

Among the papers above alluded to, there are lists of pro-

---

[1] MSS. ut suprà. During the second voyage made by Davis, "mountaines" of the supposed gold-ore were seen ; but the "glistering" deception was passed by unheeded. The illusion was dissipated.

MAMMON. *Is no projection left ?*
FACE.   *All flown, or stinks, sir.*

ALCHEMIST.

visions, and stores,[1] with an armament to consist of "four demy culverins; twelve sakers; eight mynions; one faulcon; two fowlers; forty caliuers; twenty-three barrills of Turkish powlder; shott of all sort; and ffyrworks; with other provision of Govnners stores."

The ships named to be employed, are: "THE MARY EDWARDES to be sett forth [by AL]DREMAN MARTINE and his COSS[IN]; the galeon OUGHTREDE £5000[....]; the NEWE BARKE, by estimate, furnisht victuell and men, £400": with an additional allowance, of £100, for one hundred quarters of wheat; and the bark TALBOT. This vessel was valued at £600, and the EARL of SHREWSBURY, the owner, engaged to place her at the disposal of the adventurers for half that sum, together with £500 in money: making a contribution in the aggregate of £800.

The cost of the fitting out of the "Oughtrede" and the "New Barke", would in great part be defrayed, it was calculated, thus:

"Therle of Leyr. [Leicester] and Mr. Vghtrede	3000 *li*.
Erle of Oxforde	500
E. of Lincoln	100
E. of Pembroke	200
E. of Warwicke	200
Lord Howarde	200
L. Hunsdon	200
Sir Chr. Hatton	200
Sir Fr. Walsingham . . .	200
Captn. Smythe	200
Captn. Burde	100
Captn. Frobisher	300
Edw. Fenton and his friendes . .	300
Sir Fr. Drake	700
Luke Warde	200 "

By the fragment of a letter, which escaped the ravages of a fire, to which, with the rest of the documents that have

---

[1] These documents are not in sufficient detail to enable a table of prices to be framed.

been cited, it was exposed, Sir Francis Drake appears to have
been a warm promoter of the enterprise. This letter is addressed to the Earl of Leicester, and is dated the 14th of
October 1581. The substance of the first portion is expressive
of the interest taken by the writer in the expedition, and his
ardent desire for its good success. To further the objects of
the undertaking, he offers to supply Sir Martin Frobisher
with sufficient men of his late company, that "have some
experience that waie"; and to contribute in money, one thousand marks, although he says it will somewhat try his credit,
"as now greatly indepted". Sir Francis proceeds to say, that,
should his Lordship will him to provide a ship, there is one
fitted for the action, "beinge at least 180 tunns burdẽ";
and he adds, "I will beare the aduenture of on[e] thousand
pounds, and furnishe her verie sufficientlie in verie short
time, so that there maie be ord^r geuẽ for the ouerplus of her
charge; but yf y^r L. wth Mr. Ffrobusher thinke but to haue
the little newe barke and the 2 pinñces, I will bestowe the
like aduenture therein, and uppõ yor aduise geven, I will
haue the [? ship] shethed ppared & furnished wth sufficient
pvisions to yor good likingè: whervppõ I will gladlie attend
yor aunswer herein, for that I am verie desirous to show that
dutifull service I can possiblie do in any acc̃on y^r good L.
vouchsavith to vse me; and, for y^t I am willinge to follow
the directiõ of y^r L. and Mr. Ffrobusher in eve^{r}y respect, I
shall p^y y^t som on maie be sent downe" [. . . .]. After some
lines, the sense of which is destroyed, the letter concludes
with a general assurance of the interest taken in the matter
by the writer.

The above, is the last notice that has been traced of the
intended proceedings.

§ III.

The Voyages of Master John Davis.

In the year of grace 1585, certain honourable personages and worthy gentlemen of the court and country, together with divers worshipful merchants of London and the west country, moved, it is said, by the desire of advancing God's glory and the good of their native land, associated themselves to consult on the probability of discovering the much-desired passage to the North-west. They decided, that the efforts hitherto made had failed, not from the impracticability of the design, but through neglect of the main objects of the enterprise; and they therefore determined to renew the attempt.

To carry into effect this determination, two barks were purchased. One of them, named THE SUNSHINE, of *fifty tons* burden, had a crew of twenty-three persons on board, including four musicians; the other, called THE MOONSHINE, of *thirty-five tons,* had a complement of nineteen hands. MASTER[1] JOHN DAVIS, of Sandridge in Devonshire, "a man well grounded in the principles of the Arte of Navigation", was selected "for Captaine and chiefe Pilot of this exployt"; and he had WILLIAM ESTON for his master. The captain of the Moonshine was WILLIAM BRUTON: his master, JOHN ELLIS.

---

[1] This "respective" title is retained: that of "Mister" being inappropriate to the period:

> "your father was
> An honest country farmer, *goodman* Humble,
> By his neighbours *ne'er call'd Master.*"

> *City Madam* (MASSINGER), 1632.

The Sunshine and her consort sailed from Dartmouth on the 7th of June. For some time foul winds were encountered, which opposed the progress of the vessels, and compelled them, twice, to put into Scilly. On the second occasion they were detained twelve days; but the time cannot be considered to have been unprofitably spent. M. Davis, accompanied by his master and the merchant (MASTER JOHN JANES),[1] "went about all the islands; and the captaine did plot out and describe their situation, rocks, and harboroughs, to the exact vse of Navigation, with lines and scale thereunto conuenient".

At length, the weather having moderated and the wind being fair, they started for a full due on the 28th. During their progress they fell in with vast quantities of porpoises. The master "shot at them with harping-yrons (harpoons); but the fishes were so great, that they burst the yrons". Then a pike was tried: of which "the barres were also burst off". Finally, recourse was had to a boat-hook, though with no good success. So, sport failing, the fish escaping, and the weapons being spoiled, the porpoises were let alone. "A darbie-head" was, however, caught and boiled; and "did eate as sweete as any mutton". Between the 16th and the 18th great numbers of whales were also seen.

On the 19th of July, "a great whirling and brustling of a tyde" was encountered, followed by a very calm sea. Then was "heard a mighty great roaring of the sea, as if it had bene the breach of some shoare". At this time a dense fog prevailed; so thick, that neither ship could discern the other, though they were not far asunder. Uncertainty, too, prevailed regarding the tides, and the navigators became appre-

---

[1] *M. John Janes*, " a man of good observation ", accompanied Davis in his second and third voyages. For " his sake " he also joined the expedition intended for the South Seas, the Phillipines, and China, anno 1591 : of which *Master Thomas Candish, Esquire*, was admiral ; and *Captaine M. John Davis*, rear-admiral.—*Hakluyt*, vol. iv, p. 361.

hensive : although, on sounding, no bottom could be found with three hundred fathoms of line. So a boat was "hoysed" out; and on rowing towards the "breach", it was discovered that the noise was occasioned by the rolling and grinding together of huge masses of ice. When the boat returned to the ship, the course was shaped northerly.

Next day a land-fall was made, at five hundred leagues from the Durseys, west-north-west-northerly. This land presented the appearance of a mass of stupendous mountains enveloped in snow. Neither wood, nor grass, nor earth, was visible. For two leagues off, the sea was so pestered with ice, firmly packed, that not even a boat could effect an entrance. " The lothsome view of this shore", Davis remarks, "and the irksome noyse of the yce was such, as it bred strange conceites among vs : so that we supposed the place to be wast[e] and voyd of any sensible or vegitable creatures, whereupon I called the same DESOLATION".

The locality thus indicated, is not, however, to be confounded with the CAPE DESOLATION of the modern charts ; but agrees rather with CAPE DISCORD, on the east side of Greenland, which, from what follows, it is evident the navigator had made.

The following day the wind veered to the northward; and with the change in the wind, the course of the ship was altered. " So coasting ", Davis observes in continuation, " this shore towards the South, in the latitude of sixtie degrees, I found it trend towards the West.[1] I still followed the leading thereof in the same height; and after fifty or sixtie leagues, it fayled, and lay directly North, which I still followed, and in thirty leagues sayling vpon the West side of this coast, named by me Desolation, we were past all the yce, and found many greene and pleasant Iles bordering vpon the shore ; but

[1] That is on rounding CAPE FAREWELL : " in lat. 59° 45' N., and long. 47° 56' W., according to Captain Upton."—Ross (John) Voyage to Buffin's Bay, 1818. London, 1819 : p. 224.

the hils of the maine were still couered with great quantities
of snow. *I brought my ship among those Isles, and there
moored,* to refresh our selues in our weary trauell, *in the
latitude of sixtie foure degrees* or thereabout. During their
progress to this spot, which was named GILBERT'S SOUND,
they passed through water, "very blacke and thicke, like
to a filthy standing poole", with soundings at one hundred
and twenty fathoms. On one day, the 22nd, they saw woods,
like those on Newfoundland, and met with much timber
adrift. One tree picked up by the Moonshine, had the root
attached, and was sixty feet long, with "fourteen handes
about". The 27th the weather is represented as not being
very cold; the air moderate, as in England in April; but
variable, according to the direction from which the wind
might be blowing: warm when it came from sea-ward, and
cool when coming from the land, or over the ice.

At Gilbert's Sound the ships remained from the 29th of
July till the 1st of August. The natives were numerous;
and, on this occasion, proved themselves to be "a very trac-
table people, void of craft or double dealing, and easie to be
brought to any civility or good order". At first, some apprehension was entertained of their intentions when they visited
the ship, but "familiarity" was speedily established. MASTER
ELLIS, who is reported to have been, and appears to have
been, a man of "good policie", carefully observed the gestures they made to invite intercourse, and imitated them not
unsuccessfully. By this means a good feeling was excited,
which was confirmed by the agency of the musicians. Being
brought on shore, they played a lively strain, while the mariners danced to their minstrelsy. The savages, in an extasy,
quickly joined; and, by their strange antics, added not a
little to the merriment of the party. At this anchorage was
plenty of drift wood; and the rocks consisted of "such oare
as M. Frobisher brought from Meta Incognita". There were
also "diuers shewes of study, or Muscovy glass, shining not

altogether unlike chrystall"; and a red fruit was found, sweet, full of red juice, and "the ripe ones like corinths".

On sailing, the course was directed towards the North-west; and on the 6th of August, land was discovered in 66° 40': the STRAITS which bear the name of DAVIS having been crossed. The locality in which the ships arrived was "alto-gether free from the pester of ice, and they ankered in a very faire rode vnder a brave mount, the cliffes whereof was as orient as golde". It was named MOUNT RALEIGH: where the ships lay, TOTNES ROAD: the water compassing the mount, EXETER SOUND: a foreland towards the north, DYER'S CAPE: and a foreland towards the south, CAPE WALSINGHAM. Whilst remaining here some animals were seen, which were supposed to be goats or wolves, but on nearer inspection, they proved to be "white bears of a monstrous bignesse". They were attacked, and after a sharp fight four of them were killed. The day following another bear was killed, after much shoot-ing with guns and stabbing with pikes; and on measuring one of his fore paws, it was found to be "fourteen inches" from side to side. All these animals were excessively fat. A raven was seen perched on Mount Raleigh, and there were low shrubs growing like "withies"; together with flowers resembling "primroses". The coast is represented to be destitute alike of wood, grass, and earth, and to consist of a hugh mass of rocky mountains; but the narrator observes, "the moun-taines were of the brauest stone that euer we saw".[1]

---

[1] "We found CAPE WALSINGHAM and MOUNT RALEIGH exactly in the latitude in which Davis placed them, and differing only in longitude, like all other places in this part of the world......The *Mount Raleigh* of Davis, which is the easternmost mountain on this side of his strait, is of a pyra-midical form, and exceedingly high; our observation makes it in lat. 66° 37' N., and longitude 61° 14' W. *Cape Walsingham* being in lat. 66° 37' N., and longitude 60° 50' W. [Var. 67° W.], is the easternmost land; and consequently the breadth of Davis' Strait, at its narrowest part, is about one hundred and sixty miles."—*Ross (John) Voyage to Baffin's Bay*, 1818. London, 1819. Pp. 215-216.

" *Sunday, July 4th*, 1819.—At noon we were in lat. 66° 50' 47", long.

Departing from Mount Raleigh, on the 8th, they took a southerly course, and on the 11th of August came to a foreland which was named THE CAPE OF GOD'S MERCY. Davis conceived that by rounding this cape he would come into the passage of which he was in search; and he rounded it accordingly. Steering westward, with land on his north, or starboard side, he sailed through a fine open passage, varying in width from twenty to thirty leagues: which, in a subsequent voyage, was named CUMBERLAND STRAIT.[1] It was entirely free from ice : "the water of the very colour, nature and quality of the main ocean"; and confident hopes were entertained

56° 47′ 56″, being near the middle of the narrowest part of *Davis Strait*; which is here not more than fifty leagues across. Davis, on returning from his third voyage, sets it down at forty leagues [*Nar. in Hakluyt*] , and in another place [*The Worlde's Hydrl. Discy.*] remarks : ' In the latitude of 67° I might see America, west from me ; and Desolation (Greenland), east'. The truth of this last remark has been much doubted, till the observations made on our expedition of 1818, by determining the geographical position of the two coasts thus seen by Davis, seemed to confirm the accuracy of that celebrated and able navigator."—*Parry's Voyage.* London, 1821 : p. 11.

¹ " *October* 1, 1818.—We stood off and on till daylight, when we made all sail for land. At seven we made an island......its latitude answered to EARL WARWICK'S FORELAND (lat. 62° 51¼′ N., long. 61° 12¾′ W.). Between the land seen to the westward of this, and that seen to the north, there was no land ; and we had no doubt but this was CUMBERLAND STRAIT ". Having stated the reasons which prevented him from exploring the Strait, Captain Ross, from whose narrative this note is selected, observes : "I therefore determined on steering for the southernmost land in sight ; we therefore crossed the entrance of Cumberland Strait ; and, making an allowance for indraft, steered about S.S.E." And he adds : " It will appear that, in tracing the land from *Cape Walsingham*, no doubt could be entertained of its continuity until the place where we found *Cumberland Strait* [Oct. 2, lat. 62° 00¼′ N., lat. 62° 25′ W., var. 56° W.], *which is much further south than it was laid down from the latest authorities the Admiralty were in possession of ; but it is very near the place where Davis placed it in his chart*, which has been found since our return ".— *Ross (John) Voyage to Baffin's Bay*, 1818. London, 1819 : pp. 220-222.

Enquiries have been made for the chart alluded to in the above note. The result of the enquiry is : that this interesting document (with many others of value) was *lost* on Sir John Ross's last voyage.—𝕮. 𝕽.

that the desired passage was at length found.   Having accomplished sixty leagues, a cluster of islands was discovered in
the middle of the passage, "with great sounds passing betweene them".   A council was held, and it was decided that
they had arrived at a point from which the enterprise might
be prosecuted with every prospect of success; and that it
should be proceeded in.   However, the weather became dangerously thick, and the wind fell foul, afterwards stormy;
and they were compelled, on the 23rd, to run for shelter.
This they found on the south coast of the straits.   Shortly
after they sailed for England, where they arrived on the 30th
of September.

2ND VOYAGE,   On the 7th May 1586, Captain John Davis
A.D. 1586.   left Dartmouth in the prosecution of a second
voyage.[1]   On this occasion he was placed in command of four
vessels, viz. the MERMAID, of *one hundred tons:* the SUN-
SHINE: the MOONSHINE; and the NORTH STAR, a pinnace of
ten tons.

The 15th of June they arrived at their old anchorage in
Gilbert's Sound; and the boats being sent out to seek proper ground, were met by the natives.   The scene which
ensued, was attended with pleasant circumstances, and presents the characters and proceedings of both parties during

---

[1] It is observed (*Arctic Voyages*, p. 109) : " The important discovery
of the free and open passage to the westward, between Frobisher's Archipelago, and the land now called *Cumberland's Island,* the great number
of whales, seals, deer-skins, and other articles of peltry, in possession of
the natives, which were freely offered by them to the crews of the ships,
excited such lively hopes at home for the extension of the traffic and
discovery, that the merchants of Exeter, and other parts of the west of
England, contributed a large trading vessel of one hundred and twenty
tons, to accompany the little squadron of Davis on a second voyage"......
No authority is given for this statement.   *Davis* simply states : " In this
second attempt, the marchants of Exeter and other places of the west,
became adventurers in the action "......*The World's Hydrograpl. Description, Hakluyt,* vol. iii, p. 153.

their former intercourse, in a favorable point of view. The
natives quickly espying, in one of the boats, some of the
company that had been there the year before, "presently
rowed to the boat and took hold on the oare,[1] and hung
about the boat with such comfortable joy, as would require
a long discourse to be vttered". They afterwards proceeded
to the ships, and by signs, intimated their recognition of all
the mariners they had seen before. Davis hereon landed,
and distributed presents among the "gentle and louing
savages"; and, with good feeling that reflects much credit
on him, he refused various articles that were offered in
return: explaining, that what they had received was to be
taken as a disinterested mark of courtesy and kindness.
Unfortunately, the honesty of these people was not equal to
their affectionate dispositions, or they were exposed to temp-
tations greater than they could resist. Captain Davis was
absent for some days exploring the country, and on his
return he was met with complaints, that an anchor had been
carried off; that the cables had been injured by being cut;
and that a multitude of petty thefts had been committed.
They exhibited, when disappointed of plunder, a mischievous
propensity to injure the crews by slinging stones, some of
them weighing a quarter of a pound, into the barks. The
crews were earnest with Davis to retaliate; but he seems to
have reflected wisely on the character of savage nature, and
to have been willing to make proper allowance for misdeeds,
the result, perhaps, rather of circumstances than of depravity.
He invited the savages on board, treated them kindly, and
dismissed them with presents. It was not till they renewed
the "practice of their devilish nature", that he acted against
them. A volley of stones was slung into the Moonlight, and
the boatswain dangerously hurt. The boats were then manned, and chase made after the culprits. Shots were fired,

---

[1] *Oare* for *oars*, as *billowe* for *billowes*: *caske* for *caskes*, etc.

but in vain.   The savages, pulling with great swiftness, and managing their canoes with extraordinary dexterity, escaped; and "so smally content", the baffled pursuers returned to their ships.

During his excursions on shore, Captain Davis fell in with some other savages.   They were very nimble and active, courteously assisting him and his men up and down the rocks.   In climbing, however, they were beaten by the English seamen; but in wrestling they were found to be very strong and skilful, even throwing some of the seamen from the west country, though reputed to be well skilled in the sport.   On one occasion Davis was about to row off to his ship, when he was prevented by the occurrence of a phenomenon, which was new to him, and which occasioned him some inconvenience.   "I espied", he says, "a very strange sight, especially to me that neuer before saw the like: which was a mighty whirlewinde, taking vp the water in very great quantitie, furiously mounting it into the aire; which whirlewinde was not for a puffe or blast, but continual, for the space of three houres, with very little intermission; which, sith it was in the course that I should passe, we were constrained that night to take vp our lodging under the rocks".

The date of the departure of the expedition from Gilbert's Sound is not stated; but on the 17th of July they were in latitude 63° 8', and fell in with an enormous mass of ice, having all the characteristics of land.   Davis declines enter-·ing into particulars of its size and height, lest he should not be believed.   Some idea of the magnitude of this mass may, however, be formed from the circumstance, that the navigators sailed along it till the 30th.   While in its vicinity, the cold was extreme, the shrouds, ropes, and sails, being frozen; while a dense fog loaded the air.   The people grew sick, weary, and feeble, "withall hopelesse of good successe"; and they, "very orderly, and with good discretion", but earnestly, besought their commander to abandon the enterprise.   By

good chance the difficulty was overcome. On the 1st of
August land was discovered in latitude N. 66° 33', and longitude 70° W.

Here excellent anchorage was found, and means for refreshing the crews were taken. But Davis was placed in
another dilemma. He says : " At this place, the chiefe ship
wherevpon I trusted, called the Mermayd of Dartmouth,
found many occasions of discontentment; and, being unwilling to proceed, she forsook me. Then considering how I
had giuen my faith and most constant promise to my worshipfull good friend, Master William Sanderson, who of all
men was the greatest aduenturer in that action, and tooke
such care for the performance thereof, that he hath, to my
knowledge, at one time disbursed as much money as any
other fiue others whatsoeuer, out of his owne purse, when
some of the companie haue been slacke in giuing in their
aduenture : And also knowing that I should lose the fauor
of M. Secretary Walsingham, if I should shrink from his
direction ; *in one small barke of thirty tunnes,* whereof Mr.
Sanderson was owner, *alone, without further company, I proceeded on my voyage* ". It must be observed, that the Sunshine and the North Star had quitted the expedition, to
explore between Greenland and Iceland.

Davis sailed on his solitary voyage, in his small bark of thirty
tons, on the 12th of August. The 14th, sailing west, they
discovered land in 66° 19' N, seventy leagues distant from that
they had quitted. Having stood northward for a few hours,
a southerly course was shaped, and on the 18th, land to the
North-west was discovered in latitude 65°. This was a promontory with no land south; and great hopes were entertained of a " through passage". In the afternoon of the same
day other land was discovered south-west by south. The 19th,
at noon, by observation, they were in latitude 64° 20'; but on
calculation, found they had been carried considerably out of
their course, by a strong current " striking to the west".

Landing, and ascending to high ground, Davis discovered
that he was amongst islands, which cheered him greatly.
The 28th was the eighth day they had been running along
the coast, southerly, from 67° to 57°; and they put into a fine
harbour, teeming with fish.   The shore is represented to have
been well wooded, and abounding in various descriptions of
birds, many of which were shot with bows and arrows.   On
the 4th of September, in latitude 54° N., Davis states he had
" perfect hope of the passage, finding a mightie great sea
passing between the two lands, west".   Tempestuous weather
followed, and the small bark was in extreme danger of foundering.   But she rode that storm out, and another equally
severe.   Sail was made for England on the 11th September,
and the Moonshine arrived in the west country in the beginning of October.

The Sunshine arrived at Ratcliff on the 6th of October,
having parted with the North Star in a great storm on the
3rd of September.   The latter vessel was never heard of more.

3RD VOYAGE,⎱   The third expedition under Captain John
   A.D. 1587. ⎰   Davis weighed from Dartmouth, about mid-
night, on the 19th of May, 1587.   It consisted of THE ELIZA-
BETH; THE SUNSHINE; and THE HELEN, a clinker.[1]

The old anchorage place at Gilbert's Sound was entered on
the 16th of June; and preparations were made to set up a
pinnace, which had been brought out in frame.   When it was
ready to be launched, the natives wantonly tore off the two
upper "strakes" for the sake of the nails, and the craft being
rendered useless for the purpose for which it was intended,
was given to the Elizabeth to be used as a fishing-boat.   In
consequence of this depredation, an attack was made on the
savages; but, with great cunning, they turned the vessel on
its broadside, and, under the lee, sheltered themselves from

---

[1] ? Similar to the flat-bottomed clincher-built lighters of Sweden and
Denmark.

the arrows of their assailants. Hereon, a saker was levelled against the depredators, and the gunner having made all things ready, gave fire to the piece. A marvel ensued. Anxiously on the look out, the mariners expected to see legs flying in all directions. A part of their expectations were realized. The legs disappeared with surprising rapidity; but to the mortification of the beholders, the flying members were accompanied by their proper bodies. Either from motives of humanity, or from a desire not to damage the pinnace unnecessarily, master gunner omitted to shot the piece.

The eve of departure arrived, and the courage and constancy both of the officers and crew, were put to the test. The master reported, that the vessel leaked fearfully: that the vessel "had three hundred strokes at one time, as she rode in the harbour". This intelligence greatly disquieted the parties concerned, and some were doubtful of proceeding in the ship; but, "at length", the narrator of the voyage observes, " our Captaine, by whom we were all to be governed, determined rather to end his life with credite, then to returne with infamie and disgrace, and so being all agreed, we proposed to live and die together, and committed ourselves to the ship". Resolutely carrying this determination into effect, they set sail on the 21st. Two of the vessels proceeding direct to the fishing ground discovered during the former voyage; and Davis in the third, continuing to prosecute the discovery.

The 24th, Master Davis was in latitude N. 67° 40': the 30th, in latitude N. 72° 12'; where, " at midnight, the compasse set to the variation of 28 degrees to the westward". From the 21st to the 24th, they had run along the land, which was to starboard, or on the east side; and they gave it the name of LONDON COAST. The sea being open to the northward and westward, hopes were entertained that their progress would not be impeded; but the wind shifting suddenly to the north, destroyed their hopes of making any further progress in the course they projected. After naming the point they had last attained, and from which they took their departure, HOPE SANDERSON, they shaped their course westerly, and ran forty leagues without sight of land.

From the 1st to the 14th of July, they were hampered with ice, and obstructed in their progress by foul winds; and on the 15th it was found, that either owing to some fault in the bark, or in consequence of the set of a current, they had been driven out of their course, six points to the westward. On the 20th they made MOUNT RALEIGH, and a few hours afterwards were off the mouth of CUMBERLAND STRAITS.

On account of a certain picturesqueness of language, and as a specimen of, perhaps, one of the earliest logs that can be referred to, the following passages relating to the above locality, are selected from what is entitled,

A TRAVERSE-BOOKE, *made by* M. JOHN DAVIS, *in his Third Voyage for the Discouerie of the North-west Passage. Anno* 1587.

Moneth.	Dayes.	Houres.	Courses.	Leagues.	Eleuation of the Pole		The winde	THE DISCOVRSE.
					Deg.	Min.		

July.

Noone the 19 : 24 : W. Sthy. : 13 : 65 . 30 : S., fog. | The true course, &ca. This 19 of July, at one a clocke in the afternoone, wee had sight of the land of Mount Ralegh ; and by 12 of the clocke at night wee were thwart the Streights, which (by God's helpe) I discouered the first yere.

    „   20 : — : ———— : — : — . — : ——— | The 20 day we trauersed in the mouth of the sayd streights with a contrary wind, being west, and faire weather.

    „   23 : — : ———— : — : — . — : ——— | This 23 day, at 2 of the clocke in the afternoone, having sailed 60 leagues North-west, we ankered among a huge number of iles lying in the bottome of the sayd supposed passage, at which place the water riseth 4 fadome vpright. Here, as we rode at anker, a great whale passed by vs, and swam west in among the iles. In this place, a S. W. by W. moone maketh a full sea. Here the compasse varied 30 degrees.

    „   24 : — : ———— : — : — . — : ——— | The 24 day, at 5 of the clocke in the morninge, we set saile, departing from this place, and shaping our course S.E. to recouer the maine ocean againe.

Moneth.	Dayes.	Houres.	Courses.	Leagues.	Eleuation of the Pole Deg.	Min.	The winde	THE DISCOVRSE.

July.

Noone the 25 : — : ————— : — : — . — : ——— | This 25 wee were be-
calmed almost in the bottome of the streights, and had the weather maruellous extreme hot.

„   26 : — : ————— : — : — . — : S. E. | This day being in the
streights, wee had a very quicke storme.

„   27 : — : ————— : — : — . — : S. | Being still in the
streight, wee had this day faire weather.

„   29 : — : ————— : — : 64 . 00 : ——— | At this present we got
cleere of the streights, hauing coasted the south shore, the land
trending from thence S. W. by S.

„   30 : 24 : S. S. W. : 22 : 63 . 00 : ——— | This day we coasted
the shore, a bank of ice lying thereupon. Also this 30 of July
in the afternoone wee crossed ouer the entrance or mouth of a
great inlet or passage, being 20 leagues broad, and situate between 62 and 63 degrees. In which place we had 8 or 9 *great
rases, currents or ouerfals, lothsomely crying like the rage of the
waters vnder London Bridge,* and bending their course into the
sayd gulfe.

„   31 : 24 : S. by W. : 27 : 62 . 00 : N.W. | This afternoone, com-
ming close by a foreland or great cape, we fell into a mighty
rase, where an island of ice was carried by the force of the current as fast as our barke could saile with lum wind, all sailes
bearing. This cape as it was the most southerly limit of the
gulfe which we passed ouer the 30 day of this moneth, so was
it the North promontory or first beginning of another very great
inlet, whose south limit at present we saw not. Which inlet or
gulfe this afternoone, and in the night, we passed ouer : where
*to our great admiration wee saw the sea falling down into the
gulfe with a mighty ouerfal, and roring, and with diuers circu-
lar motions like whirlepooles, in such sort as forcible streames
passe thorow the arches of bridges.*

August.

Noone the 1 : 24 : S.E. by S. : 16 : 61 . 10 : W.S.W. | The true course, &ca.
The first of August wee fell in with the promontory of the sayd
gulfe or second passage, hauing coasted by diuers courses for our
saueguard, a great banke of the ice driuen out of that gulfe.[1]

[1] *Hakluyt*, vol. iii, pp. 153, 154.

From the narrative of the voyage written by *M. John Janes*, it appears, that, the islands at the bottom of the bay where the ship was anchored, were named CUMBERLAND ISLANDS, and the inlet by which they came out LUMLEY's INLET : which has been identified by a modern author with FROBISHER's STRAITS.[1] The great cape seen on the 31st was designated, it is stated, WARWICK's FORELAND ; and the southern promontory, across the gulf, CAPE CHIDLEY.[2]   On this Fox observes : *"Davis and he* [Waymouth, a later navigator,] *did, I conceive, light Hudson into his Straights"*.[3]   The modern authority before cited expresses a similar opinion ; and there is no reason to doubt the fact.

From Cape Chidley a southerly course was taken to seek the two vessels that were expected to be at the fishing ground ; and on the 10th, in latitude 56° 40′, they " had a *frisking gale* at west-north-west".   On the 12th, in about latitude 54° 32′, an island was fallen in with which was named DARCIE's IS-LAND.   Here five deer were seen, and it was hoped some of them might be killed, but on a party landing, the whole herd, after being twice coursed about the island, " took the sea and swamme towards ilands distant from that three leagues". They swam faster than the boat could be pulled, and so escaped.   It is represented that one of them " was as bigge as a good prety cowe, and very fat, their feet as big as oxe feet ".

The 13th, in seeking a harbour, the vessel struck on a rock and received a leak : which, however, was mended the following day, in latitude 54°, " in a storme not very outragious at noone".   On the 15th, in latitude 52° 40′, being disappointed

1 *Arctic Voyages*, p. 115.

2 " *The Worshippfull M. John Chidley, of Chidley, in the countie of Deuon, esquire*", was apparently chief promoter of an expedition which sailed anno 1589, for " the famous Province of Arauco on the coast of Chili, by the streight of Magellan".   Of this expedition M. Chidley was also the General.   *Hakluyt*, vol. iv, p. 357.

3 *North West Foxe*, p. 50.

in their expectations of finding the Elizabeth and Sunshine, or of finding any token of those vessels having been in the vicinity, and there being but little wood, with only half a hogshead of fresh water on board, it was determined to shape the course homeward for England. This was accordingly done, and they arrived on the 15th of September in Dartmouth, " giuing thanks to God" for their safe arrival.

The opinion entertained by the navigator of the character of his voyage will be apparent from the letter he addressed, on his arrival in England, to the chief promoter of the voyage ; and which is to the following effect : namely,

" Good M. Sanderson, with God's great mercy I haue made my safe returne in health, with all my company, and haue sailed threescore leagues further then my determination at my departure. I haue bene in 73 degrees, finding the sea all open, and forty leagues betweene land and land. The passage is most probable, the execution easie, as at my comming you shall fully know.

Yesterday, the 15th of September, I landed all weary : therefore I pray you pardon my shortnesse.

Sandridge,
this 16 of September,   Yours equall as mine owne,
Anno 1587.   which by triall you shall best know,
JOHN DAVIS".

In his " *World's Hydrographicall description*", he further remarks : " I departed from the coast [the west side of Greenland], thinking to discouer the north parts of America : and after I had sailed towards the west 40 leagues, I fel vpon a great banke of yce : the wind being north and blew much, I was constrained to coast the same towards the South, not seeing any shore west from me, neither was there any yce towards the north, but a great sea, free, large, very salt and blew, and of an vnsearchable depth. . . . . By this last discouery it seemed most manifest that the passage was free and

without impediment toward the North ; but by reason of the
Spanish fleet, and vnfortunate time of M. Secretaries death,
the voyage was omitted, and neuer sithens attempted".[1]

§ IV.

The Voyage of Captain George Waymouth.

THIS adventure was carried into effect under the sole patronage and direction, and at the entire charge of the " Wor[ll.]
Fellowship of the M[r]chñts of London trading into the East
Indies".   Yet from the date of the undertaking to the present
day, the worshipful association have not only been denied the
credit of this " honorable acẽon"; but the merit of the enterprise has been attributed to other parties : to the Muscovia
and Turkey Companies, who had not the slightest connexion
with the matter.   This act of injustice originated with Captain Waymouth, by whom the voyage was made.   Purchas
printed, without note or comment, Waymouth's Journal, in
which the mis-statement is made.   This was in 1624.[2]   Fox,
in 1634, copied the error.   Anderson, who had no means of
ascertaining the truth, adopted the error in 1774 ; and Barrow, under the same circumstances as Anderson, revived it
in 1818.   There would be little advantage in speculating on
the motives which induced Captain Waymouth to give publicity to the mis-statement : though, it may be observed, the

---

[1] " *The Worlde's Hydrographicall Description,* 1595.   A very rare and
curious little book ; of which, perhaps, not three copies are in existence".
(*Arctic Voyages* : London, 1818, p. 116.)   It may be satisfactory to the
curious reader to learn, that the extract from this work, in which Davis
records his proceedings, is printed in the third volume of *Woodfall's edition of Hakluyt,* pp. 155-157 ; and the entire treatise is also to be found
in the fourth volume of the same collection, pp. 451-468 : London, 1811.

[2] *Purchas,* vol. iii, p. 809.

act can scarcely be attributed to inadvertence, or to want of knowledge of the truth. This, it is considered, will be evident from the following detail of circumstances in refutation of this antiquated error: which in the lapse of time, and by the mistakes of authors, has been invested with the characteristics of a venerable fact.

PRELIMINARY PROCEEDINGS.

The project was brought to the notice of the Fellowship on the 24th of July, 1601. On that day "a lr̃e written by one GEORGE WAYMOUTH, a navigat^r, touching an attempte to be made for the discovery of the North-west passage to the Est Indies", was submitted for consideration in a General Court; and it was determined to refer the matter till another meeting. Of the next deliberation, the following minute is recorded, viz.:

"A generall court holden the 7th of August 1601. Question beinge made for the sendinge out of the North-west passage, whether itt shalbe a voyage to seeke itt, or not, beinge put to handes itt was consented vnto for a vyage.

And beinge put to the question, whether the mony shouldbe levyed by the powle [poll, or head], or by the pound, itt was by erectynge of handes ordered that the mony should be levyed by the pound, accordinge to ye first adventures sett downe in the booke for ye first East Indian voyage w^{th}out supplie,[1] none to bee enforced, but every man to adventure y^t will, and to allowe xij*d.* the li. And all those that doe not subscribe his name to this adventure shalbe

---

[1] The term "supplied" is thus used in the document entitled "*A bill of Aduenture to the Company*", viz. "Whereas A.B., one of the aduenturers, and one of the brethren of the Gouernor and Companie of Merchants of London, trading into the East Indies, haueing sett downe for his aduenture li. starlinge [——], hath not onelie paied the said some to C.D., the threr. of the said Companie, but *hath supplied* accordinge to the ordenances of the Companie the *some of li. starlinge* [——] *more*, wch is after the rate of ijs. the li. of his said aduenture.—*Cot. Miscellany Book.*

exempted from this trade of the North-west. And every man to bringe in thōne haulfe by Michellmas, and the rest by Christmas next. These psones vndernamed are appointed Com̃ittees to sett downe the chardge of this voyage for 3 pinyces, and to make report vnto the next court :

<table>
<tr><td rowspan="7">Com̃ittees for the North-west pas-sadge.</td><td>Mr. Ald^{n.} Watts, governo^{r.}</td></tr>
<tr><td>Mr. William Rumney, Dep.</td></tr>
<tr><td>Mr. Cordall.</td></tr>
<tr><td>Mr. Staples.</td></tr>
<tr><td>Mr. Greenwell.</td></tr>
<tr><td>Mr. Howe.</td></tr>
<tr><td>Mr. Wiseman.</td></tr>
</table>

All this aforesaid notwithstandinge, it was in the end concluded that Mr. Gouernor should pvse [peruse] ye charters betweene this and the next court, to see whether thave [they have] authority to compell any of the Company to paye this mony towards this voyage ".

Pursuant to the authority vested in them by the preceding resolution of the General Court, the Committees assembled on the 1st of September following; and, in conference with Captain Waymouth, it was resolved, that two pinnaces would be sufficient for the purposes of the contemplated voyage : that one should be of fifty tons, and the other of forty tons; and that they should be manned with thirty men, in the proportions of sixteen to fourteen. " The chardge of all which", it is added, " by estimation will amount to the valewe of 3000li., or thereabouts". The subject of the remuneration to be granted to Captain Waymouth was next taken into consideration; and a preliminary arrangement was concluded, which is entered on the court-book, with Captain Waymouth's signature attached. Of this proceeding, a report was submitted, the next day, to a General Court ; and " they did well allowe thereof ".

At this stage of the proceedings a difficulty, which delayed the final arrangement, arose out of the following circumstances.

Although the new passage might be found by, and at the expense of the East India Fellowship, it was apprehended, that the Muscovia Company (an association already noticed in connexion with Frobisher's first voyage) would "claim the interest", and take advantage of any benefit that might accrue from the discovery. It was therefore determined to ascertain their views on the subject; and a suggestion was made, that they should cede the rights they might consider themselves to possess, for the period of fifteen years : which the East India patent had to run. The Muscovia Company refused to relinquish, what they termed, their "inheritance"; but they offered to make the discovery on their own account, and to admit as many of the East India Fellowship to participate in the undertaking, as might be willing to join them. Whether justly, or otherwise, there are no means of judging, the East India Fellowship suspected the Muscovia Company of being influenced by a desire to circumvent them: of intending to throw the burden of the charge off their own shoulders; and of being anxious to appropriate to themselves the largest proportion of profit. An offer was, however, made by the East India Fellowship, that the enterprise should be undertaken on equal terms : both the associations to share and share alike. Then the Muscovia Company withdrew their first proposition, and declared they would enter on the adventure *solely* on their own account. They asserted that the right and privilege of navigating the Northern Seas were vested in them exclusively, and they expressed their determination not to permit any interference with their claims. They declined, however, to specify any time for the commencement of the undertaking; and it seemed to the parties who conferred with them, that they were influenced by any feeling but zeal in the cause.

Strongly impressed with the advantages the discovery was

calculated to produce, both to themselves and the " Common Wealth", the East India Fellowship determined to appeal to the Privy Council. They represented to their Lordships the causes which had delayed the execution of the project, and they solicited that the Muscovia Company might be required, either, to embark in the undertaking at once, or, be called on to prove the claim they pretended to exclusive rights and privileges. The latter suggestion was adopted ; and thereon the Muscovia Company expressed their willingness to unite with the complainants. The intention was not carried into effect.

New views which were entertained by the East India Fellowship, are developed in the following extract from the minute of the proceedings of a General Court, holden on the 8th of January, $16\frac{01}{02}$, wherein it is observed, that : " for the satisfaction of the Companie touching the interest in the priveledg^s of the North-west passage wch hath bene in dispute and question betweene this Companie and the Muskovia Companie, ther hath bene the opinion of learned councell had touchinge the same, and it is resolued in lawe that the interest of the same passage is expresslie in this Companie, and it is alsoe resolued, touching the doubte that hath bene formerlie propounded whether that a generall Companie out of their generall priveledg^s thereof might graunt a part of their priveledg^s ether to an other Companie or to annie private persons, that a Companie cannot divide and dismember their priveledg^s, retaining part of them and letting out other part. So as now the doubte and questions formerlie a foote being cleared, and the interest thereof appearing to be in this Companie, Yt is finally resolued that the said voyage shall wth all expedition be prepared, as well that the shortnes of the tyme requiring expedition, as that the Companie are ingaged in their credite to the Lords to enter into it as soon as it shall appeare that they have suffitient interest in the said priveledg^s by their pattent."

Committees were therefore appointed to frame rules and regulations on the subject; and such dispatch was used, that they were completed, laid before a general Court, and confirmed three days afterwards, namely, on the 11th of January. The resolution adopted on this occasion was as follows, viz.:

" *Wheras the Queenes most excellent Ma*^{ie.} by her grac^{s.} l̃res patent vnder the great seale of England bearinge date ye xxxist day of December in the xliiijth yeare of her ma^{ie.} raigne, hath incorporated this society by ye name of ye gou^rno^{r.} and company of the me^rchants of Lo^{n.} tradinge into the East Indies, and hath given them ye sole trade of ye said Indies by all such waies and passages as they shall thinke meete to visit those parts eyther by ye way and passage already found out wch. is by the cape of bona Esperansa, or by such waies and passages as shalbe hearafter found out by ye. parts of America to enioy ye said trade for ye terme of xv^{en.} yeares from ye. feast of ye nativity of o^r Lord god 1600. *And wheras* this society in ye settinge forth of their late viage by ye cape of bona Esperansa towards the ilands of Sumat[ra] Java and other ye parts thereabouts, entendinge to trade [to] those Ilands and places for pepper, spices, gould, and other m^rchandizes wch are likest yeald the most profitable returne for ye adventurs^{rs.} in the same viage have sett forth ye greatest pte of theire adventure in english money coyned of purpose for ye said voyage and other forreine coine currant in those Ilands which moneys and coyne they could not ppare but wth great difficultie and trowble and not wthout some mislike of ye transportaĉon of treasure out of land. *They therfor* beinge desirous to vse ye priviledges to them graunted rather for the good of ye com̃onwealth of theire countrie then for theire private benefite to maintayne the trade of ye East Indies if it be possible by ye transportaĉon and vent of cloth and other the native commodities of this Realme wthout any money at all or eles soe litle as may be conveniently tollerated *Do resolve* to attempt ye discou^ry of a passage by seas into the said East Indies by yᵉ Northwest through some pte of America wᶜʰ if they shall fynd navigable then shall they by that passage arrive in the countries of Cataia and China beinge the East pts of Asia and Africa climats of that temperature wᶜʰ in all likelihood will aforth a most liberall vent of English clothes and kersies to the general advancement of trafficke of mʳchandize of this Realme of England *And to thend* to putt in execuõn as well this theire resoluõn of yᵉ discoũry of the said passage as otherwise to bringe them selves and theire trade generally to a conformitie and order *They do* according to the libertie to them given by yᵉ said lrẽs pattents for the makinge of lawes constituõns orders and ordinances for the better advancement and continuance of theire trade and traffique make ordeine and constitute these seuʳall lawes and constituõns orders and ordinances followinge vizt.

" *First it is ordered and decreed* by and wᵗʰ yᵉ generall consent of this cʳte for standinge and unchangeable decree, that wᵗʰ all convenient expedition there shalbe preparaõn made for yᵉ attemptinge of the discoũry of yᵉ Northwest passage to yᵉ East Indies, wherein shalbe vsed two shippes or pinnaces of such burthen and makinge as shalbe hearafter considered of and resolved to be fitt for yᵉ said voyage, and manned, victualled, and furnished, and provided wᵗʰ such numbers of men, municõn, furniture, victuall, mʳchandise, and other things, as yᵉ coõmittees hereafter nominated and appointed for yᵉ provision therof shall thinke meete.

" *And for yᵉ levyinge of such moneyes* as shall defray yᵉ charges of the preparaõn of yᵉ said shippes or pinaces, and all other things incident to yᵉ said voyage. *And* for the bringinge of yᵉ said moneyes, *It is ordered* that any brother of this felowshippe that hath contributed and adventured in yᵉ former voyage to yᵉ East Indies by yᵉ cape of Bona Esperanza, shall contribute to the settinge furth of this pʳsent voyage after the rate of xij*d.* at yᵉ least for euʳy pound of his

I

former adventure by him adventured, or wherein he is interested w^thout supplie. *And* if any brother of this felowshippe
shalbe willinge voluntarily to bringe in a greater contribuçon
then after the said rate of xij*d.* in ye pound of his said adventure in ye former voyage, it shalbe at his pleasure. *And* to
thẽnd to stirre vp men ye rather to enlarge theire said con-
tribuçons to this enterprise : It is alsoe ordered and agreed,
that after what rate or proporçon soeu^r any man shall contribute in this discou^ry, yf the passage be found out, that he
shall in all voyages hereafter to be made by ye said passage,
be apportioned or stinted in his adventure according to the
same proporçon or rate, and noe otherwise. *And* it is alsoe
ordered that the said contribuçon shalbe brought in by eu^ry
ye contributors in this manner, viz.: the one halfe before the
xxth day of January next comminge, and ye residue, or soe
much therof as shalbe found necessary, at ye goinge away of
ye shippes, to be paid to ye hands of Mr. Ald. Cambell, appointed Thrẽr for ye same voyage. *Prouided allwaies* that if
any brother of this felowshippe shall deny to bringe in his
aid or contribuçon at ye rate of xij*d.* in ye pound of his former adventure, or do not bring in the same at or before the
daies & tymes before limited, that then he or they that shall
make default on that behalfe, shall satisfy and pay for *a fyne*
by way of deducçon out of his stocke adventured in ye last
voyage, fyve tymes ye valewe of ye contribuçon by him pay-
able by vertue of this act. The same to be imployed to ye full
furnishinge of ye said discou^ry. And yf there remaine an
overplus to the vse of the adventurors in this intended voyage
proportionably accordinge to theire seu^rall adventures."

Two vessels, named the Godspeed and the Discovery, of the
tonnage already determined, were selected for the performance
of the intended service : and a committee to superintend the
outfit was appointed, consisting of,

Mr. Wm. Rumny, Deputy.
Mr. Rich. Staper.

Mr. Tho. Cordall.

Mr. Rich. Wyseman.

Mr. Olyver Styles.

Mr. Wm. Harrison.

Mr. Wm. Greenwell.

Mr. Nich. Leat.

Of the Outfit.

On this point some particulars have been preserved, which will be noticed *seriatim*.

I. *Instruments of* ⎱ On this account, as was agreed, the
   Navigation. ⎰ sum of one hundred pounds was allowed
to Captain Waymouth, " to furnish him self accordinge to his choyse".

II. *Provisions.* In this particular the details are not so full as might be desired. But, in the first instance, it appears, that the sum of £54. 8s. 4d. was expended in the purchase of 45 cwt. and 3 qrs. of pork, at 28s. per cwt. Then for the purchase of beef, with more pork, an outlay of £111. 5s. was incurred; and afterwards £600 for " provisions and necessaries", generally. The supply of aqua vitæ consisted of 375 gallons, 3 quarts, and 1 pint, at 3s. 8d. per gallon, besides a small item of £4 for other " strong waters". On beer £120. 3s. was expended; and on rice £6. 14s., at 26s. 8d. per cwt.

III. *Apparel.* In regard to the apparel, the accounts are minute, whether in respect to the quantity, quality, or prices of the materials. The following were the supplies, viz.: 31 pairs of leather breeches,[1] furred with white lamb skins, at 18s. 6d. per pair ; and 6 pairs of another description at 5s. 8d. per pair; 30 cassocks of the like material and similarly furred, at 19s. each; with 30 hoods to fasten to the cassocks, at 5s. 3d. each ; 30 leather gowns lined with frieze, at £1. 2s. 9d. each ;

---

[1] The quantity of material, and minor details regarding the apparel, will be found in Appendix.

with 4 of another description at 5*s.* each; 30 pairs of leather mittens, furred, at 1*s.* 6*d.* per pair; 31 pairs of wodm[ar] boot hose, at 1*s.* 3*d.* per pair; 32 pairs of socks of frize, at 5*d.* per pair; 82 pairs of neat leather shoes, at 1*s.* 8*d.* per pair; 32 pairs of neat leather boots, at 7*s.* per pair : 109 Hamborough linen shirts, at 2*s.* 7*d.* each; 47 waistcoats of (Welch) cotton, or "plane", at 3*s.* 6*d.* each; 12 pairs of "knyt" wollen hose of sundry colours, at 2*s.* 10*d.* per pair; 19 pair of stockings, at 1*s.* 4*d.* per pair; 48 dozen of leather points at, 1*d.* per dozen; 3 white capoches, 13*s.* 6*d.*; 7 pettycotes, 18*s.*; 5 dobletts, £1. 7*s.*; 3 mandillions, 13*s.* 6*d.*; 3 mandillions cantis, 3*s.* 6*d.* These articles, including the sum of £6 for chests and cords, cost in the aggregate, £80. 12*s.*

IV. *Muster-roll* } A list of the persons embarked in the *and wages.* } expedition, with the pay attached to their respective ranks, has been framed from the Court-minutes, the accounts of disbursements, and some miscellaneous documents.[1] Except in some instances of the rating of the men, respecting which the information is defective, the list may be considered correct. The original agreements entered into by seventeen of the crew are preserved. Of these persons four make their marks, three write their initials, and ten affix their signatures.[2] This presents a favourable view of the state of education in the time of Elizabeth : that is, as far as regards writing, and, it may be presumed, reading. Writing and reading were not, however, the sole tests of efficiency. It will be perceived by reference to the autographs, that a well-trained seaman, though unlettered, was rated above and considered entitled to better pay than the man, his inferior in the profession, though excelling him in the mechanical part of education.

V. *Miscellaneous.* Of these charges there are several. Among them are the following, viz.:—For the expenses of Captain Waymouth on his journies to and from the "West Countrey"

---

[1] See Appendix.   [2] Ibid.

to hire seamen, £6 ; for the travelling expenses of " 12 men
that were hired in the West Countrey comming vp to London,
£12"; for " 4 bedds, 18s."; " to Mr. Seger for writing her
Matie lr$ to the Emperor of China and Cathay, £6. 13s. 4d.";
for " a case wth 2 dage [pistols] for Captain Waymouth's ship,
£1"; also " a doble sovringe of gold" valued at £20s. 5d.;
and " 2 pec^s of 5s." which cost 10s. 2d.

Captain Waymouth : his entertaynm^t

The preparations for the voyage being complete, " Articles
of Agreement" were entered into between the Governor and
Company of the East India Fellowship, and Captain Waymouth.

The document commences by stating the reasons which have
induced the Wor^{ll} Fraternity to enter on the undertaking; with
what they have done to render the expedition efficient. It is
observed: " THE GOU^R NO^R and COMPANIE of the M^rchants of
London trading into the East Indies, vpon greate deliberacõn
had and taken of the longe tedious course wch hath been hitherto
houlden by all such as doe trade or sayle from theis pts of the
world into the East Indies alonge the Coaste of Europe and
Africa by the Cape of Bona Esperansa and of the greate adventures wch are borne in soe longe a voyadge by many kindes
of daungers offered there in and being moued wth greate hope
that there is a possibilitie of discou^ry of a neerer passadge into
the said East Indies by seas by the way of the Norwest yf the
same were vndertaken by a man of knowledge in Navigacõn
and of a resolucõn to put in execucõn all possibilitie of indus-
trie and valo^r of the atteyninge of so inestimable benefitt to
his native countrie and his owne ppetuall hono^r HAUE to that
end enterteyned GEORGE WAYMOUTH a man in their opinion
qualified and ffitt to vndertake and attempt the pformance of
this discouerie vnto whome they haue deliu^red before hand the
sõme of one hundred pounds to furnish him selfe wth convenient instrumen^{ts} of navigacõn according to his owne choyse,

and vnto whose direccon they haue comitted two shipps the one called the Discou[R]Y the other the GODSPEEDE being manned victualled prepared and ffurnished wth all things necessarie and convenient for such a voyadge and therein bestowed and supplied all kinds of provisions according to his own desier, whereby both the said George Waymouth and his Companie are prouided of victualls apparell and furniture for the space of 16 monnethes and haue alsoe laden abourd the said shippes a convenient pporcon of m[r]chandize".

Next the services agreed to be performed by Captain Waymouth, are specified in the following terms, viz. :

The Covents. a-greed upon, viz.
" George Waymouth doth promyse, &ca., that he and his companie shall and will be redie by the [?] day of [?] next ensuing the date hereof [the 8th of April] to departe from the porte of London, and as wynd and weather will pmitt shall and will directlie sayle

Captaine Waymouth & his comp. to sayle towardes ffretod Davis, & soe forward by the norwest to the kingdomes of Cataya or China or the backe side of America.
towards the coaste of Groineland into that pte of the seas w[ch] is described in sundry generall mapps by the name of ffretain Davis, and shall passe on forwarde in those seas by the Norwest, or as he shall finde the passadge best to lye towards the parts or kingdom of Cataya or China or the backe side of America, w[th]out geveng ouer the proceedinge on his course soe longe as he shall finde those seas or any pte thereof navigable and any possibilitie to make way or passadge through them.

Not to returne of one whole year att the least.
And shall not him selfe retourne or voluntary suffer any of his companie to retourne backe againe vnto or towards the coaste of England for any lett or ympedim[t] whatsoeuer, untill he and they haue bestowed one yeare att the least from the time of their depture in going forward seeking sounding and attemptynge the pformc of this intended voyage.[1] * * * And further

---

[1] The object of an intervening clause is sufficiently expressed in the

that the said George Waymouth shall wthin 10 daies after
his retourne into England, whether he doe

A journall of their
p'ceedings to be de-
liuered to the com-
panie by the Capt.
wthin 10 daies after
retourne. pforme the said discou'y or not, wthout con-
cealm^t of any thinge wch he hath discou'd
in the viadge, deliuer a declarc̃on in writing
vnder his hand vnto the Gou'nor of the said
Companie or his deputie, conteyninge a report of all and
euery his p̃ceedings in the viadge worthie of note or memory
for the good of the Companie and for the helpe of such as
shall be disposed hereafter to proceed in the same passadge,
and shall be redie from tyme to tyme duringe the space of
40 daies after his arriuall and retourne to London, upon
warninge and som̃ons geven him in that behalfe to come
before the Gou'nor and deputie of the said Company for the
tyme being and the Comitties and such others of the Company as yt shall please the Gou'nor and dep. to call vnto
them, and shall trulie relate vnto them such things as passed
in the said viadge whereof they or any of them shall desier
to be enformed, wthout denyall or refusall in that behalfe,

Not to discouer
his p'ceedings in
the voyadge other-
wyse then to the Go-
u'nor & Company. and shall not discouer the secreets or course
of his p̃ceedings in the viadge to any other
p̃son or p̃sons whatsou^r then to the said
Gou'nor deputie and Com̃itties."

*Then the remuneration to be granted to Captain Waymouth
in case he should succeed, is stated in these terms :* " The
Gou'nor and Companie of the M^rchants of London trading

to the said Capt.
after proofe he hath
discou^red the said
passadge. to the East Indies for them and their successors doe in considerac̃on of the premyses
promyse, &ca., to and wth George Waymouth
to satisfie and pay vnto [him] or his assignes,
wthin ffortie daies after his retourne into England, and after

marginal note, to the following effect : " Tolleration of such as the Companie shall appointe to keepe registers of the goods and observac'ons of
their p'ceedings in the viadge for the benefite of posteritie". The parties
alluded to were pursers or merchants.

sufficient proofe and testimoniall by him made, that he
hath passed through the Northwest passadge into the East
Indies, and arrived at any porte w^{th}in the dominions of
the kingdomes of Cataya, China, or Japan, the some of ffiue
hundred pounds of lawfull English money w^{th}out fraude or
coven."

*Finally, in the event of failure, any claim to reward is waived
by the navigator; and wherefore.* Thus "the said George Waymouth doth promyse and agree that vnless in this intended
viadge he shall discou^r and passe through the said Northwest

The said Captn.   passadge, and shall make sufficient proofe
doth disable him   and give good testimoniall that he hath
selfe from all de-
mands for his sal- passed through the same passadge and ar-
lary and painestak-
inge if he discou^r riued in some parte of the East Indies in the
not.   dominions or kingdoms of Cataya, China, or
one of them, that then neyther he nor his assignes shall
or will demaund or requier of the said Gou^rnor or Companie,
or any of them any salary wages or reward for his viadge or
travell in the discou^y of the said passadge in reguard the said
viadge was vndertaken by the said Gou^rnor and Companie
ptelie by his psuacõn and vpon his resolucõn to adventure his
travell and lyfe therein for the good of his countrie to w^ch
his resolucõn the said Companie were content to add the
adventure of the setting forth of the viadge to their greate
charge".

SUMMARY OF THE VOYAGE.[1]

A.D. } Captain Waymouth sailed from Ratcliff in the river
1602. } Thames, on the 2nd of May; and was off the Start,
the northern point of which bore west, on the 1st of June, in
latitude N. 59° 30'. On the 18th a great island of ice was
descried from the main-top mast, which extended as far as the
eye could reach to the northward; and about 2 P.M., in latitude N. 59° 51', the southern part of Greenland was sighted,

[1] Purchas, vol. iii, p. 809c.

bearing north at a distance, estimated, of ten leagues. Two
days afterwards, with Cape Desolation, twenty-four leagues
N.N.E. by calculation, the phenomenon noticed by Davis was
observed. Streams of black water, "thicke as puddle", were
intermixed with blue sea, which is represented to have been
as clear as glass. In the thick water, shoals were apprehended; but on sounding, no ground was to be got in 120
fathoms. A course more or less westerly was then followed
till the 28th, when land was sighted, which was at first taken
to be the coast of America, but proved to be Cape Warwick,
or Earl Warwick's Foreland, to the northward of Resolution
Island. In lat. N. 63° 53', land, also represented to be America, was again seen. It lay S.W. by W., about five leagues
off, the nearest approach that could be made, in consequence
of the ice which lined the shore. This was on the 8th of July.
The following day a violent storm was encountered; and on
the 17th, they were in considerable danger of being crushed
among "four great islands of ice, of a huge bignesse". During the day, especially towards the afternoon, a dense fog
prevailed. At nine in the evening a great noise was heard,
"as though it had been the breach of some shore". Being
desirous of ascertaining the cause, Waymouth "stood with
it, and found it to be the noyse of a great quantity of ice,
very loathsome to be heard". The fog had now become so
dense, that they could not see the distance of two ships'
length, and it was thought expedient to shorten sail; but,
"When the men came to hand them, they found the sayles,
ropes, and tacklings, so hard frozen, that it did seem very
strange, being in the cheefest time of summer".

The next day was clear, with intense frost. "In the forenoone", the narrator observes, "when we did set our sayles,
we found our ropes and tacklings harder frozen then they
were the day before: which frost did annoy vs so much in
the vsing of our ropes and sayles, that wee were enforced
to breake off the ice from our ropes, that they might runne

K

through the blocks.   And at two of the clocke in the afternoone, the wind began to blow verie hard, with thicke fogge,
which freezed so fast as it did fall vpon our sayles, ropes
and tackling, that we could not almost hoyse our sayles, or
strike our sayles, to haue any vse of them.   This extreme
frost and long continuance thereof", he adds, " was a maine
barre to our proceeding to the northward, and the discourag-
ing of all our men"; and, probably it was owing to these circumstances that the following occurrence, a mutiny among
the crew, took place, which had the effect of completely frus-
trating the objects of the voyage.   This event is thus related:

The p^rticulers of ye Mutinie.

The nineteenth day [of July 1602], the wind was north and
by east, and our course to the eastwards.   The same night
following, all our men conspired secretly together, to beare vp
the helme for *England,* while I was asleepe in my cabin, and
there to haue kept me by force, vntill I had sworn vnto them
that I would not offer any violence vnto them for so doing.
And indeede they had drawne in writing, the causes of their
bearing vp of the helme, and thereunto set their hands, and
would haue left them in my cabin: but by good chance I vn-
derstood their pretence, and preuented them for that time.

The twentieth day, I called the chiefest of my company into
my cabin, before Master *John Cartwright,* our preacher,[1] and
our Master, *William Cobreth,* to hear what reasons they could
alledge for bearing vp of the helme, which might be an overthrow to the voyage, seeing the merchants had bin at so great
charge with it.   After much conference, they deliuered me
their reasons in writing :

Concluding, that although it were granted, that we might
winter betweene 60 and 70 degrees of latitude, with safetie
of our liues and vessels, yet it will be May next before wee

[1] This personage, who had travelled in Persia, was associated by the
worshipful fraternity with Captain Waymouth, to further the objects of
the voyage ; but his character appears to have been mistaken.

can dismore them, to lanch out into the sea.   And therefore
if the merchants should haue purpose to proceede on the discouerie of the north-west parts of *America ;* the next yeare
you may be in the aforesaid latitudes for [from] *England,*
by the first of May, and so be furnished better with men and
victuals, to passe and proceede in the aforesaid action.

Seeing then that you cannot assure vs of a safe harbour to
the northward, we purpose to beare vp the helme for *England*;
yet with this limitation, that if in your wisedom, you shall
think good to make any discouery, either in 60 or 57 degrees,
with this faire northerly winde, we yeeld our liues, with your
selfe, to encounter any danger.   Thus much we thought
needefull to signifie, as a matter builded vpon reason, and not
proceeding vpon feare or cowardise.

Then we being in latitude of 68 degrees and 53 minutes,[1]
the next [day] following, about eleuen of the clocke, they
bare vp the helme, being all so bent, that there was no meanes
to perswade them to the contrary.   At last vnderstanding of
it, I came forth of my cabin, and demanded of them : Who
bare vp the helme ?   They answered, ONE AND ALL.   So they
hoysed vp all the sail they could, and directed the course
south and by west.

The two and twentieth, I sent for the chiefest of those
which were the cause of the bearing vp of the helme, and
punished them seuerely,[2] that this punishment might be a
warning to them afterward for falling into the like mutinie.
In the end, vpon the intreatie of Master *Cartwright* our
preacher, and the Master *William Cobreth,* vpon their sub-
mission, I remitted some part of their punishment.

———

Immediately after punishment had been inflicted on the
mutineers, a large island of ice was fallen in with, and the

---

[1] " This cannot be ".—*Fox*, p. 49.

[2] " This doth not appeare [reasonable] that he could punish, and yet
suffer them to carry the ship backe ".—*Fox*, p. 49.

boats were hoisted out and the crews set to work to obtain a supply, to convert into fresh water, of which they were in great need. While they were engaged in this service, which proved difficult on account of the hardness of the ice, the "Iland gaue a mightie cracke two or three times, as though it had beene a thunder clappe, and presently began to overthrow", so that the boats narrowly escaped being overwhelmed.

In lat. 61° 40′ N., var. 35 W., where "the needle did decline, or rather incline, 83 degrees and a halfe", Waymouth states he entered an inlet, which, from the circumstance of its not being much pestered with ice, he felt convinced afforded a better prospect of the passage than Davis's Straits. He represents the inlet as being forty leagues broad; and adds, that he sailed in it "one hundred leagues west and by south": which Fox declares to be "no such matter"; and which another author, adverting to what is now known on the subject, pronounces to have been "impossible".[1] From the 5th to the 14th of July, the navigator appears to have been ranging along the coast of Labrador, where, on the 10th, variation 22° 10′ W., he saw many islands. On the 15th he was in lat. 55° 31′, var. 17° 15′ W.; and the day following saw "a very pleasant low land, all islands", in lat. N. 55°, var. 18° 12′ W. On the 17th he entered, and sailed up, an inlet for thirty leagues, in sanguine hope of having found the desired passage; but he was doomed to disappointment. In this inlet, which has been identified with Sleeper's Bay or Davis's Inlet,[2] Waymouth encountered his last peril, and escaped in safety. The fly-boats were assailed by a furious storm, which terminated in a whirlwind of extreme violence, that rendered them, for a time, completely unmanageable; and though very strongly built, they took in so much water, for want of spar-decks, that they narrowly escaped being swamped. As soon as the weather cleared up, the course was shaped for England.

[1] *Arctic Voyages*, 1818 : p. 168.	[2] Ibid.

It is to be observed, that the voyage of Waymouth was a complete failure. The highest latitude attained by this navigator on the west coast of Greenland, was 24 leagues S.S.W. from Desolation; and when he had crossed Davis's Straits, there is no proof of his having been higher than 63° 53′ N., though he asserts he had reached 68° 15′ N., when the mutiny broke out. From the day he made Cape Warwick, which was on the 28th of June, to the day of the above named occurrence, namely the 19th of July, the journal is vague and confused. For many consecutive days all notice of the work done is omitted; and, when noticed, the information is scanty and unsatisfactory. Every land that Waymouth sighted is denominated "AMERICA", though there is no proof of his having been, at any period, on any part of that coast, except when cruising, during the latter part of the voyage, along the shores of LABRADOR.   Fox (*N. W. Foxe*, page 50) remarks : " Hee neyther discovered nor named any thing more than *Davis*, nor had any sight of *Greenland*, nor was so farre north ; nor can I conceive he hath added any thing more to this designe ; yet these two, *Davis* and he, did, I conceive, *light Hudson* into his *straights*".   In this opinion Sir John Barrow concurs, and adds : " Little or nothing can be drawn from his narrative, except that he was among the islands to the northward of Hudson's Straits, and probably those of Cape Chidley".[1]

PROCEEDINGS SUBSEQUENT TO THE VOYAGE.

Captain Waymouth arrived in Dartmouth on the 5th of August 1602 ; and his journal, which was transmitted from that place, was read at a Court of the Committees held on the 16th of September.

As might be expected, considerable disappointment was experienced at the result of the voyage, and enquiries were quickly instituted to " sattisfy the Company of their returne

[1] *Arctic Voyages*, p. 168.

soe suddenly ".   The first person questioned was MASTER
CARTWRIGHT, *the Preacher*.   In answer to the enquiries to
which he was subjected, he referred to the journal of the
voyage that had already been submitted, and professed his
inability to give any explanations on account of his ignorance
of navigation.   JOHN DREW, *the Master of the Godspeed,* Captain Waymouth's consort, was the second party examined.
He directly charged *"Cartwright the minister"* with being
the originator of the mutiny already alluded to ; and he
ascribed the failure of the voyage to that occurrence.   He
declared the preacher to have been the cause of the mutiny,
on the authority of the boatswain, the gunner, and the carpenter, of the Discovery, the ship which Captain Waymouth
commanded ; and he expressed his conviction, that if those
parties were called on, they would " averr soe much before
the Company".   JOHN LANE, *master's mate of the Godspeed,*
alleged that the Preacher " did confesse to him and justifie
that he was the pswader and mover of the company [crew of
the Discovery] to retourne for England and to geave ouer
the voyage ".   In consequence of these representations, it
was resolved, that *" the said Cartwright "* should be required
to give up " the gowne and apparell delivered him to haue
beene vsed yff the voyage had beene made to the partes of
Cathaia and China".   It was also determined, that, if the
preacher should prove refractory on the demand being made,
that opinion should be taken of "some learned counsel what
accõn would best lye against him for compelling the render-
ing thereof".   How the matter terminated does not appear.

Besides the above parties, Captain Waymouth was subjected to examination : not only by the Court of Committees
of the East India Fellowship, but by the Lords of the Privy
Council.   His explanations are not on record; but it appears
he submitted a written statement, in which he represented
certain inlets to exist, by which the contemplated passage
might be effected ; and his reasons were deemed so satisfac-

tory, that it was determined, that, "being very competent ",
he should be employed on a second voyage. The project,
however, after a protracted discussion, which lasted from
the 24th of November 1602 to the 24th of May 1603, was
abandoned : apparently, from pecuniary considerations; and
orders were issued for the sale of the Discovery and the Godspeed. The price was fixed at "li. 300 for one vessell wth his
inventorie, and the like for the other".[1]

§ V.

𝕍𝕠𝕪𝕒𝕘𝕖 𝕠𝕗 𝕄𝕒𝕤𝕥𝕖𝕣 𝕁𝕠𝕙𝕟 𝕂𝕟𝕚𝕘𝕙𝕥.

IN the year 1606 a resolution was taken to send out a further
expedition in search of the North-west passage, which was
placed under the command of JOHN KNIGHT, who, the year
before, had been employed by the King of Denmark in exploring a portion of the Greenland coast. For his aid, the
commander was furnished with a document, entitled "A passe
to John Knight for the discouery of the Norẘest passage".
It was to the following effect, viz. : " *To all those* to whome
theis presents shall come, of what degree and condicõn soeu[r],
we the Companie of English marchants for the discou[r]y of
new trades, and of the East India Companie, send greetinge.
Whereas w[th] the consent and likeing of his ma[tie] and the
privie counsell, we haue intertayned the bearer hereof *John
Knight* and his companie to vndertake and attempte the
pformance and discou[r]y of s[r]teyne [certain] places, as we
haue geuen him order, and have prepared and solie cõmitted
a small shipp called the HOPEWELL [*of fortie tunnes*][2] vnto the
chardge of the said John Knight to the same end and pur-

---

[1] Court Book.—*E. I. Mss.*
[2] Purchas, vol. iii, lib. iv, ch. xvi, p. 827. The Hopewell was a *pinnace.*

pose, & to noe other effect. *Theis are therefore* to intreate & desier you, & eu[r] of you to ₚmitt and suffer the said John Knight w[th] the said shipp and companie freelie and quietlie to passe w[th]out any yo[r] lett, hindrance, or molestacõn. *In testimonie* whereof wee haue caused the seu[r]all seals of o[r] Companies herevnto to be fixed. London, the 10th of April 1606. And in the 4th year of the reigne of o[r] Sou[r]eigne Lo. *James*, by the grace of God K. of greate Britain, Ffraunce, and Ireland, defendo[r] of the faith", etc.[1]

A.D. 1606. On the 18th of April, the Hopewell sailed from Gravesend. The voyage did not prove, however, one of discovery. The results were the loss of the master and of some of the crew: peril, excessive toil, with severe hardship to the rest of the people; and unmitigated disappointment to the projectors.

The Hopewell arrived at the Orkneys on the 26th of April, and was detained there for fourteen days by contrary winds. Captain Knight represents the Orkney men to be hardy and expert seamen. He shipped two before starting. His account of the country and habitations agrees with that given in the narrative of the second voyage made by Frobisher.

After a most tedious and uninteresting passage, the vessel arrived off some broken land, in latitude 56° 25' N: much ice driving to the southward. The wind was fresh and the commander made fast to a piece of ice; but falling calm, he endeavoured to row in between the masses. This was an unfortunate attempt. He became hampered. The weather fell thick and foggy; and, to add to his trouble, a furious storm arose. Enormous masses of ice were driven about in all directions, and though the bark escaped the danger of being absolutely crushed, it could not be prevented by any degree of skill or energy (and neither seem to have been spared) from

---

[1] Court Miscellany Book.—*E. I. Mss.*

being severely damaged. This was on the 14th of June. Sight of land appears to have been lost till the 19th, when it is described as being seen again, rising like eight islands, in latitude 56° 48′ N., variation, 25° W. A cove was found in which the ship was brought up, and made fast by hawsers laid out on shore. Misfortune pursued the ill - fated man. On the 24th, there ensued a severe storm from the northward. A tremendous surf rolled in, bringing with it hugh masses of ice. Not only were the warps that held the ship snapped, but the rudder was knocked away from the stern-post. To avoid further damage, the ship, half full of water, was hauled to the bottom of the cove.

So far is from the journal of the commander. The particulars which follow are derived from an account written by " Oliver Browne, one of the company".

On Thursday the 26th of June, Captain Knight, hoping to discover a convenient harbour, set forth with his mate, Edward Gorrill, and three hands well armed with muskets, pistols, swords, and targets, to explore a large island which lay about a mile from the Hopewell. The party landed, leaving two men in charge of the boat that had conveyed them. One had his trumpet with him, for he was a trumpeter ; and the other was provided with a musket. The boat keepers watched the exploring party over a high hill. The poor fellows disappeared, never to re-appear. From ten in the forenoon till eleven at night, the watchers kept at their post. The trumpeter sounded oft and loudly : in vain. His companion fired repeatedly : also in vain. Then they rowed sorrowfully back to the ship and imparted their heavy tidings to their comrades, which filled them with dismay. The extremity in which they were placed, was at once comprehended by the mariners. They apprehended they had lost their master, on whose skill and science they depended for their safety. Four stout hands were also wanting, reducing their number to eight. Their ship was in a wofull plight; and

L

though they had begun to set up a shallop, it was far from
being in a serviceable condition. All night they lay in a tent
on the shore between two rocks, keeping strict watch lest they
should be surprised by an enemy; and anxiously striving to
catch any sound that might indicate the approach of those
whose return was so anxiously desired. *"But they came not
at all"*.

The day following an attempt was made to land on the
island, the scene of the disaster which has been narrated,
that a search might be made for the missing men. But the
attempt proved ineffectual, and the party by whom it was
made experienced much difficulty, and no little danger, in
making their way back to the ship.

The 28th came, bringing fair weather, and efforts were
made to clear the vessel: to save and mend all things that
could be saved and mended; and, as she lay bruising and
beating on the rocks, to lighten her as much as possible.
During the succeeding night, the oppressed crew were subjected to a visitation of a new and serious description. They
were attacked by savages, who set on them furiously with
bows and arrows; and at one time succeeded in obtaining
possession of the shallop. However, the eight mariners,
with a fierce dog, showed a resolute front, and the assailants,
upwards of fifty in number, were finally driven off. The
savages are represented to have been "very little people,
tawnie coloured, thin or no beards, and flat nosed". They
are also described as being "man-eaters"; but for this imputation there appears to be no warrant, except in the imagination of the parties on whom the attack was made.

The ship during this time remained fast in the ice, which
extended far and wide; and the carpenter busied himself in
completing the shallop. He " did tench her in some places,
but neither calked her nor pitched her"; yet she was moved
down to where the ship lay. To free the ship, they set to
work with broad-axes and pick-axes, and by dint of hard

labour and unflagging perseverance, they succeeded in clear-
ing a passage. They towed the ship into clear water, but
they found her "very leake"; the shallop in the same condition ; and what was worse, they "had never a rudder to
stirre [? steer] the shippe withall". This was on the 30th of
June. "The first and second dayes" of July, the narrator
pitifully remarks, "we continued also rowing vp and down
among the floating and driuing ice, *with little hope of recouer-
ing our countrey*".

Having, on the 3rd, a gale of wind from the north, and
a strong current, they drifted to the south, and made fast to
an island of ice. Then they proceeded to stow all things
within board, to make the vessel stiff, as they had no other
ballast. The hanging of the rudder next engaged their attention. Their courage had hitherto been hardly tried : their
ingenuity was now severely tested. They had no proper
materials to make either gudgeons or pintles. In this dilemma they were fain to break up the master's chest, and to
take off all the iron bands, with which to fasten on two pick-
axes, the only substitutes they had for pintles. As an additional security, they rove a cable through the middle of the
rudder, "to keepe it too with two tackes". Thus they "had
some steerage, though it was but bad": as may be easily
imagined. This eased them, for " *before they had been forced
to row till they were all sore and weary*".

The 4th of July they were fairly under weigh ; but they
were in great danger of foundering, owing to the extreme
leakiness of the craft. So leaky, indeed, was she, that if the
crew omitted to pump her but for one half-hour, she could
not be cleared with a thousand strokes. They romaged diligently and found many leaks, which they contrived to stop ;
but it was long before they could discover the one that was
the chief source of their trouble. At last it was discovered
close abaft the fore-foot, where the keel was splintered in
three or four places; and as it could not be got at internally,

being under the timbers, they had recourse to the expedient which is technically denominated *fodering*. The narrator says: "Then did we take our maine bonnet, and basted it with occum [oakum] and put it ouerboord, right against our leake, which eased vs some foure or fiue hundred stroakes in an hour". This, though it may be considered but a small relief, was acceptable to the overlaboured people: for this is the condition in which they then were. One man was very sick, another had "splitted" his hand sorely; and all were so sore with rowing and pumping, that they were scarce able to stir. "*But that they must perforce*". To labour they were compelled, in spite of their unlabouring condition.

The adventures and sufferings of these stout-hearted fellows were now drawing to a close. Shaping their course towards Newfoundland, with a strong current in their favour, they made *Fogo* on the 23rd of July. At that place they were most hospitably entertained. Having refitted, they left on the 22nd of August, full of grateful feelings towards their generous friends; and arrived at Dartmouth on the 24th of December.

——————

§ VI.

Voyage of Master Henry Hudson.

SIR JOHN WOLSTENHOLM, Sir Dudley Digges, and others, being firmly persuaded of the existence of a passage to the north-west, which had hitherto been diligently sought and invariably missed, determined to send out an adventure on their own account. A vessel called the DISCOVERY, *of fifty-five tons*, was accordingly purchased, and supplied with victuals for six months. The master appointed, was HENRY HUDSON; who had considerable reputation as a navigator, having previously made three voyages to the northward. One had been

directed along the east coast of Greenland : one had been
intended to find a passage, eastward, between Spitzbergen
and Nova Zembla, which failed ; and one had, in the first
instance, been directed also to the north-east, but was eventually diverted to the coast of America, and led to the discovery of Hudson's river.

A.D. 1610.   The DISCOVERY sailed from Gravesend on the
17th of April ; and on the 9th of June arrived off
Frobisher's Straits. Keeping a westerly course, Hudson saw a
flat, open country in latitude 60° N., which he named DESIRE
PROVOKED. This was on the 8th of July. On the 11th he
reached some rocks and islands, which he designated ISLES
OF GOD'S MERCY. They were in latitude 62° 9′ N. The next
place noted was HOLD WITH HOPE, a bay, in latitude 61°
24′ N. Then, between 61° 33′ and 62° 44′, he saw a land,
which he named MAGNA or NOVA BRITTANIA. On the 2nd
of August he came up with a head-land, that he called SALIS-
BURY'S FORELAND. Sailing on W.S.W. for fourteen leagues,
he encountered a great whirling sea ; but whether caused
by the meeting of streams, or by water-falls, he was unable
to decide. A few leagues beyond, he reached the western
limit of the passage, now known as HUDSON'S STRAITS, which
he had been navigating from off Frobisher's Straits ; and
passed out by the southern channel : lying between the
N.W. point of the portion of Labrador now called East
Main, and a group of islands opposite. Hudson named the
head-land on the main CAPE WOLSTENHOLM, and the nearest
point on the islands CAPE DIGGES. Beyond the channel
the land was found to trend to the southward ; and the prospect of a large sea, now known as HUDSON'S BAY, was opened.
This was in latitude N. 61° 20′.

ABACUK PRICKETT, one of the ship's company, adds in his
narrative, that the following places were also discovered and
named, viz. PRINCE HENRY'S FORELAND : KING JAMES'S CAPE :

QUEEN ANNE'S FORELAND; and MOUNT CHARLES (now ascertained to be an island). The positions of these places are not given in the narrative; but they may be traced in the maps of the period.

Hudson's journal terminates abruptly on the 3rd of August; and after that the progress of the vessel cannot be traced with any precision. The only place named is MICHAELMAS BAY, but no locality is assigned to it. The following is the summary given by Abacuk Prickett, in his narrative above alluded to. He says: "Having spent three moneths in a labyrinth without end, being now the last of October, we went down to the east, to the bottome of the bay; but returned without speeding of what we went for. The next day we went to the south and the south-west, and found a place whereunto we brought our ship and haled her aground: and this was the 1st of November. By the 10th thereof we were frozen in". Somewhere about this place, *Captain James*, a later navigator, is represented to have wintered.[1]

It was not till the 18th of June in the following year, 1611, that an attempt to move the ship was made. About six days afterwards, when nearly clear of the ice, a mutiny broke out. Dissension had long prevailed in the vessel; and privation had added to the discontent on board. The originator of the mutiny was ROBERT JUET, a truculent and turbulent fellow, who had been superseded in his rating of master's mate by ROBERT BYLOT. The spirit of mutiny was speedily caught by one HENRY GREENE, and, eventually, he became chief of the mutineers. The motives by which Juet was actuated, may be comprehended though not justified. Irritation and disappointment may have induced feelings of revenge on his part. Nothing can be adduced to palliate the infamy of Greene's conduct. He was well educated, but utterly destitute of principle. Prodigal and profligate, he had brought himself to the verge of ruin. He was saved

---

[1] *North-west Foxe*, p. 77. 4to. London: 1635.

from destruction by Hudson, who, on shore, gave him shelter in his house; and, afloat, gave him a berth, hoping and intending to improve his fortune. Without any motive, except such as an evil and depraved nature may be conceived to engender, Greene turned against his benefactor, and became, of all the mutineers, his most implacable foe. Greene it was that doomed Hudson to lingering misery, certain to terminate in a terrible death. It was in consequence of his decision, and under his superintendence, that the master and his son were exposed, in a frail vessel, to the tempestuous and ice-encumbered sea. HENRY HUDSON *the master*, JOHN HUDSON *his son*, and *six others of the crew*, who were either sick or disabled, were brutally driven from their cabins and forced on board the shallop. A seventh, a hale and stout man, followed. He was the carpenter, JOHN KING by name. Honestly refusing to participate in the guilt of the majority of the crew, and nobly resolving to share, whatever it might be, the fate of his commander, he left the ship for the shallop, unmoved by the entreaties of his otherwise merciless comrades. The victims were no sooner on board, than the shallop was cut adrift, and the ship went away under full sail. She was hove to, however, shortly afterwards, to be the more conveniently searched for plunder; but the shallop appearing to come up, "they let fall their mayne-sayle, and up with their top-sayles, as if to flee from an enemy". In a short time sight was lost of the shallop; and, for ever.

Retribution was shortly afterwards visited on some of the principal among the mutineers. HENRY GREENE, WILLIAM WILSON, JOHN THOMAS, MICHAEL PIERCE, ANDREW MOTTER, and ABACUK PRICKETT, were taken at disadvantage by a party of savages. Henry Greene was slain on the spot. Wilson died the same day on which the attack was made, "cursing and swearing in the most fearful manner". Pierce survived two days, and then gave up the ghost. "Thus", says Prickett, who described himself to have been severely wounded in

the fray, "have you the tragicall end of Greene, the captaine
as he was called, and his three mates, being the lustiest men
in the shipp".

The residue of these "stony-hearted men", as Foxe not
inaptly terms them, escaped not without experiencing sufferings of the severest description.   Provisions soon fell scant,
though they started from the mouth of Hudson's Straits with
three hundred fowls on board, which they had succeeded in
killing, besides a proportion, rather slender however, of other
provisions.   First, they were reduced to the liquor in which
they seethed their fowls, for a mid-day meal; and half a bird
each, at night, for supper.   Next, they burned the feathers
from off the fowls, which, as they could not be plucked, had
previously been flayed; and the garbage was considered too
precious to be thrown away.   Next, they were fain to crush
the bones of the fowls, and fry them in candle-tallow, which,
mixed with vinegar, was deemed "a good dishe": though the
greatest " daintie" was a pound of candles allowed to each
man every seven days.   Juet, to cheer them, reported that
they were within sixty or seventy leagues of the coast of Ireland, though he knew it was two hundred leagues distant ;
and he died of absolute starvation before the distance was
accomplished.   The rest of the crew, from sheer debility,
were compelled to sit at the helm ; and the progress of the
vessel was retarded in proportion as she was badly steered.
Bylot, the master, was compelled to do the duty of a seaman,
and to neglect his own duty.   The tackling went to rack.
The last fowl was in the " steepe-tub"; and grim famine
stared the forlorn and despairing wretches in the face, when,
to their inexpressible joy, land was discovered.   It proved to
be "near the Durses in the bay of Galloway".   But the
sufferings of the crew did not terminate at once.   They had
no money to purchase necessaries, and no one would trust
them.   At length, by pawning their best anchor and cable,
they obtained wherewithal to procure provisions, and to hire

people to navigate the ship to England. There they arrived shortly after.

It may be presumed, that as they were subsequently engaged in the same service, Prickett and Bylot succeeded in exculpating themselves from blame in regard to their connexion with the mutineers. But Foxe, at the conclusion of his summary of the voyage, observes significantly: " *Well,* Prickett, *I am in great doubt of thy fidelity to* Master Hudson".

---

§ VII.

Voyage of Sir Thomas Button.

The proceedings of this voyage are involved in what appears to be needless mystery. *Purchas* complains he could not obtain any information on the subject; and *M. Briggs* was also kept, to a great degree, in the dark, although he was eminent for his scientific acquirements, deeply interested in the success of the enterprise, and intimately acquainted with the navigator. For what is known respecting the proceedings, thanks are due to the inquisitiveness and industry of *Luke Fox,* who sought, and obtained information from some of the companions of Button, if not from the navigator himself, and also from Sir Thomas Roe, an energetic promoter of the North-west project. The information thus acquired was first printed in the *North-west Foxe,* A.D. 1635.

Subsequently the INSTRUCTIONS under which Sir Thomas Button sailed were recovered. They are considered to be drawn up with considerable skill, to be interesting in various particulars, and to advert to points not devoid of value, even in the present day. That the reader may form a judgment of the character of this document it is subjoined.

M

CERTAINE ORDERS AND INSTRUCÕNS set
downe by *the most noble Prince Henry of
Wales,* this 5 of Aprill 1612 vnder his
highnes signature and signe manuell and
deliuered vnto his Seruant Captaine Thomas
Henry P.   *Button* generall of the Company *now imployed about yᵉ full and perfect discouery of
the North-west passage* for the better go‑
uernment as well of the shipps committed
to his charge as of the personns in them
imployed vppon all occasions whatsoever.

1. **That** it maie please Almightie god to preserue you and
your charge from danger, and if it shall seeme good vnto his
wisedome to give a blessing of successe vnto this hopefvll and
important enterprize, LET there be a religious care dailie
throughout your shippes to offer vnto his diuine Maᵗⁱᵉ the
Sacrifice of praise and thanks-giving for his fatherlie goodnes
and protecõn. Especiallie prouide that the blessed daies
wᶜʰ hee hath sanctified vnto his service be Christianlike obserued with godlie meditacions.

2. **Let** noe quarelling or prophane speeches, noe swearing
or blaspheming of his Holie name, noe drunkennes or lewde
behaviour passe vnpunished, for feare of his most heavie in-
dignaõn.

3. **Let** there be a perticuler note taken of all suche as
shall shew themselves most willinglie obedient vnto you,
most dilligent and industrious in their charges, most resolute
and constant in the prosecution of this Acõn : That thereby
we being informed at your returne, maie esteeme accordinglie
of their deservings.

4. **Let** there be faithfull and true registring everie daie of all
the memorable accidents of the voyage and that by as many
as shalbe willing, especiallie by the most skilfull and discreete
personnes, whome we would have once everie 10. or 12. daies

to confer their Notes for the better perfecting a Jornall, w^ch
we expect at your returne.

5. **More** perticulerlie when you shalbe cleare of the Landes
end, be carefull to have kept a true accoumpt of y^r wayes to
GROINLAND, and from thence to the STREIGHTS mouth, and to
observe in what Latitude it lieth, what face the coast beareth,
what Sea setteth into it, and when you are within it, howe
the coast doth trend, the contynuance and course of the ebbe
and fludd, what height it riseth, from whence it cometh, and
with what Moone ; what Current, Eddie, or overfall you finde,
what Islandes or Rockes, and howe bearing, and last of all
your soundings wch you must trie with good store of faddome
once at least everie ffourth glasse, and oftener amongst broken
landes Rocks Shole and white waters. Yet remembring that
the waie is alreadie beaten to DIGGES ISLAND, rather then
lose tyme we would have you hasten thither, and leave the
perfect observaçon of theis thinges to the PINNACE in her
returne.

6. **As** often as occation offers itselfe, especiallie when you
shalbe forced to sende on lande, for we would not have that
you your self should quitt your shippe, Let some skilfull man
with good instrument obserue the ELEUATION, the DECLINATION,
the VARIATION of the compasse, and if you arryve time enough,
the begynning and ending of the ECLIPSE, that will happen on
the 20th of May next. ESPECIALLIE if you should winter let
there be carefull and painefull watching to observe the instant
of the coniunctions of anie of the planets, or the distance of
the Moone from anie fixed starre or starres of note. All w^ch
we would have entred into a Booke, and presented me at
your returne.

7. **Let** there be care by y^r order and direction for keeping
of your shippes in consorte all your course, wherein we wishe
you to make all the haste you can to the STREIGHTS MOUTH,
but we think your surest way wilbe to stand vpp to ISELAND
and soe over to GROINLAND in the heighte of 61 soe to fall

downe with the current to the most Southerlie Cape of that
land lyeing in about 59 called CAPE FAREWELL, wch pointe as
the Ice will give you leave, you must double, and from thence,
or rather from some 20 or 30 L. to the Northward of it, you
shall fall over DAVIS HIS STRAIGHTS to the westerne Maine;
in the height of 62 Degrees or thereabouts you shall finde
HUDSONS STREIGHTS wch you maie knowe by the furious course
of the Sea and Ice into it, and by certaine Islandes in the
NORTHERNE SIDE thereof as your Carde shewes.

8. Being in: We holde it best for you to keepe the NOR-
THERNE SIDE as most free from the pester of Ice at least till
you be past CAPE HENRY, from thence follow the leading Ice
betweene KING JAMES and QUEEN ANNES FORELANDS, the distance of which two Capes observe if you can, and what harbour or Rode is neir them, but yet make all the hast you maie
to SALISBURY HIS ISLAND betweene wch and the Northerne
continent you are like to meet a great and hollowe billowe
from an opening and flowing Sea from thence. Therefore
remembring that your end is West we would have you stand
over to the opposite Maine in the Latitude of some 58 degrees,
where riding at some headland observe well the flood of it
come in SOUTHWEST, then you maie be sure the passage is
that waie, yf from the NORTH or NORTH WEST your course
must be to stand vpp into it, taking heed of following anie
flood for feare of entring into BAIS, INLETS, or SANDS [? *sounds*],
wch is but losse of time to noe purpose.

9. By the waie: if your SHIPPES within the STREIGHTS
should sever, we think DIGGS ISLAND for the good Rode and
plentie of refreshing that is there wilbe your fittest RANDE-
VOUS. And if it should fall out that the WINTER growe vppon
you before your finding a thoroughfare into the SOUTH SEA,
we think your safest waie wilbe to seeke southward for some
place to winter in, for we assure our self by Gods grace you
will not returne, without either the good Newes of a passage,
or sufficient assurance of an impossibility.

10. You must be careful to prevent all Mutynie amongst yo[r] people, and to preserve them as muche as maie be from the Treacherie and villanie of the SALUAGES, and other Easterne [?] people; where ever you arrive have as little to doe with them as maye be, onlie if the STRAIGHTS it self afford noe sufficient strength [?], you shalbe happie in finding out some convenient parte on the back of AMERICA or some Island in the South Sea for a haven or staçon for our shippes and marchandizes hereafter; but yet spend as little time as maie be in this or any other searche, saving of the passage till you have dispatched the PYNNACE wth advertisement of your entrie into the SOUTH SEA, wch must be done as sone as you shalbe thereof assured.

11. Last of all: see that you and all vnder yor charge, doe faiethfullie obserue and followe all such further directions and instrucçons as shalbe given by the ADUENTURERS. And to the end it may appeare what care we haue of the Action and howe acceptable everie mannes good indevour and service therein wilbe to Vs, LET theis be perticerlie read once everie Moneth, if it can be, to your whole Companie.

(L. S.)[1]

CAPTAIN, afterwards SIR THOMAS BUTTON, had the reputation of being not only well skilled in the knowledge of sea-affairs, but in other respects a talented man. Associated with him was a relative, of the name of GIBBONS, with a friend called HAWKRIDGE. These parties joined the service as volunteers, and both bore high characters as navigators : though when tried on subsequent occasions, they cannot be considered to have sustained the good opinion that was entertained of them. The ships fitted out for the new voyage were : THE RESOLUTION, commanded by SIR THOMAS BUTTON; and the DISCOVERY, commanded by CAPTAIN INGRAM.[2]

---

[1] This document is printed from a rare *facsimile* of the original MS. C.R.

[2] The coincidence in the names of these vessels with the names of those

A.D.   The equipment of the vessels, including provisions
1612.   for eighteen months, being in every respect complete, the expedition sailed early in the month of May.

The first account given of Sir Thomas Button's progress
is, his being off the south shore within *Fretum Hudson,* and
near *Hope's Advance.* From thence he proceeded to the
north shore, and in the vicinity of some islands (subsequently
named by Baffin *Savage Islands*), made a trial of the tide:
which he found to come from the S.E., flowing three fathoms;
and then, directing his course to what is termed the south
channel, between *Salisbury Ile* and the south shore of the
Straits, he anchored at *Digges Island.* In this locality he
stayed eight days, to set up a pinnace that had been carried
out in frame. "And here it was", it is observed, "where
the villaines *Greene* and *Jewett* were slaine, after they had
exposed *Master Hudson*". The statement is probably correct, as both *Bylot* and *Prickett,* who sailed with that unfortunate navigator, were attached to the present expedition.
Here also, it appears, five of Button's people were killed by
the savages, in revenge for the seizure by the English commander of some of their large canoes: two of which only
were restored.

From Digges Island the navigator proceeded north-westerly, and fell in with land, to which he gave the name of
CARY's SWANS'-NEST.[1] The next land-fall was made in about
latitude 60° 40′ N., and was called HOPES CHECK'D, because,
it is supposed, "there his expectation was crossed". This
land was seen on the 13th of August, on which day a violent
storm also occurred; and the ships' heads were put southerly.
The weather continuing boisterous, it was deemed necessary

under the celebrated COOK, when employed on the same service, but on
the opposite side of America, has been remarked by the author of the
Arctic Voyages, p. 196.

[1] According to Foxe, fifty-eight leagues on the west side of Southampton Island, from the point named CAPE COMFORT by Baffin.—*N. W. Foxe*
(*The Probability of the Passage*), p. 257.

to seek a harbour, in order to repair damages. The desired haven was found "in a small rile or creeke", on the
north side of a river, in lat. 57° 10′ N. To the river the
name of PORT NELSON was given, after the master of the
Resolution, who died and was buried there. The circumja-
cent land was called NEW WALES, and the bight, where the
river disembogued, BUTTON'S BAY.

Thus, it will be perceived, Sir Thomas Button was the first
navigator by whom Hudson's Bay was crossed from east to
west. To him must also be awarded the merit of being the
first Englishman by whom the eastern side of that portion of
America was visited; and there seems to be no just reason
why he should be deprived of the credit of the action: which
is virtually the case by the name of his bay being expunged
from modern maps and charts.

Having determined to winter in Port Nelson, Sir Thomas
proceeded to take precautions for protecting his ships from
danger of " storme of snowe, ice, raine, or what else might
fall", by throwing up substantial " barracadoe" of fir-wood
and earth. The river, "not a mile broad",[1] was not, however, completely frozen over till the 16th of February; and
during the intervals of mild weather, which were not un-
frequent, the people were employed on shore in procuring
game. By this means "they were supplied with great store
of white partridges, with other fowle"; and Foxe states, he
had heard it credibly reported, that the company killed
"1800 dozen" during their sojourn. After the 16th of February, however, the weather appears to have been very severe. Many of the men perished, although three fires were
constantly maintained, and the survivors were reduced to a
very sickly condition : the general himself being among the
number of the " disabled".   "God a mercy for nothing, for I
had not above eight sound men", was the pertinent reply given
by the Prince's servant to Luke Foxe, on its being remarked

1 Note.—*N. W. Foxe*, p. 119.

he could not be certain of the tide he took at Nottingham island, at his return from Port Nelson, because he had not sent a boat on shore.[1]

When there was no occupation for the people on shore, or when they were confined by the inclemency of the weather to the ships, the general, considering " that the best way of preventing men from murmuring, discontent, and secret conspiracy, is to divert them from dwelling on their unpleasant situation",[2] wisely and skilfully devised means to keep their minds employed. He propounded questions, to which he required written answers, "concerning the route of their late navigation; and engaged them in comparing each other's observations as to the courses they had run, the set of the tides, and the latitudes of the places they had touched at".[3] Thus, as is justly observed by the author above quoted, by apparently consulting them on what was best to be done, and what course should be pursued during the approaching spring, he contrived to make every man in the ship feel himself of importance, and succeeded in inducing a personal interest in the future success of the voyage. Following the example of Foxe, " such answers as came to my hands, I do hereby, reader, freely impart for thy better understanding".[4]

The ice began to break up on the 5th of April 1613, giving the companies of the vessels an opportunity of taking an abundance of fish "as bigge as mackrils"; but the ships were not moved from their winter berths for the space of nearly two months after that day. On sailing, a north-westerly course was taken, according to a suggestion that had been made by *Josias Hubart* the pilot of the Resolution:[5] which, in the opinion of the author of the *Arctic Voyages*, " shews the sound notions entertained by this man respecting the true mode of searching for the passage";[6] and which induces

---

[1] Foxe in reply to his detractors.—*N. W. Foxe*, p. 249.

[2] . [3] *Arctic Voyages*, 1818: pp. 198-199.   [4] See APPENDIX.

[5] See Hubart's paper : APPENDIX.   [6] P. 199.

Master Fox, in a marginal note, to remark, "well guest, Hubart". Arriving "in 60°, they found a strong race of tide runinge sometymes eastwarde sometymes westwards, wherevpon Josias Hubbarde, in his platt, called y^t place HUBBART'S HOPE".[1] The 23rd of July, HOPE'S ADVANCE, which was seen and named on the former part of the voyage, was again fallen in with; and on the 26th, UT ULTRA was made in latitude 62° 42' N.

The highest degree of latitude that was attained, appears to have been 65°, on the 29th of July; and then the course was shaped towards the southward. On the 4th of August, MANSEL'S ISLANDS, or as they are erroneously called in some charts, MANSFIELD ISLANDS, were discovered in latitude 61° 38' N. It is also believed by Fox, that Sir Thomas Button had previously named the extreme point of Southampton Island, lying to the westward of Carey's Swans'-Nest, CAPE SOUTHAMPTON, and that on the east of it, CAPE PEMBROKE.

Digges Island was next made, and thence the course was directed towards England. On this part of the voyage, the following remarks are reported, by Fox, to have been made by ABACUK PRICKETT. " He saith, they came not through the maine channell of *Fretum Hudson,* nor thorow *Lumley's Inlet;* but through into the *Mare Hyperborum* betwixt those Ilands first discovered and named *Chidley's Cape* by *Captain Davis,* and the North part of *America,* called by the Spaniards, who never saw the same, *Cape Labrador,* but it is meet by the N.E. point of *America,* where was contention among them, some maintaining (against others) that them Ilands were the *Resolution,* which *Josias Hubbart* withstood, untill he stood himselfe into the danger of displeasure; but at length it proved a new Streight, and a very streight indeed to come through, which resolved all doubts: but hereupon all their

---

[1] Note on a map in *Purchas* (vol. iii, p. 848) connected with a paper by M. Briggs.

plots and journals". It is a source of regret, that these documents are not to be obtained.

Sir Thomas Button appears to have felt acutely the disappointment occasioned by his failure to discover the passage of which he had been in search, but he does not despair of ultimate success. On the contrary, he expresses himself as feeling assured, " That God that made us all of dust, will not fail to raise up some good spirits for the further prosecution of this businesse : as that by their honest endeavours, and religious resolutions, they will effect that which is not ripe for his sickle". He trusts that, " God, which best knowes what the truth of his endeavours have been in this action, will not faile to give a blessing to some that followe ; and for his part he desires to be blest no otherwise than as he hath sincerely laboured ; and therefore he must conclude and ever beleeve according to the word, that *Paul* plants, *Apollo* waters, and *God* gives the increase. So that until his good will and pleasure is, all that we doe cannot in this aught else prevaile".[1]

The ill-success of Sir Thomas Button, moreover, was not regarded to give " sufficient assurance of an impossibility". On the contrary, assurances were derived from the voyage, of the practicability of the discovery ; and they are embodied by Thomas Harriott in the following

THREE REASONS TO PROVE THAT THERE IS A PASSAGE FRŌ THE NORTHWEST INTO THE SOUTH SEA.

i. The tydes in Port Nelson (wher Sir Tho. Button did winter) were constantly 15 or 18 foote, wch is not found in any Baye Throughout the World but in such seas as lye open att both ends to the Mayne Ocean.

ii. Euery strong westerne winde did bring into the Harbo^r where he wintered, so much water, that the neap-tydes were

---

[1] Fox, on the authority of a fragment of Sir Thomas Button's journal, communicated to him by Sir Thomas Roe.—*North West Foxe*, p. 134.

equall to the spring-tydes, notwithstanding that the harbo[r] was open only to the E.N.E.

III. In coming out of the harbo[r] shaping his course directly North, about 60 degrees, he found a strong race of a tyde, setting due East and West, w[ch] in probabilitie could be no other thing, than the tyde coming from the west and returning from the east.[1]

But the truth of the theory remains yet to be proved.

§ VIII.

The Voyage of James Hall.

JAMES HALL, who had been employed by the King of Denmark in the years 1605, 1606, and 1607, was engaged in the year 1612 to take charge of an expedition which was promoted by a new association of English adventurers, that had been organized by MASTER ALDERMAN COCKIN.[1] From remarks, however, that occur in the narrative, it would appear that the voyage was undertaken less for the purpose of discovering the North-west passage, than to take advantage of the reputed discovery, by the Danes, of mines, whether of gold or silver is not stated, on the west coast of Greenland.

A.D. 1612. } The expedition consisted of two small vessels called THE PATIENCE and THE HEART'S EASE. When the ships started, is not apparent; but, on the 1st of July, they were in a place called COCKIN'S SOUND. From thence they pro-

---

[1] Mathematical Papers of Thomas Harriott (*Brit. Mus.*) vol. 8-6789 (*Addl. Mss.*).

[2] "*Richard Cockain and Co*" subscribed the largest amount contributed to the first voyage made by the Company of Merchants of London trading into the East Indies; and a "*Master William Cockin*" was one of the first Committees of the Fellowship. (See Appendix.)

ceeded towards the river "where the supposed mine should be". The weather, however, proving stormy, with the wind from the northward, they were constrained, on the 21st, to put into RAMELSFORD; and here the master, Hall, was slain by a savage: who, " with his darte, strooke him a deadly wound upon the right side". The unfortunate man was the only person assailed; and he is supposed to have fallen a victim to revenge, from the fact of his having been associated, on a former visit, with the Danes: who, it is said, " out of that river carried away five of the people, whereof never any returned againe; and in the next river killed a great number".

After the interment of the master, the company went northward, and entered CUNNINGHAM'S RIVER, where they found " divers places where the Danes had digged "; and collected " a kinde of shining stone": which, on being tried by the goldsmith, James Carlisle, proved to have "no mettall at all in it"; and to be utterly worthless. The stone is described as being " like vnto Muscovie studde, and of a glittering colour".

From Cunningham's river, the course was retraced to Ramelsford, in latitude N. 67°, which is described as being one of the fairest rivers to be seen on the coast of Greenland, and as lying in E. and E. by S.

On the murder of the master, the natives withdrew altogether from trading with the English, and it was therefore resolved to return home. Hull was made on the 17th of September.

It has been remarked: " The little that is known of this voyage appears to have been written by WILLIAM BAFFIN; and it is chiefly remarkable for its being the first on record, in which a method is laid down, as then practised by him, for determining the longitude at sea by an observation of the heavenly bodies." It is justly added: "The method he made use of sufficiently proves that Baffin possessed a very considerable degree of knowledge in the theory, as well as prac-

tice, of navigation".[1] Baffin's account of his method, which
may be compared with another account given in the narrative of his voyage of 1615, is as follows :

"WEDNESDAY THE 8TH OF JULY 1612, in the morning I
perceived the sunne and moone, both very fair aboue the
horizon, as I had done diuers times before. At which time
I purposed to find out the longitude of that place, by the
moone's comming to the meridian line: which I did vpon an
iland neere the sea, hanging at the extreames two threeds
with plummets at them, instead of an index and sights.

"THURSDAY THE 9TH day, very early in the morning, I went
on shoare the iland, being a fine morning, and obserued till
the moone came iust vpon the meridian. At which very
instant I obserued the sunne's height, and found it 8° 53′ N.,
in the eleuation of the pole 65° 20′. By the which, working
by the doctrine of sphericall triangles, hauing the three sides
geuen, to witt, the complement of the pole's eleuation; the
complement of the Almecanter; and the complement of the
sunne's declination; to find out the quantity of the angle at
the pole: I say by this working I found it to be foure of the
clocke, 17′ and 24″. Which, when I had done, I found by
mine ephemerides, that the moone came to the meridian at
London that morning, at foure of the clocke, 25′ and 34″ :
which, 17′ 24″ subtracted from 25° 34′, leaueth 8° 10′ of time
for the difference of longitude betwixt the meridian of London and the meridian passing by this place in Groenland.
Now the moone's motion that day was 12° 7′, which, con-
verted into minutes of time, were 48′ 29″; which by working
by the rule of proportion, the worke is thus : if 48′ 29″ (the
time that the moone cometh to the meridian sooner that
day then she did the day before) give 360 (the whole circumference of the earth), what shall 8° 10′ give? to witt, 60° 30′,
or neere thereabout; which is the difference of longitude
betweene the meridian of London and this place in Gro-

[1] *Arctic Voyages*, p. 201.

enland, called Cockin's Sound, lying to the westward of London."

There is, however, a great discrepancy between the longitude of Cockin's Sound given by Baffin, and that given by Sir John Ross in his voyage of 1818. In the chart prefixed to that voyage, and in the table of latitudes and longitudes annexed,[1] the longitude of Cockin's Sound is made 53° 00' W. There is, however, another statement made by Sir John Ross, which differs from the chart and table. In page 35 it is remarked, " we saw land south of Cokin's Sound. . . . . It bore E. by N. to South, being about fifty miles distant, according to the judgment of the master . . . . though I thought it not more than thirty-eight". The ship, when this remark was made, was in longitude 55° 42' W. If this be the correct reading, Baffin's apparent error is somewhat reduced; but still the difference is great, and is totally at variance with all other instances in which his accuracy has been tested. Such instances will be noticed in connexion with his voyages of 1615 and 1616.

-----

§ IX.

Voyage of Captain Gibbons.

CAPTAIN GIBBONS, it will be recollected, accompanied Sir Thomas Button on his voyage in 1612, as a volunteer; and it is evident the knight entertained a very high opinion of his relative. Sir Thomas " saith, albeit that hee is so neere in blood, as that modestie will not allow of his speaking too much of his merit, yet hee will boldly say thus much of his sufficiency, as that he is not short of any man that ever yet

-----

[1] TABLE. " Coquin's Sound, *latitude* 53° 00', *longitude* 65° 38'": which although not noticed in the *errata*, is evidently a typographical blunder for lat. 65° 38', and long. 53° 00'.

he carried to sea. All that he can say of him further is, that for his countrie's, and for the aduancement of this business they had in hand, he could wish his body were answerable to his other abilities, which, were it, not himselfe, but many, and his country most, would be the better for it."[1] With this strong testimony in his favour, given by a competent judge, Captain Gibbons undertook the advancement of the business; and failed most wofully.

A.D. 1614. } CAPTAIN GIBBONS was placed in the command of the DISCOVERY, the consort of the Resolution in his previous voyage. Neither the date of his departure, nor that of his return, is recorded; but the voyage was made in the course of the year 1614.

Of the result of the voyage, all that is known is thus laconically communicated by Master Fox. " Little " he says, " is to be writ to any purpose, for that hee was put by the mouth of *Fretum Hudson,* and with the ice driven into a bay called by his company GIBBONS HIS HOLE, in latitude about 57° upon the N.E. part of STINENIA, where he laid twenty weekes fast amongst the ice, in danger to have been spoyled, or never to have got away, so as the time being lost, hee was inforced to returne".[2]

The bay in which Gibbons was caught, is supposed to have been that now called NAIN, on the coast of Labrador.[2]

Although the name of the Worshipful East India Fellowship is not mentioned in the printed relations of the voyages connected with the North-west enterprise, it has been ascertained from the records, that their assistance was not withheld. The particular voyages to which the contributions were apportioned have not, however, been traced.

---

[1] *North West Foxe,* p. 134. *Ib.* p. 137.   [2] *Arctic Voyages,* p. 205.

It is recorded that, in December 1614, SIR THOMAS SMITH, the Governor, took an opportunity to remind the Court of Committees, " that three yeares since[1] this Coumpanie did aduenture £300 p. annum for three yeares towardes the discou^ry of the Norwest passage". Having adverted to the failures that had occurred in connexion with the enterprise, and having also alluded to some property belonging to the company, that had been brought home in a vessel engaged in one of the unsuccessful attempts, he proceeds to observe : " The hope and pbabilitie notwthstandinge of findinge it hereafter doth incouradge many of the pticuler Aduenturers to proceede and vndertake a voyage this yeare, wch he thought fitt to acquaint this coumpanie wthall, to know their opinions what they intend to do therein : whether to joine in any parte of the said aduenture; hopeing that they will not refuse to aduenture againe that remaynder wch is come home, and somewhat more towards ye same discou^ry". The resolution of the Court on this proposition is recorded in the following terms, viz.: " This Courte considering that it were dishonorable for such a bodie to withdrawe their hand from so worthie a worke for a small matter of charge, wch will not exceede a noble a man in their pticulers, and the honor and benefitt will be greate yf yt may be found. They were therefore contented to ioyne for a certain some besydes the remaynder : wch they gaue freely by erecõn of hands. And the question being putt likewise for three seuerall somes, They did by like erecõn of hands resolue vpon the aduenturinge of twoe hundred pounds, so there may bee no expectation of any further supplie".

---

[1] The records of this period are not attainable.   C. R.

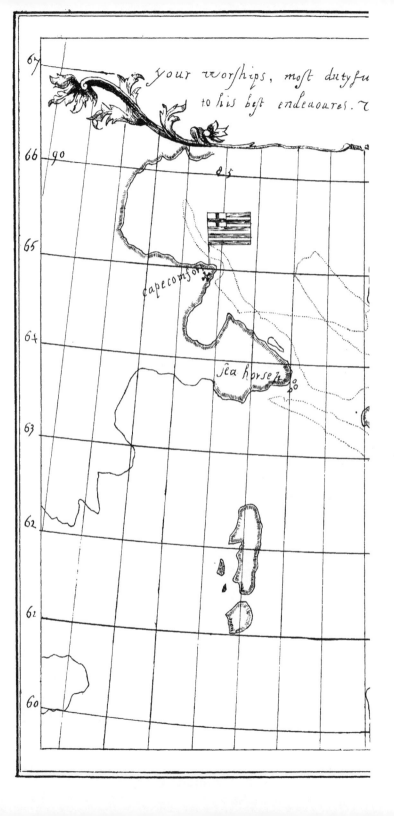

your worships, most dutyfu

to his best endeauores.

67

66   90

85

65

cape comfort

64

sea horse

63

62

61

60

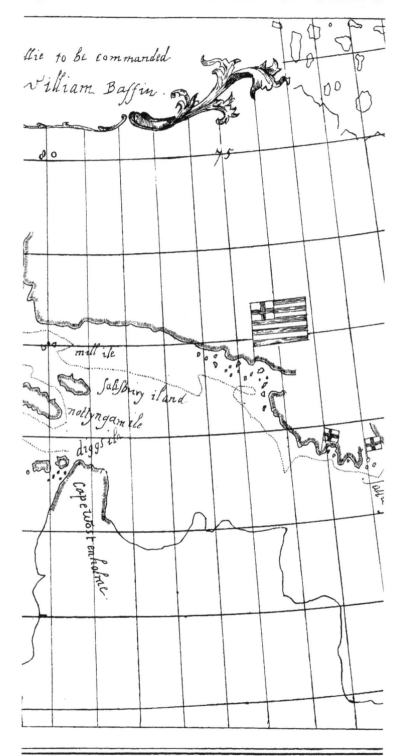

ttie to be commanded
William Baffin.

00   75

mill ile
Salisbury iland
nottyngam ile
diggs ile

Cape worstenholme.

Drawn by J. Wharton Rundall.

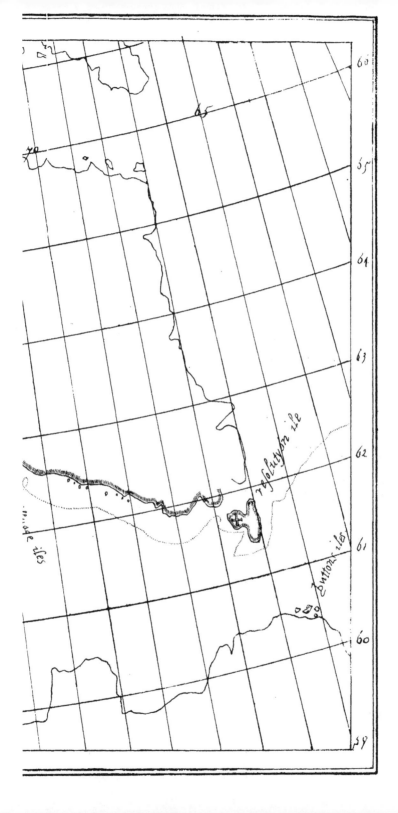

resolution ile

...ge iles

butons iles

§ X.

Voyages of Bylot and Baffin.

THE only printed documents relating to these voyages, that possess any claim to originality, are those which are to be found in Purchas, and which were, professedly, printed from communications made by Baffin. One of these is a narrative of the procedings in the first voyage, performed during the year 1615, now ascertained to be an incorrect version. The second is a narrative of the voyage of 1616 : which may be faithful or not. The third is a short explanatory letter, relating to the later voyage, addressed to Sir John Wolstenholme.

In addition to the above, Purchas was furnished with other documents prepared by Baffin, and essential to the right understanding of those that are printed. They were : I. THE BRIEF JOURNALS : exhibiting the daily courses of the ship, with the winds, latitudes, longitudes, and variation of the compass ; and II. CHARTS : shewing the tracks that were followed, and fixing the localities of the discoveries that were made. These documents, which, as before observed, are essential to the right understanding of such of the documents as are printed, being deemed " somewhat troublesome and too costly to insert ",[1] were excluded by Purchas from his compilation. By this proceeding, not only was interesting information suppressed ; but occasion has been given to impeach the character of Baffin.

It is with feelings of no ordinary satisfaction therefore, that, as regards the voyage of 1615, the compiler of this volume is able to communicate a correct version of the narrative, which, hitherto, has been printed in a mutilated form only ; and to give publicity to the other documents, which have not appeared in any printed form. These papers, with an additional letter

---

[1] *Purchas*, vol. iii, p. 848. (Marg. note.)

addressed to Sir Thomas Smith, and other adventurers in the enterprise, are now given in their full integrity, from the autograph originals preserved in the Library of the British Museum, and are published with the permission of the Trustees of that Institution.[1]

I.

TO THE

RIGHT WORSHIPFVL AND TRVLYE HONORABLE *Sir* THOMAS SMITH: *knight. Sir* DUDLY DIGGES: *kt. Mr.* JOHN WOLSTENHOLME: *esquire. and the rest of the worthy* ADUANCERS *and* ADUENTURERS *for the* FINDINGE OF A PASSAGE *by the* NORTH WEST.

THE AUNTIENTE (*Right Worshipfull*) had so much regard to the worthies of those tymes, that any waye sought the good and preferment of theare countrye and common wealth wheare they lyued, That ingratytude was so far from them, they honoured, yea with diuine honoure, those to whome theire countrye was any way obleeged. But wee which liue in an age, whome the poets tearme an jron age, are so far from honouringe our worthies with due prayse, that many had rather seek occation of slander then otherwise, although not agaynst theare persons, yet agaynst theare acctions.

You are the worthyes of our tyme, whose many fould aduentures are such, but espetiall this of the north west, which are not discouraged with spendinge and losse of many hundreth poundes, ney rather many thousand pounds; reapinge no other profitt butt onlye bare reports, and those little auaylable to the purpose. But I feare if I should take on me to sett forth your due prayse, I should come so far short of the marke I aymed at; that it weare better for me to leaue it undoone, then badlye doone: knowinge that who so seeketh to amend

---

[1] *Additional Mss.* 12,206.

With great pleasure I acknowledge the courtesy of MR. COOLEY, the Honorary Secretary of the Hakluyt Society, in communicating to me the existence of original papers connected with Baffin.   T. R.

APELLES pictture had need be some good artist, and who so seeketh to sett forth the worthie prayse of our LONDON MARCHANTS, had need bee more then a good rethoritian. But what neede I spende tyme hearin, when neuer dyinge fame hath, and will, enroule your names in TYMES CHEEFEST CHRONICLE OF ETERNYTIE : where no ENUIOUS MOMUS shall have power to rase out the smallest tytle thereof.

And seinge I haue beene imployed, and haue reaped some profitt from your purses, I might be counted a uery bad seruant if I gaue not in some accounte howe we spent our tyme. Such as it is, I present it to your worshipps vewe : whearin I haue indeuoured to set doune our proceedinges in so short a methode as conueniently I coulde, referringe our pertyculer courses, latytudes, longitudes, windes, leagues we run, and variatyon of the compas, to the breefe table or Jurnall in the beginninge of the booke, wheare euery of these is sett in their seuerall collombes, with the tytles at the heade.

And whereas in the collombe tytle TRU COURSE, in many places is sett a number betweene the letters, as on the last day of *Aprill*, is N. 20 E, which is north 20 degrees eastward, or allmost north north east : the tru waye that the shipp had room that 24 houers, the variatyon of the compas, and other accidentes alowed. Also there is a collombe wheare is sett downe the longitude, wheare we weare ech day at noone (although not usual in Jarnales) that theareby ech seuerall uariatyon of the compas, and any other accidente may be the more redylie found without protractinge all or parte of the voyage : in which variatyons I hope I haue not much erred from the truth, comminge nearer then some which haue beene imployed that way heretofore.

And because your worships may more redylie see and perseue howe far we haue beene, I haue heare followinge placed a small mapp, and it is to be noted that within the ILE OF RESOLUTYON, wee sawe no more land, then that I haue colored with greene, besides ilands. And heare is traced out our ships waye, with the red prickle lyne, notynge euery place wheare we came on shore (to make tryall of the tyde) with a red crosse, and for the tyme of high water at those places they are on the next page.

Thus bouldly haue I presumed on your worships clemencie in two respectes, the one in consideration of your selues, beinge so well acquaynted with these matters (as hauinge payde so deare for them) would in respect (not of the writer) but of the accion, vouchsafe the readinge thereof; the other, that beinge in duty bounde to be at your worships pleasure, I knowe not howe to shewe my selfe more dutyfull affected, then by giuinge in an accounte, how we haue spent, or mis-spent, our tyme; beseechinge your worships to accept them, not as my worke, but as my will and affection. And so with my daylie prayers to GOD for your health and prosperous successe in all your accions, I rest,

YOUR WORSHIPS, most dutyfullie to be commanded
to his best endeuoures, WILLIAM BAFFIN.

The LONGITUDE *and* LATYTUDE *of* SUCH PLACES *wheare we haue beene on shore within* RESOLUTION ILAND *& what Moone doth make a full sea, or the* TYME OF HIGH WATER *on the* CHAINGE DAYE. *And allso there distance from* RESOLUTION ILAND.

	[1] *	[2] *	[3] *	[4] *	[5] *
	° ′	° ′			
Resolution Iland .	66 . 26	61 . 30	E S.E.	7½	legues.
Saluage iland	72 . 00	62 . 30	S E. 4 E.	8¾	58
nine legues ½ beyond .	73 . 00	62 . 40	S.E.	9	67½
Broken ilands	74 . 30	63 . 46	S.E. by S.	9¾	87
North Shore	80 . 30	64 . 40	S.S.E.	10½	142
6 leagues short of Cape Comfort	85 . 20	64 . 45	S. 5 E.	11¾	180
At Cape Comfort	85 . 22	65 . 00	S. 5 E.	11¾	186
Sea Horse Poynt	82 . 30	63 . 44	S. by E.	11¼	154
Sir Dudly Diggs iland	79 . 40	62 . 45	S.S E.	10½	123
Nottyngam iland	80 . 50	63 . 32	S.S.E.	10½	13 †

---

* BLANK IN THE ORIGINAL. ? 1, *Long.:* 2, *Lat.:* 3, *Bearing:* 4, *Time:* 5, *Distance.*

† This corner of the page is torn.

II. THE BREEFE IOURNALL.

Dayes.	THE Tru course.	Leagues.	windes by the compas.	La ty-tude.	Longitude from London.	Vari aty on.	
APRIL.				° ′	° ′	° ′	
7	...	...	...	...	...	... E.	This morne wee sett sayle from Silly.
8	...	...	...	...	...	...	Wee came to anchor this eveninge att Padstowe.
18	...	...	S.E.	...	...	7 . 00	This morninge wee sett sayle from Padstowe.
19	...	...	S.E.	50 . 30	7 . 00	...	
20	W. ⅓ N.	41	E.S.E.	50 . 30	7 . 00	6 . 50	
21	W. by N. ¼ N.	37	E.S.E. : S.S.E.	50 . 38	10 . 15	...	
22	N.W. ⅓ N.	45	E.S.E. : E.N.E.	51 . 12	13 . 00	...	
23	N.W. by W.	50	E.N.E.	52 . 44	15 . 20	5 . 30	
24	N.W.W. ¾ N.	44	E.N.E.	54 . 05	19 . 20	1 . 16	
25	W.N.W. ½ N.	24	N.N.E.	54 . 50	22 . 40	...	
26	N.W. by W.	36	E.N.E.	55 . 25	24 . 35	...	
27	N.W. by N.	13	E.N.E. : N.W.	56 . 28	27 . 24	...	
28	N.w. by W. ⅓ w.	10	N.W. : E.N.E.	57 . 00	28 . 00	...	
29	N. 29 w.	24	E.N.E. : w.	57 . 30	28 . 15	...	
30	N. 20 E.	10	variable but w. ward	58 . 30	29 . 25	...	
				59 . 00	29 . 00	...	
MAYE							
1	N. by w.	17½	W.N.W.	59 . 50	29 . 26	1 . 30 w.	
2	W.N.W. ¼ w.	24½	W.N.W. : S.E.	60 . 24	31 . 40	...	
3	w. by N.	35	S.E. : S.W.	60 . 43	35 . 15	...	
4	W. 3 s.	25½	S.S.E.	60 . 40	38 . 00	...	This afternoone a storme att south-east.
5	W. 26 s.	25½	S.S.E.	60 . 04	40 . 24	9 . 24	We suppose a currante sett to the south-west.
6	W. 12 s.	28	S.S.E. : S.E. : N.E.	59 . 45	43 . 00	10 . 30	This forenoone wee sawe land.
7	s.w. by s.	21	N N.W. : N. : W.	58 . 56	44 . 15	...	This night a storme.

Dayes.	THE Tru course.	Leagues.	windes by the compass.	La ty-tude.	Longitude from London.	Vari aty on.	
				° ′	° ′	° ′	
8	w . 13 s.	13	w. by N.	58 . 46	45 . 20	11 . 30 w.	Cape Farewell bore north 15 leg. east at noone.
9	w . 25 s.	7	N. by w.	58 . 32	46 . 00	12 . 00	
10	w . 15 N.	15	N.N.E.	58 . 40	47 . 30	...	
11	w . 20 N.	38	E.S.E. : S.E.	59 . 16	51 . 00	...	
12	w . 20 N.	39	S.S.E. : S. by E.	59 . 48	54 . 40	...	
13	w . 18 N.	45	S. : S. by E.	60 . 30	58 . 50	...	
14	N.W.	9	N.w. : N. by E.	60 . 50	59 . 30	...	
15	W.N.W.	15	N.N.E.	61 . 00	61 . 00	19 . 26	At noone we put into the ice.
16	W.N.W.	4½	E.	60 . 58	61 . 15	20 . 18	
17	W.N.W.	26	E.N.E.	61 . 27	63 . 40	...	
18	...	...	S.S.E.	...	...	...	
19	...	...	S.S.E.	...	...	...	
20	...	...	S. by E.	...	...	...	
21	...	...	w.s.w.	...	...	...	
22	...	...	W.N.W.	61 . 20	64 . 33	22 . 36	This eveninge at 8 a clock we weare forth of the ice.
23	...	13	W.N.W.	61 . 18	64 . 26	...	
24	N.E. by N.	12½	N.N.W.	61 . 50	63 . 30	21 . 00	
25	N.E. by N.	21	N. by w.	62 . 20	62 . 40	...	At 5 a clock this afternoone, we saw the iland of Resolu-tion.
26	w .	...	N.E. : E.	62 . 21	64 . 40	...	
27	...	...	E. : E.N.E.	62 . 12	65 . 20	23 . 40	
28	...	...	w. by N.	61 . 40	66 . 30	...	
29	...	...	w. by N.	...	...	...	
30	...	...	S.S.E.	...	...	...	This morne we weare sett within the entraunce of the Strayts.
31	...	...	N.N.W.	61 . 18	66 . 50	24 . 6	Wee came to anchor on the west side of Resolution ile.
IVNE 1	...	...	w.N.w.	61 . 20	66 . 56	24 . 8	Att noone we sett sayle.
2	...	...	E. : N.N.W.	...	...	...	

							Remarks
3			N.w.	61 . 35	67 . 56		We came to anchor at Saluage iles, at 8 a clock this night.
4	w. 4 N.	10½	w.s.w.	61 . 38	68 . 04		This morne we set saile, and in the afternoone came to anchor agayne 9 leagues w.n.w. of
5	N.W. 6 w.	17	s.s.e. : w.s.w.	62 . 10	69 . 34	26 . 26	This eueninge we sett sayle.
6	w.n.w. ¼ N.	19	w.s.w.	62 . 32	71 . 30	27 . 10	
7	s.w. by s.	4	w.n.w. : N.w.	62 . 21	71 . 40		
8	N. 40 w.	5	N.w.	62 . 27	72 . 00	27 . 20	
9	N.w.	1⅛	N.N.w.	62 . 30	72 . 06		
10	w.n.w.	9½	E. : N.w.	62 . 40	73 . 04		
11			N.w.	62 . 40	73 . 04		
12			w.n.w.	62 . 40	73 . 04		
13	w.n.w.	9	variable.	62 . 48	74 . 00		This eueninge we anchored among diuers iles.
14			N. : N.N.w.				
15			s.s.e.	63 . 22	74 . 05		At eleuen a clock we sett sayle.
16			s.s.e. : w.n.w.	63 . 26	74 . 45	27 . 45	We made fast to a piece of ice wheare we stayed 8 dayes.
17			N.w. by w.	63 . 26	74 . 45		
18			variable.	63 . 40	76 . 14		This daye I obserued the moones comminge to the meridian and found the longitude 74° 5′ west from London, and 91° 35′ from Wittenberg.
19	w.n.w.	12½	s.e.			28 . 30	
22			N.N.w.	63 . 28	76 . 18		
24			N.w. by N.	63 . 28	76 . 20		
25			N.w. by N.	63 . 18			
26							
27			s.e.	63 . 30	76 . 32		This evening we set sayle ; hauinge had calme whether since the 19 daye.
28			s.e.	63 . 30	77 . 32		
29	w.n.w.	13	s.e.	63 . 42	78 . 30		
30	w. 3 s.	5	variable.	63 . 40		28 . 34	Att noone we sawe Salisburie island.
Ivly 1	w.	11½	s.s.e.	63 . 40	79 . 45	28 . 10	
2	N. 31 w.	6¼	N.N.w.	63 . 55	80 . 10	28 . 28	
3	w. 24 N.	10	w.s.w.	64 . 05	81 . 13		This morne we weare by a smale iland, we called it Mill ile. At night our ship was in great distress with ice.
4	N.w.	28	s.w.	64 . 54	82 . 45		
5	N.w. by N.	5	N. : N.N.w.	65 . 00	83 . 00		

Dayes.	THE Tru course.	Leagues.	windes by the compas.	La ty- tude.	Longitude from London.	Vari a tyon.	
6	N.E.	5	N.N.E.	65 . 10	82 . 40	28 . 20	This eueninge we anchored near the north shore.
7	S.E. by E.	11	N.W.	64 . 48	81 . 28	:	
8	S.	3½	W.	64 . 46	81 . 28	:	
9	S.E.	3	W. : N.W.	64 . 36	80 . 40	:	
10	S.W.	5	S.W.	64 . 24	81 . 04	:	
11	W. 6 N.	18	W.S.W. : N.N.W.	64 . 30	83 . 08	:	We sent our bote ashore 6 leagues south of Cape Comfort: att 6 a clock this eueninge we returned.
12	W. 3 N.	12	W. : W.S.W.	64 . 33	84 . 48	:	
13	N. 36 W.	17½	S.W.	65 . 18	85 . 56	:	
[14]	...	...	S.E.	65 . 18	85 . 56	:	We anchored neare Cape Comfort. At night wayed anchor.
[15]	...	...	S.E.	65 . 02	85 . 22	:	We came to anchor at Sea Horse Point this eueninge.
[16]	w.s.w.	...	Variable.	63 . 54	82 . 50	:	This morne we wayed anchor and stood for Nottinghams ile, wheare this night we anchored.
17	w.s.w.	6½	N.W. by W.	63 . 38	82 . 00	:	
18	w.s.w.	8½	N. : N. by E.	63 . 36	81 . 00	:	
19	...	...	N.W.	:	:	:	
20	...	...	S.W. by s.	:	:	:	
21	...	...	W.N.W.	:	:	:	
22	...	...	N.N.W.	:	:	:	
23	...	...	N.N.W.	:	:	:	
24	...	...	Southward.	:	:	:	
25	...	...	W.S.W. : W. by S.	:	:	:	We passed betweene Nottinghame and Salisburies ile.
26	...	...	N.N.W. : N. : N.N.E.	63 . 30	80 . 00	:	At night came to anchor.
27	E.N.E.	2	E. : E.N.E. : N.E.	:	:	:	This day stood ouer for Sea Horse Point agayne.
28	E.N.E.	13	N.E.	62 . 44	:	:	This morne we returned for Digges ile.
29	...	...	N.E.	62 . 44	80 . 05	:	We came to anchor at Digges ile, foule wether.
30	...	...	N.E. by N.		80 . 05	:	We wayed and sett sayle for homewards.
31	E. 8 N.	18	S.	62 . 56	75 . 45	:	

Avg.									
1	E. by s.	15	s.sw. : s.w.	62 . 46	76 . 5	:	This afternoone we came to anchor on the north shore among diuers ilands, 30 leagues within Resolution ile.
2	E. 19 s.	38	s.w. : N.w. by w.	62 . 16	72 . 6	:	
3	E. 17 s.	19	N.w. : s.E.	62 . 20	70 . 15	:	This day we sett sayle.
4	...	...	...	... ...	...	19 . 30	We past by the ile of Resolution, but sawe it nott.
5	E. 32 s.	45	N.w.	61 . 00	65 . 30	:	
6	E. 20 s.	46	N.w.	60 . 20	61 . 00	:	
7	E. 18 s.	43	N.w.	59 . 36	57 . 00	:	
8	E. 13 s.	29	N.w. : s. by w.	59 . 14	54 . 14	:	
9	E.	26	S.S.w. : s.	59 . 15	51 . 40	:	
10	E. 7 s.	32	N.N.w.	59 . 4	48 . 52	:	We came through som smale ice, of Cape Farewell, but saw no land.
11	E. 34 s.	46	N.w.	57 . 32	45 . 40	:	
12	E. 7 s.	40	w.s.w.	57 . 18	42 . 00	:	
13	E. 8 s.	38	w.s.w. s. by E.	57 . 6	38 . 25	:	
14	E. 40 N.	20	S.E. by E.	57 . 42	36 . 56	:	
15	N. 22 E.	11	E. by s.	58 . 15	36 . 35	:	
16	S.S.E.	7	E.	58 . 5	36 . 15	:	
17	E.N.E.	8	S.E.	58 . 20	35 . 35	:	
18	N. 30 E.	22	S.E.	59 . 20	34 . 30	:	
19	S. 25 E.	9	E.S.E. : E.	58 . 52	34 . 8	:	
20	S. 40 E.	14	N.N.E.	58 . 18	33 . 15	:	
21	S. 20 E.	20	E. : E.S.E.	57 . 22	32 . 30	:	
22	S.	4	E.	57 . 8	32 . 30	:	
23	S.S.E.	14	N.E.	56 . 30	32 . 6	:	
24	E. 25 s.	21	N.N.E.	56 . 5	30 . 20	2 . 00 E.	
25	E. 30 s.	36	N. by E.	55 . 10	27 . 35	:	
26	E. 35 s.	38	N.N.E.	54 . 00	24 . 52	:	
27	S. 29 E.	39	N.E.	52 . 40	23 . 42	:	
28	S. 30 E.	18	N.E. by E.	52 . 18	23 . 5	:	
29	S. 30 W.	10	E.N.E.	51 . 25	23 . 30	:	
30	N. 30 E.	3	E.S.E.	51 . 32	23 . 25	:	A sore storme.
31	S.E.	20	N.E.	50 . 46	22 . 15	:	

[*Note.* Here the journal ends, at the bottom of a reverse page. Whetherleft incomplete, or whetherthe concluding portion be lost, must be left to conjecture.]—T. R.

III.

A Tru Relatyon of such thinges as happened in
*fourth voyage for the discouery of a passage to the
north west, performed in the yeare*
1615.

After so many sundrye voyages to the north westward, to
the greate charge of the aduenturers, The last being under
the command of *Captaine* Gibbins, in which by som sinister
accident, was little or nothinge performed. Yett the right worshipfull, *Sir* Tho. Smith, *knight:* Sir Dudly Digges, *knight;*
Mr. John Wostenholme, *esquire; Mr.* Alderman Jones, with
others, beinge not theare with discouraged, this yeare 1615
sett forth agayne the good shipp called the Discouerare,
beinge of the burthen of 55 tonn, or theare aboute, (which
ship had beene the three former voyages on the accion).

March.

The cheefe mr. and commander, vnder God, *was* Robert
Byleth, *a man well experienced that wayes, (hauinge
beene imployed the three former voyages) my selfe beinge
his mate and assotiate, with fourteene other men and 2
boyes. This ship being in redines, vpon the* 15th *daye*
15 *of March came abourd* Mr. John Wostenholme, *esquire,
one of the cheefe aduenturers, and with him* Mr. Allwin
Carye *(husband for the voyage). Who hauinge deliuered
our mr. his commission, and reade certayne orders to be
obserued by vs in the voyage, giuing vs good exortations,
and large promyses of reward, as treble wages to all, if
the accion weare performed, they departed, charginge vs
to make what speede we could away. So the next day,*
16 *beeing thursdaye, we wayed anchor at* St. Katherins,

17 *and that tyde came to* BLACK WALL, *and the next day to*
18 GRAUES ENDE ; *and the morrow after to* LEE.
19 *Sondaye the* 19 *it blu hard at south west and by south,*
yet this daye we came to anchor neare the BOOY *on the*
NOURE ENDE. *The* 20 *daye the winde variable, but by* 2
a clock this afternoone we came to the NORTH FORLAND,
22 *wheare we stayed all the* 22 *daye, which day we wayed and*
23 *that night anchored in the* DOUNES. *The* 23 *in the morne*
we wayed anchor, the winde att east, and east and by south :
26 *thus with indifferent windes and wether we came to anchor*
in SILLY *the* 26 *daye.*

APRILL.

7 *Heare we stayed for a fayre winde till the* 7 *day of Aprill,*
being Good Frydaye, which day we wayed anchor in the
morne, the winde south south east. We had not stoode on
our course aboue 10 *or* 12 *leagues, but the wind came to*
south, then to south south west and blu extreme hard, which
encreased so sore, that we weare not able to beare any sayle
at all.
8 *The next morning we stood for* PADSTOW *in* CORNEWALL,
because we could not fetch Silly agayne, and about 10 *a*
clocke we came to anchor in the entrance of the harbour,
9 *and the next daye, being Easter Sonday, in the forenoone*
we moored our ship in the harboure. Heare we stayed till
the 19 *daye, hauinge had much foule wether and contrary*
windes. While heare we stayed we found much kindness at
the handes of Mr. RICHARD PENKEWILL, *who, beinge will-*
inge to further vs with what things we wanted, or that
place could afford, as with beefe and porke, and also with
a capstand which we wanted, haueing broke ours in the
storme when we came from Silly. And also he was de-
sirous his eldest sonn should goe alonge with vs, to which
our mr. and the rest of the company agreed, because he
19 *layd in all prouition fitt for the voyage. So the* 19 *of*

Aprill in the morne we wayed anchor, the winde south east
a good gale, we keepinge our courses as in the breefe Jarnall
you may more conueniently see. And seinge fewe thinges of
note happened in our outward bound voyage, I refer all
other thinges to that table before noted.[1]

MAYE.

6 We haueing had an indifferent good passage, vpon the 6
of Maye we sawe land on the coste of GROYNLAND on the
east side of CAPE FAREWELL; and that night we had a
storme. So keeping a southwardly course to gett about
the ice which lay on that coste, we kept on our course tyll
the 17 daye of Maye : all which forenoone we sayled
through many greate ilands of ice. Som of them were
200 foot aboue water, as I proued by on shortly after,
which I found to be 240 foote high aboue water. And if
reporte of some men be tru which affirme that there is but
on seuenth part of it aboue water, then the height of that
peece of ice I observed was 140 [? 280] fathoms, or 1680
foote, from the top to the bottome. This proportion doth
hould I knowe in much ice, but whether in all, or no, I
know nott.[2]

---

[1] The italic print denotes the matter *omitted* by Purchas. *Material
alterations*, or *additions*, in the version given by Purchas, will be noticed
in foot-notes.

[2] *Dimensions of ice-bergs.* August 25, 1818 (lat. 76° 10′ N., long. 78° 30′
W., var. 109° 58½′ W.). " I made fast to an ice-berg...This berg was one
hundred and four feet high, six hundred long, and four hundred feet broad."
...September 11, 1818 (lat. 70° 34½′ N., long. 67° 46½′ W., var. 75° 00′ W.).
" At eight this morning we discovered the largest iceberg we had ever
seen at such a distance from land (7 leagues)...Lt. Parry reported to me
that it was four thousand, one hundred, and sixty-nine yards long; three
thousand, eight hundred, and sixty-nine yards broad; and fifty-one feet
high, aground in sixty-one fathoms : and that it had nine unequal sides.
Its appearance was much like that of the back of the Isle of Wight, and
its cliffs exactly resembled the chalke cliffs to the west of Dover."— *Voyage of the Isabella and Alexander (John Ross)*, pp. 159-201. London: 1819.

17 This 17 of May aboute noone, wee weare come to the firme
ice as it shewed to sight, *although in deede it was many*
peeces drauen together : wheare our mr. asked my opinion
conseninge the puttinge into the ice. My judgment was
it would be best for vs to stand somwhat more north ward,
to se if we could find any more likley place, for heare we
could not disserne wheare to put in the ships head. Hee
answered we weare as for [far] to the north ward as the
south end of RESOLUTION ILAND, and now had all the south
channell southward of vs ; and through much ice we must
goe. Supposinge that, if we could gett som 3 or 4 leagues
within the ice, at euery tyde it would open and we should
gett somthinge on our waye, it being now fayre wether,
and if it should chance to blo hard, we should then be
forced to enter in. *I could not much say agaynst his opynion,*
beinge indeede in the latitude of 61 *deg.* 26' *and hee knew*
the manner of this ice better then my selfe, so presently we
resolved to put into the ice. (This first entrance I liked not
uery well, the ice being so uery thick, and by all our accounte
and reconinge we were 30 *leagues from shore, which after*
we found to be tru).

After we weare entred a little into the ice, it was not
longe before we weare fast sett vp, but sometymes of the
tyde the ice would a little open, then we made our way as
much to the north west as we could, yet we playnlie found
that we weare sett to the southward, *although the wind*
weare southwardly.

22 Nowe vpon the 22 daye the wind came to north north-
west, then we determined to gett forth agayne, fearinge
the wind should com to the north east, for then it would
be hard for vs to fetch any part of the Straytes mouth :
seinge this aboundance of ice and knowing that it must
haue some time to dissolue, our mr. was determyned
to run up DAUIS STRAYTES and to spend some 20 dayes
therein, to trye what hopes that wayes would afford,

supposinge by that tyme we myght come near RESOLUTION
ILE. This purpose of our mr. contynued no longer but tyll
we weare forth of the ice, which by God's assistance was
22 the 23d daye about 8 a clock att night, the wind at N.W.
and by W. When we weare cleare of the ice, we stood
to the northwarde, as much as the ice and winde would
suffer vs, running about 13 leg. north east and by north ;
by the next day at noone, beinge in the latytude of 61° 50′
and fayre wether.

25 The 25 daye we made our waye and course weare as
we did the daye before, namely N.E. and by N., 13
legues.[1]

26 The 26 daye all the forenoone fayre wether and could, but
in the afternoone it blew uery hard, and close haysey wether, that about 2 a clock we weare forced to take in our
sayles. All the tyme that we sayled this daye we passed
through much ice, lyinge in longe driftes and ledges,
hauing made a west way about [?] leagues.[2]

27 The 27 daye aboute 4 in the morninge we sett sayle.
Most parte of the day proued close and foggy, with much
snowe, freesinge on our shroudes and tackle, that the like
we haue not had this yeare ; but toward 5 a clock in the
afternoone it cleared vp and we sawe the ILAND of RESO-
LUTION, it bearinge west from vs about 13 or 14 leagues,
and at night moored our ship to a peece of ice.[3]

28 The 28 daye, beinge Whitsondaye, it was fayre wether,
but the winde at west and west by north, that we weare
forced all this daye to make our shipp fast to a peece of ice,
yet we playnlie perceued that we sett more into the straytes

---

[1] [About twelve leagues and an halfe, our latitude at noone 62 degrees
20 minutes. At sixe a clocke the winde was north north east. P.]

[2] [Having runne about twenty one leagues true vppon a west course.
And note when I put this word true, I meane the true course, the variation of the compasse and other accidents considered. P.]

[3] [The winde being at west. P.]

with one tyde of floud, then we sett forth in 2 ebbs, although the wind blu contrary.

29 The 29 the winde variable and fayre wether.   About eleuen a clock we sett sayle and tacked too and fro along
30 the iland.   And the next morne, about two a clocke, the winde came to the south south east, but we hauinge so much ice we could doe but little good nowe we had a faire wind.[1]   This night (or rather eueninge, because it was not darke,) we were sett *within the poynt of the iland, so that nowe we weare* within the straytes, playnly prouinge what is sayd before, namely that one tyde of floud setteth more in, then two tydes of ebb will sett forth.[2]
31 The last daye of Maye also faire weather, the wind for the most part north north west.   The afternoone being cleare, we saw the point of the South shoare[3] bearing from vs south by the compas, which is indeed south south east, somewhat eastward, because here the compas is varied to the west 24 degrees.

IVNE.

1 The first day of June some snowe in the forenoone, but afterward it proued very faire, the wind west north west; and perceiuing the ice to be more open neare to the shore we made the best waye we could to get in, and to com to anchor if the place weare conueniente; seeinge the wind was contrary and also to make tryall of the tyde. And by seuen a clock we weare at anchor in a good har-

---

[1] [The wind continued all this day and night a stiffe gale.   P.]

[2] It was a subject of constant surprise to the officers of the *Fury* and *Hecla*, to find those vessels, represented to be dull sailers, make considerable way during the ebb-tides, when beating against a fresh wind from the westward ; and the circumstance caused *Captain Parry* to entertain no doubt of the accuracy of the remark made by the early navigators [from Baffin to Luke Fox] : of the flood-tides running stronger than the ebbs on this coast.— *Voyage of the Fury and Hecla* (*Parry*), 1821, etc. p. 19.   London : 1824.

[3] [Called *Button's Iles*, P.]

bour, on the west side of RESOLUTION ILAND, wheare an
east south east moone maketh a full sea, or halfe an houer
past seuen on the chainge day, as seamen acounte.   At
this place the water doth rise and fall about 22 or 23
foote ; the compas doth vary 24 .. 6′ west, and it is in longitude west from LONDON 66 degrees 35′.   The latytude
of the north ende of the iland is 61 .. 36′,[1] *and the latytude
tude of the south end is* 61 .. 26′.   The bredth of the south
channell, or the distance betweene the iland and the south
shore is 16 leagues, and the bredth of the north channell
is aboute 8 miles in the narrowest place.

Vpon this iland we went on shore, but found no certaine
signe of inhabitants, but only the tracke of beares and
foxes.   The soyle is only rocks and stonie ground, hardly
any thinge growinge thearon which is greene.   It is indifferent high land to the north, hauinge one high hill or
hummocke to the north east side, but toward the south
ward it falleth away uery low.

2 The 2 June in the forenoone the wind came to east
south east with snowe and foule wether.   About noone
we wayed and stood vp along by the iland[2] to the north
ward.   This afternoone it proued foule wether, but toward
eueninge it cleared vp and we saw the north shore.   But
heare to wright of our often mooringe to ice, takinge in
sayles, and fast inclosinge, would prooue but tedious to
the reader, as it was troublesom to vs ; so therefore I
referre it: but our course, and waye we made from noone
to noone may be seene else wheare.

We continuing our courses so neare to the north shore as
conueniently we could, with much variable wether and
8 windes, but stedfast in contynuance among ice, till the 8

---

[1] " We had now only advanced within five or six miles of *Resolution
Island,* which by our observations, lies in lat. 61° 20′ 40″, long. 64° 55′ 15″."
— *Voyage of the Fury and Hecla (Parry),* 1821-23, p. 8.   London : 1824.
[2] [So well as the ice would giue vs leaue to gett.   P.]

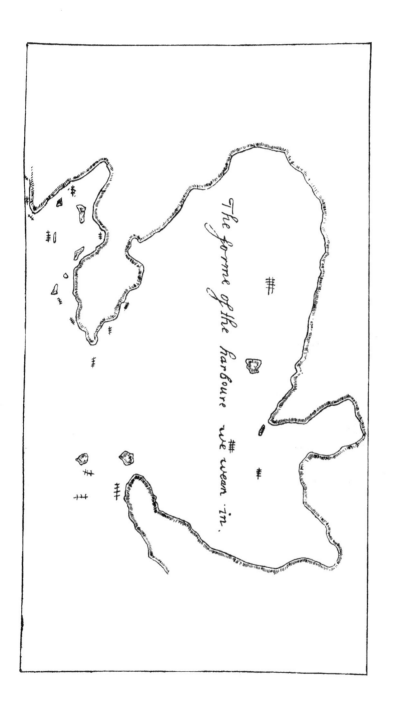

The forme of the harboure we wear in.

daye. Then hauinge the winde contrary to vs, being somewhat neare a poynt of land (or rather a company of ilandes),[1] we determyned to come to anchor[2] among them *if possible we could. About* 6 *a clock we weare come to anchor*, and as we weare busy *in makinge vp our sayles and fittinge our ship*, we hard a great houlinge and noyse, as we supposed of doggs vpon the ilande neare to vs.

So soon as the ship was moored, we sent our bote somewhat nearer the shore, to see if they could perceue any people, who returninge, they tould vs they sawe tentes and botes, with a number of doggs, but people they sawe none.

Then by and bye we went to prayer, and after our men had supt, we fitted our bote and selues with things con-uenient; then my selfe and seuen other landed, and went to the tents, wheare finding no people, we went to the top of the hill (being about a flite shot of) wheare we sawe one great cannoo, or bote, hauinge aboute fourteene personns in it; they being on the furthest, or north west side theareof, beinge from vs somewhat aboue a musket shott of. Then I called vnto them, (using some words of *Groyn-landish* speeche), makinge signes of frendship. They did the like to vs; but seeing them *to be* fearefull of vs, and we not willinge to trust them, I made another signe to them, shewinge them a knife and other small thinges : which I left on the top of the hill, and returned doune to their tents agayne.

Beinge returned to theare tents, we found some whale finnes to the number of 14 or 15,[3] which I tooke aboard, leauinge kniues, bedes, and counters insteede thereof. And among other of theare househould, I found in a

---

1 [Which after we called *Savag Isles*, hauing a great sound, or in-draught, betweene the north shoare and them. P.]

2 [Neere one of them, being the eastermost saving one. P.]

3 [Fortie or fiftie with a few seale-skinnes. P.]

smale lether bagg a company of little images of men;
and one the image of a woman with a child at hir backe:
all the which I brought awaye.

Among there tents (being fiue in number) all couered
with seale skinnes, weare runninge up and done, about 35
or 40 dogs, most of them mussled.   They are most of
them about the bigness of our mungrell mastives, being a
brinded black culler, lookinge almost like wolues.   These
doggs they vse instede of horses, or rather as the *Lappians*
doe theare deare, to draw theare sledes from place to place
ouer the ice.   Theare sleds beinge shod, or lined, with bones
of great fishes to keepe them [from] wearinge, and the
doggs have collers and furniture uery fittinge.

These people haue their apparell, botes,[1] tentes, with other
necesaryes, muche like to the inhabitaunte of Groyneland, sauing that they are not so neate and artefitiall,
seminge to bee more rude and vnciuill, raynginge vp and
doune as theare fishinge is in season.   For in most places
wheare we went ashore, we sawe wheare people had
beene, although not this yeare, but wheare theare dwell-
inge or abode in winter is, I cannot well coniecture.
9 The next morninge we fetcht 2 botes ladinge of stones
aboard, because our ship was very light, keepinge a good
watch on shore, for feare the people should come doune
vpon vs while we weare busie.   By noone our ship was
fitted.   Then afterward we marched aboute the island,
but could see no people.

This iland lyeth in the latytude of 62 .. 30' and in
longitude west from *London* aboute 72 degrees,[2] being
60 leagues within the entrance of the straytes.   Here

---

[1] [Boots. P.]

[2] By the observations made on board the *Fury* and *Hecla* (July 24,
1821), this anchorage was made 2½ miles to the northward, and 1° 52' to
the eastward of the position assigned to it by Baffin. Variation 52° 37'.
— *Voyage of the Fury and Hecla (Parry)*, 1821, etc. P. 16. (*Chart*.) London : 1824.

the compas doth varye 27.30′, and a south east 4 degrees east moone maketh a full sea. It doth ebb and flowe almost as much water as it doth at RESOLUTION ILE ; and heare the floud commeth from the eastward, although our Master was confidente to the contrary.

10 The 10 daye,[1] in the morninge, we set sayle, the winde north, which contynued not longe, but was very variable tyll noone, and then it came to north west, we hauinge sayled along by the shore, about 9½ leagues north north west, the ice lyinge so thicke in the offen, that we could not gett of. Then perceuinge a good harbour betweene the mayne and 2 smale ilandes, we went in with the ship, wheare we moored her, and stayed till the 12 day at night.

In this place it is high water on the chaunge day, at 9 a clock, or a south east moone maketh a full sea.[2] Here the floud commeth from the south east, as it did at SALVAGE ILAND,[3] *and because our Mr. was conceued otherwise, I tooke our surgeon (a man of good iudgment) to the top of the ile, where most apparently we saw the tru sett of the tyde by the ice dryvinge in the offen. For all the tyme the water doth rise by the shore, the ice did sett in to the straytes ; and as soon as the water fell it returned. But the truth of this was made more apparent by other places after ward.*[4]

12 The 12 day after we had doone som busines in our ship, as cleared our pumps and such lyke, seinge the ice to driue in more then vsuall it did before, about 8 a clock we set sayle, it being almost calme. Shortly after the winde came to south west and by south, which contynued but till 12 a clock ; then it came to west with snowe and foule wether.

---

1 [At sixe a clocke. P.]
2 [The latitude of the place is 62 degrees 40 minutes. P.]
3 [Although our master was perswaded otherwise. P.]
4 [In this place is no sign of people, as we could perceive. P.]

13 The 13 aboute noone we tooke in our sayles, and made
the ship fast to a peece of ice, beinge some 9 leagues
14 from our last harbour. All this daye and the next the
wind was contrarye, and foule wether, we driuinge too
and fro with the wind and tide.

15 The 15 in the morne, the wind came to the south south
east; then we set sayle, and made the best waye we could
through the ice, and in the afternoone it blu uery much
winde, and was foule wether, so that at 8 a clocke we
weare forced to take in our sayles and to make the
ship fast to ice agayne, it beinge a storme and amounge
much ice.

16 The 16 day, lying still in the ice, the wether close and
hasye (as it hath beene these six dayes) we being neare a
greate company of ilandes, and the wind at north north
west, this afternoone wee stood toward these ilandes:
and at night came to anchor neare one of them, in
a small coue, the better to defend the ship from danger of
17 the ice. In this place we stayed all the next day : but
18 vpon the 18 being Sonday, at eleuen a clocke we set sayle,
it beinge allmost calme, we makinge the best way we could
gett from a monge those ilands, being more safe further
of then neare them : for these iles lye in a bay (as it
weare), being many of them, and euery one hath his
seuerall sett and eddy, carryinge the ice to and fro, that
a ship is allwaye in danger of some hurte. The latytude
of the place is 63 .. 26' ; and west from *London*, neare
74 ..[1] 25' : the compas doth vary 27 .. 40';[2] and a south
east and by south moone[3] maketh a full sea.

19 *This evening and the next forenoone, we had a fine gale of*
wind at south east, we standinge alonge the lande, it being
all broken ground and ilandes to the sea ward. By noone
weare come to the poynt of those ilandes, and being not past

---

[1] [72. P.]   [2] [46. P.]
[3] [And a quarter of an houre after nine on the chainge day. P.]

*a league or 4 miles distant, we weare fast sett vp with ice,
the wether very fayre and allmost calme.   This poynt of
ilands I after called Fair Ness,*[1] *by reason of the fayre
wether we had at this place, for from this* 19 *daye till the*
27 *daye (yea tyll the* 30) *the wether was so faire, cleare
and calme, that it was more then extraordinary in this
place, and we so fast closed vp with ice, that many tymes
one could not well dip a payle of water.*

*And some dayes while heare we stayed we shott at butts
with bowe and arrows, at other tymes at stoole ball, and
some tymes at foote ball.   And seinge I haue begun to
speake of exercise, I think it not amiss to relate one dayes
exercise of my owne.*

While we weare thus fast inclosed with ice, and the
21 *wether fayre and cleare (as is sayd before)* vpon the 21
daye I sawe both the sonn and moone very cleare. Then
thinkinge it a fit tyme to be doinge of somthinge to im-
ploy myself vpon, I fitted my instruments to take both
the Almycanter and Azimuth of the sonn and also of the
moone : fearinge I should not see them so well agayne.
Which obseruations I think it not much unfitt heare to
sett doune (although I neuer wrought it, because I had
another the next daye, better to my contentment, otherwise I would have spent some tyme in this), as heare they
followe :

		deg.				deg.
The	Sonns Almycanter ...	25 . 5		The	Moones Almycanter	32 . 5
	Sonns magne. Azimuth	29 . 00			Mones Azimuth ...	43 . 00
	w. of N.				s. of w.	

butt heare is to be noted that the moones Almycanter
and Azimuth weare taken 4 minites 30 seconds of tyme
after the sonns.

22 The next morne being fayre and cleare, and allmost as

---

[1] [This evening, and the next morning, we had a faire steering gale of
winde at south east, wee standing along by the land, it being all small
broken ilands, to a point of laud about twelve leagues in distance from

stedy as on shore, it was no neede to bid me haue my instrument of uariation in redynes to take the time of [the]
moone's comming to the meridian, hauinge my quadrant
redy to take the sonnes Almicanter, it being indifferent
large, as of 4 foote semydiameter.   I hauinge[1] taken the
uariation of my needle this forenoone and dyuers tymes
before, which was 28..30′ W.   Nowe hauinge all things
in redynes (for I had tyme jnough) for it would be after
foure in the afternoone before any thinge could be doone;
so hauing wayted till the moone was precisely on the
meridian, and that instant tooke the height of the sonn,[2]
which was 26° 40′. *The latytude of the place is* 63..40′, and
the sonns declination for that tyme 23 degrees 6 minites.
By which three things giuen I found the houre to be fiue
a clocke 4′. . 52″. . 1‴. . 4⁗ or 76 degrees 13′. . 16″ of the
equinoctiall afternoone. Nowe according to *Searle's Ephe-
meris,* the moone came to the meridian at LONDON at 4
a clocke 54′. . 30″: and after *Origanus*, the moone came to
the meridian at WITTENBERGE at 4 a clocke 52′. 5″, the same
day. Nowe hauinge this knowne, it is no hard matter to
finde the longitude of the place sought for.   For according to the moones ordinary meane motion, which is 12
degrees ech day, which is in tyme 48 minites: and [?] to
this account, if the moone be on the meridian at 12 a
clock this day, tomorrowe it will be 48 minites past 12.

Nowe I hauinge the time at this place found by obseruation, which was 5 a clocke 4′. . 52″. . 1‴. . 4⁗ (but in this I
neede not be so precise): and at LONDON 4 a clocke 54′. .

the ile wee put last from : which point I called BROKEN POINT, it being
indeede a point of broken iles. On the nineteenth day, by twelue a clocke
at noone, wee were about foure miles from the point before named, fast
inclosed with ice, very faire weather ; and well might wee haue called
this point FAIRNESSE, or, POINT.   P.]

[1] [Haue. P.]

[2] [The sunnes Almicanter, at the instant when the moone was on the
meridian, was 26 degrees.   P.]

30″: which substracted from the former leaueth 10′..22″
..1‴..4‴; and the moone's motyon for that 24 houers
was 12¹..38: which conuerted into tyme is 50′..25″..
20‴. This beinge knowne the proportion is as follows : If
50′..25″..20‴ giue 360 what shall 10′..22″..1‴..4‴ giue?
The fourth proportionall will be 74 degrees 5′ which is
the longitude of this place west from LONDON : because the
moone was later on the meridian at this place by 10′..22″.

*And by the same forme of working by Origanus Ephemerides,
the distance is 91 degrees 35 minites west from the place Origanus Ephemerides is supputated for, but for to decide which
is the truer I leaue to others : but neyther of them is much
different from my supposed longitude according to my iurnall
which was 74..30′.*[2] And seeing I am entred to speake of
celestiall obseruations, I will note another which I made
at sea the twenty six of April, by the moones comminge
in a right, or strayte, line with two[3] starres; the one was the
Lyons heart, a starre of the first magnitude ; the other a

---

[1] [22. P.]

[2] [And by the same working of *Origanus Ephemerides,* the distance is
91 degrees, 35 minutes west of west. But whether be the truer, I leaue
to others to iudge :—and in these workings may some errour be committed, if it be not carefully looked vnto : as in the obseruation, and also in
finding what time the moone commeth to the meridian at the place where
the ephemerides is supputated for, and perchance in the ephemerides
themselves: in all which the best iudicious may erre ; yet if observations
of this kinde, or some other, were made at places far remote, as at the *Cape
Bonasperanza, Bantam, Japan, Noua Albion,* and *Magellan Strayts,* I suppose wee should haue a truer Geography than wee haue. P.]

Alluding to *Broken Point, Captain Parry* remarks : " This headland
is memorable on account of a *lunar observation made off it by this able and
indefatigable navigator* [*Baffin*], giving the long. 74° 05′, which is not a
degree to the westward of the truth." The accuracy of Baffin's "supposed
longitude, 74° 30′, according to his journal ", is equally remarkable ; and
would no doubt have attracted the attention of his "*able and indefatigable*" *successor,* if the circumstance had been stated in the printed narrative to which alone Parry had access.— *Voyage of the Fury and Hecla,*
1821-23. P. 21. London : 1824.

[3] [Fixed. P.]

starre in the *Lyons rumpe,* beinge of the second bignes.
These 2 stars makinge a right line with the outward edge.
or circumference of the moone, at the instante I tooke the
height of one of them, namely the *Lyons harte,* because I
would haue the houer of tyme:[1] but in this obseruation it is
good to attend for a fit tyme: as to haue the moone in a right
line with two starres not far distante, and those not to be
much different in longitude, because then the moone will
soone alter the angle or position, and such a tyme would
also be taken when the moone is in, or neare, the 90 degree of the eclipticke aboue the horizon, for then there is
no paralax[2] of longitude, but only of latytude : but who
is so paynfull in these busines shall soone see what is
needefull, and what is not : but the notes I tooke are as
followeth :

Lyons heart ♌	Right assention 146[3] deg. 28 min. 30 sec.	
	Declination ... 13 deg. 57 min. 30 sec.	
	Longitude ... 24 deg. 29 min. 45 sec.	
	Latytude ... 00 deg. 26 min. 30 sec.	
	Almycanter ... 33 deg. 40 min. 00 sec.	
Lyons rumpe ♍	Right assention 163 deg. 23 min. 00 sec.	
	Declination ... 12 deg. 38 min. 00 sec.	
	Longitude ... 5 deg. 53 min. 45 sec.	
	Latytude ... 14 deg. 20 min. 00 sec.	
The Moone	Paralax ... 00 deg. 47 min. 46 sec.	
	Latytude ... 03 deg. 20 min. 00 sec.	
	Almycanter ... 37 deg. 00 min. 00 sec.	

Latytude of the Place, 56 deg., 43 min., 00 sec.
After Tycho Brahe.

These notes I haue set doune, that if any other be
desirous to spend a little tyme therein they maye ; my
selfe haue spent some therein, and more I would haue
spent, if other busines had not letted.   I haue not heare
set downe the pertyculer worke, because I found it not

[1] [The circumference, or outward edge, of the moone, being in a right
or straight line with these two starres before named : at the instant I
tooke the altitude of the south ballance, which was 2 degrees 38 minutes,
because I would haue the time. P.]

[2] [Paralell. P.]

[3] [46. P.]

altogither to my mynde. The working of this proposition
I receued from Master *Rudston.*[1]

But if it had pleased God, that we had performed the
accion we intended, I would not feare but to haue brought
so good contentment to the adventurars, concerninge the
tru scituation of notable places, that smale doubt should
haue beene thereof: but seeinge so smale hopes are in
this place, I haue not set doune so many obseruations as
otherwise I would.

We lying heare inclosed with ice, hauinge fayre and
27 calme wether (as before is said) till the 27 day at eueninge;
which tyme we sett sayle, the winde at south east an easie
28 gale. All the 28 and 29 dayes, we made the best waye
29 we could[2] through the ice. At noone this day we sawe
SALISBURY ILAND.[3]

30 *The last of June the wind variable ; but our daylie object
was still ice. All this day we stood toward the foresaid
iland.*

IVLY.

1 The first of *July* close, haysie, wether, with much raine,
the winde at south south east. By noone this daye we
weare some 3 leagues from SALISBURY ISLAND; but hauinge
much ice by the shore stood alonge to the northward; and
the next morninge we weare fayre by another smale ile (or
rather a many of small ilandes), which we afterward called
MILL ILAND by reason of the greate extremetye and
grindinge of the ice, as this night we had proofe thereof.
At noone beinge close by this ile we took the latytude
thereof, which is near to 64 . . 00', *but how it lyeth may be*

---

1 In the *Appendix* will be found the method used at this period for
ascertaining the variation of the compass : followed by a letter addressed
by *Master Rudston* to *Master Thomas Harriott*, the expounder of the
method.

2 [But the nine and twentieth day the ice was more open then it had
been these ten dayes before, and at noone...... P.]

3 [It bearing due west from vs. P.]

R

better seene in the mapp then heare nominated with writinge.
Heare driuinge to and fro with the ice most parte of this
daye till 7 or 8 a clocke, at which time the ice began
somewhat to open and separate.   Then we set sayle and
hauinge not stood[1] past an houer : but the ice came driuinge with the tyde of floud from the south east with such
swiftnesse, that it ouerwent our shippe, hauinge all our
sayles abroad and a good gale of winde, and forced her
out of the streame into the eddy of these iles.

The ilande or iles, lying in the middle of the channell,
hauinge many sounds runninge through them, with dyuers
points and headlands, encountering the force of the tyde,
caused such a rebounde of water and ice,[2] *that vnto them
that saw it not is almost incredible. But our ship being
thus in the pertition, between the eddy which runne on
waye, and the streame which runne another, endured so
great extremytie, that vnless the Lord himselfe had beene on
our side we had shurely perished ; for sometymes the ship
was hoysed aloft ; and at other tymes shee hauinge, as it
were, got the vpper hand, would force greate mighty peeces
of ice to sinke doune on the on side of hir, and rise on the
other. But* GOD, which is still stronger then either *rocks,*
ice, *eddy,* or streame, preserued vs and our shippe from
any harme at all. *And I trust will still contynue his love
to vs, that we may performe some more acceptable seruis to
his glory, and to the good of our common welth.*

This continued till towards high water, which was
aboute one a clocke. Then with no smale trouble we got
into the channell and stood away to the *north ward.*[3]

---

[1] [Along by the ile, on the east side thereof. P.]

[2] [(Which ran one way and the stream another) our ship hauing met
the ice with the first of the floud, which put her so neere the shoare, that
she was in the partition betweene the ice, which the eddy caused to runne
one way, and the streame the other, where she endured great distresse ;
but God, which is still stronger than either ice or streame, preserued vs
and our shippe from any harme at all. P.]

[3] [North-*west*-ward. P.]

When we had past some distance from the ilande we had the sea more cleare of ice then it was since we came into
3 these straights; and sayled all the next day through an indifferent cleare sea, with the wind at south west : but towards 8 a clocke at night, we weare come agayne into much ice, it being thicker and bigger than any we came amonge yet. This place[1] is distant from Mill ilande som 26 leagues, and the tru course north west and by west.[2]
4 The next morne we sounded, and had ground at 120 fathoms, soft osey ground. Then standinge more north-
5 erly, the fifth day in the forenoone we had ground at 80 fathoms, which day the winde came to the north, and we settinge som thinge more southward, had ground at 110 fathoms. Thus seeing this great aboundance of ice in this place, and notinge that the more we get to the *north-ward*,[3] the more shoalder the water was, the ice also beinge foule and durtye, as not bred far from shore, our mr. determined to stand to the eastward, to be certainely informed of the tyde.
6 The sixth day in the forenoone (as we stood to the east-ward) we broke in a planke and two tymbers in the ships bow, which after we had mended we proceeded[4] forward.
7 The next forenoone, we saw the shore, it being but low land *(in respect of the other)* and *toward this side* the sea is *more* should *then at other places* : but excellent good channell ground, as smale stones and shels ;[5] and also heare is a very great tide both of ebb and floud. But no other floud then that which commeth from Resolution

1 [Where we began to be inclosed againe. P.]

2 [After wee were fast in the ice, we made but smale way, yet we per-ceiued a great tyde to set to and fro. P.]

3 [North-*west*-ward. P.]

4 [For to get to the east side, which we called the north shore, because it is the land stretching from *Resolution*, on the north side of the straits. P.]

5 [Some twelue or fourteene leagues from shore but the further off more osey. P.]

ilande ; for about 7 a clocke, we beinge neare the shore,
hoysed forth our bote, then 5 other and myselfe wente
on shore found it ebbinge water. We staied on shore
about an houer and a halfe, in which time the water fell
about 3½ foote, *all the ice in the offen settinge to the southward*. A south south east moone maketh a full sea, or
halfe an houre past tenne[1] *on the chainge day*. Here we
sawe no signe of people to be this yeare, but in yeares
heretofore they have beene, as we might well see by
dyuers things, as wheare their tents had stood, *and such
like ;* perchance theare tyme of fishing was not yet come,
theare being so great aboundance of ice.

8. 9. The 8 day the winde was at west, and the next almost
calme, we *keepinge*[2] not far from the shore, our mr. determined to stand over for NOTTYNGAM ILAND, to make
triall of the tyde theare ; but the winde being at south
west we weare forced all this day to[3] *tack to and fro,
whereby we had more proofe of the settynye of the tyde*.
Towards the night the winde came to the north north
west ; then we stood away to the westward (leauing the
search of Nottyngam ile) hauing a great swellinge sea out
of the west with the winde which had blowne : which
put vs in some hope.

11 The eleuenth day, in the forenoone, we sawe land west
from vs, but no ground at 130 fathoms : so standinge
alonge by the land which here lay about north west and

12 by north. And by the next morne we weare thwart of a
bay, *or sound runninge into the land. In the bottom thereof
the ice was not yet broke vp.* Then standing ouer[4] *that
bay* towards a faire cape, or headland, in the afternoone
it was almost calme, and we beinge almost a league from
shore hoysed forth our bote and sent six of our men to
see howe the tyde was by the shore.[5] They went from

---

[1] [As seamen account. P.]   [2] [Reeking. P.]   [3] [Turne. P.]
[4] [To the northwards. P.]   [5] [And from whence it came. P.]

the ship at 5 a clocke and came aboord agayne at 8, who brought vs word that it was falling water, and that it had ebbd while they weare on shore somewhat about 2 foote. Also they affirmed that the floud came from the northward in this place, the which we also sawe by the ship driuinge to the northward, and it being calme (the cause thereof I suppose to be the indraft of the bay) but this put vs in great hope of a passage this waye, wherefore our Mr. named the poynte of land that was some 6 leagues to the northward of vs CAPE COMFORT. It lyeth in the latytude of 65de. 00'[1] and is 85de. 20'[2] west from LONDON, and heare we had 140 fathoms water not a league from shore.

13 There our sudden hopes weare as soon quayld, for the next morninge hauinge dubbled the cape, when we supposed (by the account of the tyde) we should be sett to the northward, it beinge little or no winde, we weare sett to the contrary, and that day hauinge a good gale of winde we had not proceeded on our course past 10 or 12 leagues, but we sawe the land trendinge from the cape, round aboute by the west tyll it bore north east and by east, and very thick pestred with ice, and the further we proceeded the more ice and shoalder water, with smale showe of any tyde.[3] We seeing this, our mr. soone resolued heare

---

[1] [26 minutes. P.] According to *Parry*, lat. "64° 54'".— *Voyage of the Fury and Hecla*, 1821-23, p. 33. London: 1824.

[2] [86 degrees. P.] According to *Parry*, long. "82° 57'".—*Ibid.*

[3] [At sixe a clocke this afternoone we sounded and had ground in 130 fathoms, soft osey, hauing had at noone 150 fathoms. P.]

In this vicinity, at 7 P.M. on the 5th of August 1821 (lat. 65° 22' 50" N., long. 81° 24' 00" W., var. 55° 05' 30"), *Captain Parry* found the tide set E. by S. at the rate of half a mile an hour ; and by observation, he ascertained and confirms the truth of Baffin's remark respecting "the small show of any tide".

The following day, the *Fury* and *Hecla* were two miles and a quarter (lat. 65° 28' 15" N.) to the northward of the locality in which Bylot and Baffin left off their search for the North-west passage, with the land bearing N.E. by E. "The same land", *Captain Parry* observes, "which we had now in sight, proved to be one of several islands, and I gave it the

could be no passadge in this place, and presently we bore
vpp the healme and turned the ships head to the southward. *This was about 6 a clock. The land which we sawe
beare north and north east was about 9 or 10 leagues from
vs, and shurely without any question this is the bottom of
the baye, on the west side; but howe far it runneth more
eastward is yet uncertayne.*

14 The 14, the winde was for the most part at south east, so
that we could make but small waye backe agayne; and the
15 next morninge very foule wether, we comming to anchor
in a smale coue near Cape Comfort, on the north west side
thereof.   Heare we found (as on the other side) a south
½ east moone maketh a full sea, *or halfe an houre past* 11
on the chainge daye : but howe the floud doth set we could
not well see, it beinge so foule wether at sea, *and so fogge.*
In the afternoone the wind came to north by west, then
we wayed anchor, and stood along by the land to the southward, with a stiffe gale of winde and very hasey.   By the
16 16 at noone we met with a great quantitie of ice lying som
7 or 8 leagues within the point of the land.   Among this
ice we saw som store of MORSE, *som vppon the ice and other
in the water, but all so fearefull that I thinke little good
would be expected in hope of killinge them.   They are so
beaten with the* SALUAGES *they will not suffer nether ship nor
bote to com neare them.*   By eight a clocke we were com
to this southern point, which I called SEA HORSE POINT,
wheare we anchored open in the sea, the better to proue
the sett of the tyde.

Heare we found, most apparently to all our companies
sight, that in this place the tyde of floud doth come from

name of BAFFIN ISLAND, *out of respect to the memory of that able and
enterprising navigator".*   On the 15th of the same month, the expedition
was within a league of *a remarkable headland on Southampton Island,*
which was named by Captain Parry, CAPE BYLOT, as being "probably the
westernmost land seen by that navigator".—*Voyage of the Fury and
Hecla,* 1821, etc. pp. 31-33-37.   London : 1824.

the south east, and the ebb from the north west, *being the certaynest sett of tyde we haue yet made proofe of; playnelie perceuing the sett of the ships ridinge at anchor, and also by the settinge of the ice. And for our better assurance, our mr. went himselfe on shore to make proofe thereof. The tyme of high water on the chainge daye is about eleuen a clocke, somethinge past : kepinge a proportion of tyme in all places as we have beene at since we came into the strayts, all concurringe of the floud to come from the south east, and no place else, sauinge 6 leagues short of Cape Comfort, but the cause thereof I suppose to be nothing but the indraft of the baye.*

17 *The next morning our mr. asked our opinion whether it weare better for vs to seeke out some harboure heareaboute to see if we could kill any of those* MORSE *we sawe, or presently to go for* NOTTYNGAMS ILANDE *to make proofe of the tyde of floud theare, which was the place wheare formerly was affirmed the floud to come from the north west.*

My answear and most of the companies was, that seeinge we are bound for discouery, it could not be our best waye to spend any tyme in search for these morse, they being so fearefull and beaten with the saluages. And yf we should kill some fewe of them they would not be worth the tyme we should spend. Seeinge we knewe not wheare to harboure our ship, and when shee is in harboure, we haue no other bote but our ships bote, which we dare not send far from the ship. And those morse we sawe weare in the sea, and what tyme or wheare they would com on shore was vncertayne.

These thinges considered I thought it better to go for NOTTYNGAM ILANDE, *and so to prosecute our uoyage as theare we shoulde finde occation, and if theare our hope of passadge was voyde, and the weather prooue fayre, we might soon com back to this place agayne, it beinge nott past 16 leagues distante.*

When I had spoke, our mr. sayd he was also of that minde,

and so we wayed *anchor presently* and stood ouer with a
stiffe gale of winde, which continued; and toward night
very foule wether, and a sore storme. By tenne a clocke
we weare com to anchor on the north west side of Nottyngam Ile, where are 2 or 3 smale iles lye off from the
greater, which make very good sounds and harbours.
About this ile we found som store of ice, but nothing in
comparison of that which heretofore we haue had.

We staied about this island till the 27 day, hauinge
much foule wether, many stormes, often foggs and vncertaine windes. Dyuers tymes we set sayle to goe to that
side of the ile where the ship rode when Captaine Button
was in her: findinge in other places of this ilande the floud
to com from the south eastward, and the tyme of high
water on the chainge daye to be at half an houer past ten,
and not at halfe an houer past seuen, as some supposed.
In these ten dayes we staied about this ile, we fitted our
ship with ballast, and other necessaries we had neede of;
and then proceeded as followeth.

26 The 26 daye, being indifferent faire wether, we passed between Nottyngam Ile and Salisburys Ilande at the south
point thereof (I mean of Nottyngam Ile), wheare are many
small low, *broken*, iles, without the which had beene a fit
place for vs to haue anchord, to haue found out the tru sett
of the tyde. But our mr. desirous to com to the same place
wheare they had rode before, stood along by this ile to the
westward, and came to an anchor in the eddy of these
broken groundes, wheare the ship rode at no certaintie of
tyde at all.

27 The next morning the wether proued very foule with
much rayne and winde, so that our *kedger*[1] would not
hold the ship,[2] but was driuen into deepe water, that we
weare forced to set sayle, the winde beinge at east, and
then east-north-east, and at noone at north-east, still

---

[1] [Reger. P.]   [2] [At eightie fathoms' scope. P.]

foule weather. Being vnder sayle, we stood away towards SEA HORSE POINT. Our mr. (as I suppose) was
perswaded that there might be som passadge between
SEA HORSE POINT and that land which they called SWAN
ILANDE : so this afternoone we saw both SEA HORSE POINT
and NOTTYNGAM ILE. The distance is about 15 leagues,
bearinge the one from the other north west and south east.

28   The 28 in the morninge we weare neare the former
point, *being somwhat southward of it*, trendinge away west
south west so farre as we sawe ; and very much pestred
with ice. At seuen a clocke we tacked about & stood
south east and by south.

29   The next day at eleuen a clocke we came to anchor at
DIGGES ILE, hauinge very foule weather. At this place
wheare we rode, it lyeth open to the west, hauinge two
of the greatest iles which breake off the force of the floud
till the tyde be well bent ; for after the water beinge risen
by the shore about an houer and a halfe, then the ship
doth wind vpp and ride truly on the tyde of floud all the
tyde after. Now the tyme of high water on the chainge
daye is halfe an houer past ten,[1] *nearest eleuen, whom*
hearetofore was taken to be halfe an houer past seuen, or
an east south east moone, by which mistake I suppose hath
growne the erroure at Nottyngam iland, affirminge the floud
to com from the north west, makinge account that it would
be high water at both places alike (as indeede it is), but the
mistakinge of the tyme was all, for it is an easey thinge to
make a man beleeue that which he desireth.

30   The 30, being fayre weather, about noone we set sayle,[2]
wheare we presently perceued the saluages to be close
hid on the top of the rockes ; but when they see we had
espyed them, dyuers of them came runninge downe to the
water side, calling *and weauinge* vs to com to anchor,

---

[1] [Or neerest thereabout. P.]

[2] [And stood along close by Digges Ile. P.]

which we would haue done if conueniently we could. But
heare the water is so deepe, that it is hard to find a place
to ride in, which we seeinge, lay to and fro with our ship,
while som of our men in the bote killed 70 fowle, for in
this place is the greatest quantitie of these fowle (whom
we call WILLOCKS), that in few places else the like is to be
seen: for if neade were we might haue killed many thou-
sands, almost incredible to those which haue not seene it.
Heare also we had sufficient proofe of the tyde, as we lay
to and fro with the ship, but when our men weare com
aboord agayne, we set all our sayles for homeward, makinge the best expedition we could.

AVGVST.

3   But on the third of August we were forced to com to
anchor agayne about thirtie leagues within RESOLUTION
4,5 ILAND, on the north shore. The next daye we set sayle,
and the 5th in the forenoone we past by RESOLUTION
ILAND, without sight thereof: thus continuing our course
(as in the breefe iournall may be seene) with much contrarie windes and foule wether.

SEPTEMBER.

6   We had sight of CAPE CLEERE in Ireland the sixt of
September. The next morninge by daylight we were faire
by SILLY, and that night, at two a clocke the next morne,
we came to anchor in PLYMOUTH SOUND, *without the loss
of one man. For these and all other blessings the Lord
make vs thankfull.*[1]

*And now it may be that som expect I should give my opynion
conserninge the passadge. To those my answere must be, that
doubtles theare is a passadge. But within this strayte whome*

---

[1] [With all our men liuing, hauing onely three or four sicke, which
soone recouered. P.]

is called Hudson's Straytes, I am doubtfull, supposinge the con-
trarye. But whether there be, or no, I will not affirme. But
this I will affirme, that we haue not beene in any tyde then that
from Resolutyon Iland, and the greatest indraft of that commeth
from Dauis Straytes; and my judgment is, if any passadge with-
in Resolution Iland, it is but som creeke or in lett, but the mayne
will be vpp fretum Dauis ; but if any be desirous to knowe my
opynion in pertyculler, I will at any tyme be redy to showe the
best resons I cann eyther by word of mouth, or otherwise.

FINIS.

It has already been observed, that through the suppression
of information, communicated by Baffin, of his proceedings,
occasion has been taken to impeach his character. In connexion with this second voyage, allegations have been urged
against Baffin,[1] which, if capable of being substantiated, would
render him untrustworthy as a narrator, and destroy his reputation as a navigator and discoverer.

It is alleged, he has given " a most vague, indefinite, and
unsatisfactory account" of a most important voyage, "*pur-
porting* to have reached many degrees of latitude beyond any
preceding navigator", and made in a direction "where the
passage must be found if it has any existence". In connexion with this voyage, it is observed: "he has given neither
course, nor distance, nor variation of the compass, except
once ; and no one longitude whatever". It is added : " so
vague and indefinite, indeed, is every information left, which
could be useful, that each succeeding geographer has drawn

---

[1] *A Chron. Hist. of Voyages into the Arctic Regions.* By *John Barrow*,
F.R.S. London : 1818.

'BAFFIN'S BAY' on his chart as best accorded with his fancy". Severe as these strictures are, it must be confessed they may be applied with justice to the narrative printed in Purchas. But at the same time it is to be remarked, that Baffin does not profess to give, in "that place", a complete report of his proceedings. On the contrary, he admits that some particulars are omitted, to avoid "tedious repetition"; and for the details thus omitted, he refers to his "Breefe iournall". This explanation has been overlooked : at least, it has not been made the subject of notice.

On the authority of an ambiguous phrase it is alleged: "it would almost seem as if Baffin was averse from discovery on this voyage, when he had reached only the latitude 70° 20', beyond which even Davis had been". The fact is : when Baffin arrived in the latitude of 70° 20', he experienced disappointment by the absence of an indication of success, on which the old navigators placed great reliance. He had calculated, that as he increased his northing, he would find the height of the tides increase ; but in this place he found they did not rise more than eight or nine feet, which was considered to be but "a small rise"; and this circumstance, he states, gave him "some *dislike* of the passage". Probably Baffin meant nothing more, than this circumstance induced him to have a *misgiving* of the ultimate success of the undertaking. It is impossible to decide which construction is correct ; yet, that which does not involve an imputation may be preferred.

Next : a complaint is made of "the slovenly manner in which he runs over the numerous '*sounds*' in a very high degree of latitude": which is further described as being "quite vexatious". A doubt is insinuated of the existence of these sounds. It is said: "they were, perhaps, nothing more than huge ice-bergs, or, at any rate, passages made by an archipelago of islands". Yet, a page or two preceding that in which the insinuation is hazarded, a passage is to be fonnd, quoted from Baffin's narrative, to this effect: "all which sounds and islands the map doth truly describe". Were this document in existence, there could be no pretence for insinuating a charge of want of veracity against Baffin; and it seems difficult to justify an insinuation of that description against him, because the evidence of his trustworthiness has been suppressed by the act of another: rather it may be deemed matter of surprise, that such a course should have been pursued by any one cognizant of the facts of the case. Indeed, implicit reliance does not appear to have been placed on the sufficiency of the grounds on which the insinuation is hazarded; and an attempt is accordingly made to strengthen the position, by an endeavour to convict Baffin on testimony given by himself. It is asserted: "so much aware" was Baffin of the delinquency imputed to him, that he deemed it necessary to address an apologetic letter on the subject, to Sir John Wolstenholme. The correctness, or otherwise, of this assertion may be tested by consulting the letter itself, which follows the summary of the voyage.

Finally, it is said: "Baffin drew off from the main land of America, to the eastward, from the very spot where, of all others, a passage is most likely to be found": which is purely conjectural. It is added: "but he is not to blame for not then possessing that knowledge which Cook, and Hearne, and Mackenzie, have since supplied".[1] It may be observed, however, that, had Baffin been engaged on an exploring voyage some century and a half later, at the point he drew off he could not have derived any information from the researches either of Cook, Hearne, or Mackenzie. A glance at the map will show at once the respective tracks of those parties, and how they bore in relation to each other.

It must candidly be allowed, however, that in this "intolerable deal" of objurgation, a palliative, though infinitesimal in quantity and of no very commendable quality, is to be detec-

1 " *These be good humours indeed !* " ANCIENT PISTOL.

ted. Every source of reprehension having been exhausted, it is admitted: " Purchas, however, is blameable to a certain extent, for the meagreness of Baffin's journal". But an acknowledgment that Purchas is partially to blame for the meagreness of the journal, smally compensates for the grave charges that have been brought against the navigator.

All that has been said, it may be urged, and truly urged perhaps, does not establish the absolute trustworthiness of Baffin, though the inaccurate views of a critic may be demonstrated, and the object of his criticism proved to be deserving of greater forbearance than he has experienced. But the reputation of Baffin is supported by other, and indisputable testimony.

While the strictures that have been the subject of notice, were in progress of publication, two most able and enterprising men, CAPTAIN SIR JOHN ROSS, R.N., and CAPTAIN SIR WILLIAM EDWARD PARRY, R.N., were, league by league, pursuing the track *purported* to have been followed by the old navigator ; and the commander of the expedition, Sir John Ross, sums up the result of his investigation in the following terms : " In re-discovering Baffin's Bay, I have derived great additional pleasure from the reflection that I have placed in a fair light before the public, the merits of a worthy man and able navigator ; whose fate, like that of many others, it has not only been, to have lost, by a combination of circumstances, the opportunity of acquiring during his life-time the fame he deserved ; but, could he have lived to this period, to have seen his discoveries expunged from the records of geography, and the bay, with which his name is so fairly associated, treated as a phantom of the imagination".

Of the correctness of the latter representation, the reader may satisfy himself by inspecting the "*Map*" prefixed to "*The Chronological History of Voyages into the Arctic Regions*". That map will be searched in vain for a trace of "*Baffin's Bay*". The particular instances in which Sir John

Ross confirms the accuracy of the old navigator, will be found appended, in their appropriate places, to the summary of the voyage.

A.D. 1606. The second voyage was performed in the same ship, set forth by the same adventurers, and commanded by the same officers, that were engaged in the first. For the conduct of the expedition, the following instructions were issued, namely: "For your course you must make all possible haste to *Cape Desolation*; and from thence you, William Baffin, as pilot, keep along the coast of Greenland and up *Fretum Davis*, until you come toward the height of eighty degrees, if the land will give you leave. Then, for feare of inbaying, by keeping too northerly a course, shape your course west and southerly, so farre as you shall thinke it convenient, till you come to the latitude of sixtie degrees; then direct your course to fall in with the land of *Yedzo*, about that height, leaving your further sayling southward to your owne discretion, according as the time of the year and windes will give you leave; although our desires be, if your voyage prove so prosperous that you may have the year before you, that you goe so farre southerly as that you may touch the north part of *Japan*, from whence, or from *Yedzo*, if you can so compasse it without danger, we would have you to bring home one of the men of the countrey; and so God blessing you, with all expedition to make your return home againe".[1]

The Discovery, with a complement of seventeen officers and men, sailed from Gravesend on the 26th of March; but at the outset, the voyage was retarded by foul weather, which rendered it necessary that shelter should be sought, first, in Dartmouth, and afterwards in Plymouth. It was not till the 19th of April that a final start was made. From that day they made a fair passage, during which nothing of moment occurred, till the 14th of May, when land was sighted in latitude 65° 20′ N. on the west coast of Greenland, and within Davis's

1 Purchas, vol. iii, p. 842.

straits. Being visited by some native fishermen, Baffin gra-
tified them with various trifling presents; and they accompanied him to a distance "with great loue", expressing much
disappointment when they found it was not his intention to
anchor in their vicinity. Although the wind was contrary,
the navigator "plyed to the Northward", and at length
anchored in a fair sound in latitude 70° 20′ N., near the LON-
DON COAST of Davis. At this anchorage, Baffin was disappointed by finding the tides to have but a small rise, only
eight or nine feet. He states, the circumstance gave him
" some dislike to the passage": an expression which, as already
noticed, has been construed to his prejudice, though without
justice.

After a stay of two days at the above place to take in water,
and for other purposes, Baffin pursued his course toward the
Northward, reaching HOPE SAUNDERSON, the extreme point of
Davis's navigation, on the 30th of May. Hereabouts his
progress was impeded by the ice which had accumulated
greatly; but by the 1st of June he got into clear water. The
wind, however, was contrary, and shelter was taken among a
cluster of islands, which are placed in latitude 72° 45′; and to
which the name of WOMAN'S ISLANDS[1] was given. A party of
natives were seen, but they fled on the appearance of the ship,
though some females were afterwards discovered, who had

[1] *July the 3rd*, 1818, in lat. 71° 33′ N., long. 56° 2′ W., *Sir John Ross*
was abreast of *Hope Saunderson*, and in sight of *Woman's Island*, which
were made by observation more north and further west than they then
appeared in the Admiralty charts. *Baffin's* lat. of Woman's Island,
72° 45′, is adopted in the table of latitudes and longitudes appended to
the voyage.—*Appendix*, p. xcviii.

It may not be irrelevant to notice, that on the following day (July 4
1818) lat. 72° 30′ N., long. 56° 37′ W., the variation taken on an ice-berg
was 81° 1′ W.; and on board, the ship's head being W. by N. ½ N., 98 W.,
making the deviation 18° on that point of the compass. On the 7th, the
dip, or inclination of the needle ashore, was 84° 9′ 15″, the lat. being 74°
2′ N., the long. 58° 45′ W., with variation as before.— *Voyage of the Isabella and Alexander*, 1818, pp. 58, 59. London: 1819.

concealed themselves behind rocks; and among them was one, apparently, not under four-score years of age. To the credit both of Baffin and his people, it must be observed, that the poor people discovered by them were treated with so much kindness, that the fugitives were induced to return, and good fellowship was established.

These people are represented to have been but very poorly off, living on dried seals' flesh, which they devoured raw; and for which they apparently had a relish, as they expressed dislike to the ship's provisions after having tasted them. Their clothing consisted of the skin of the same animal, which was also used for tents and for covering their boats, being skilfully prepared for the purpose. The women differed from the men in their apparel, though in what particulars is not stated; and their faces were marked with a series of black streaks, or lines. These marks, which it may be presumed were intended to be ornamental, were ascertained to be made by raising the skin of young persons and introducing a black pigment. They are indelible. From their gestures, these people were supposed to worship the sun. The dead were found to be buried on the hill-sides, where the living also dwelt; and the corses were covered with stones, but too slightly to be entirely concealed. However, it is stated, the piercing air, "keepeth them from stinking savour". Both men and dogs, it was found, were buried in the same manner.

The navigators sailed from Woman's Island with fair weather and a foul wind. However, they "plyed it up" along the ice, between which and the shore was a kind of channel from seven to eight leagues broad, till the 9th of June, when they reached latitude 74° 15'. At this point the ship became greatly pestered with ice, and was brought to anchor among some islands about eight miles from the main. From thence an endeavour was made to work to the westward, but the ice presented an insuperable obstacle, and the way was retraced to latitude 73° 45' N. where good shelter was found. This

T

spot was named HORN SOUND, and as the ice was observed to melt very fast, it was determined to wait there patiently till the passage should become free. Much surprise is expressed at the remarkable rapidity with which the icy rampart disappeared; and, taking advantage of the circumstance, the voyage was resumed on the 18th. No difficulty was experienced in proceeding northerly. The islands already noticed were passed, and in latitude 74° 40′ N. an offing was gained of about twenty leagues to the westward. During the remainder of the month, little way was made, though some progress, day by day, was effected. The weather was variable, but frost and snow frequent; and " on Midsummer day", the narrator states, " our shrouds, roapes, and sailes were so frozen, that we could scarce handle them : yet", it is added, "the cold is not so extreme but it may be well endured".

On the 1st of July, in latitude 75° 40′ N. an open sea was entered, which " anew revived the hope of a passage". Next day, a fair cape, or headland, was fallen in with in latitude 76° 35′ N., which was named SIR DUDLEY DIGGES CAPE.[1] Twelve leagues onward, a fair sound was discovered, which was named WOLSTENHOLME SOUND.[2] An island, named WOL-

---

[1] *August* 17, 1818 (lat. 75° 54′ N., long. 69° 15′ W.). " In the evening we had an easterly breeze, and *Cape Dudley Digges*, which Baffin describes as being easily known by a small island off it, in sight. The island has a conical shape, and is very rugged......it was found to be bold and deep on the outside; but on the inside there was a rippling, which led us to judge the water there was shallow."......*August* 18, 1818 (lat. 76° 12½′ N., long. 69° 54¾′ W.). "*Cape Dudley Digges* was found to be a few miles to the southward of the situation in which Baffin has laid it down. It appeared to form a precipice of about eight hundred feet in height, was perfectly clear of snow, and presented a yellowish vegetation at top, behind which, at the distance of eighteen miles, there appeared to be high mountains covered with snow."—*Voyage of the Isabella and Alexander (Ross)*, 1818, pp. 140-1. London : 1819.

[2] *August* 18, 1818, 4 P.M. (lat. 76° 25′ N., long. 71° 00′ W., var. 103° 10′ W.) " We passed *Wolstenholme Sound* about 2 P.M., and found it completely blocked up with ice. It seemed to be eighteen or twenty leagues in breadth......We found the entrances to this inlet, and the general form

STENHOLME ISLAND, is described as lying in the centre of the sound and forming two entrances. Baffin sought shelter under the island, but the currents ran so strong that within two hours, although a couple of anchors were laid out, the ship drove; and it became necessary to get under sail, and stand out to sea. In this sound, are represented to be many inlets, or bays; with good opportunities for whale fishing.

The 4th, a great storm came on in the morning from west by south. At the outset, the fore-course was blown away; and the gale continuing to blow with undiminished violence, it was at length found necessary to take in all sail and "lye adrift". On the storm ceasing, the ship was found to be embayed in a large sound; and, sail being made, the course was directed to the S.W. side. An anchorage was met with in a cove, or small bay; but the wind blowing furiously over the tops of some neighbouring hills, both anchor and cable were lost, and way was made into the sound again. A calm afternoon enabled the ship to get to sea. From the abundance of whales which were seen this place was called WHALE SOUND; and it is represented to be in latitude 77° 30′ N.[1]

On the 5th, some progress was made; till encountering a great bank of ice backed with land, the ship was put on a southerly course, to an island which was named HAKLUYT'S ISLAND,[2] and which is described as being situated between Whale Sound and another great sound which was designated SIR THOMAS SMITH'S SOUND.[3] "It runneth," Baffin observes,

and appearance of the land, to agree extremely well with the description of it given by Baffin, as well as did its bearings and distance from Cape Dudley Digges."—*Voyage of the Isabella and Alexander (Ross)*, 1818, p. 156. London: 1819.

[1] *Whale Sound* (lat. 77° 15′ N., long. 71° 20′ W., var. 102 00′ W.: *Appendix*, xcviii). "We tacked, and stood to the N.E., to get a better view of Whale Sound and the land near it, and we soon discovered there was no navigable passage in that direction."......

[2] ......"After this we resumed our course to the westward, and *Hakluyt's Island* of Baffin was seen, appearing very near the mainland."

[3] "*Smith's Sound*, discovered by Baffin, was distinctly seen, and the

" to the north of 78° and is admirable in one respect, because in it is the greatest variation in the compasse of any part of the world known ; for by divers good observations, I found it to be above five points, or fifty-six degrees, varied to the westward, so that a north east and by east is true north, and so of the rest".[1] Next, on the 8th, some islands were fallen in with,

capes forming each side of it were named after the two ships, *Isabella* and *Alexander* ; I considered the bottom of this sound to be eighteen leagues distant, but its entrance was completely blocked up by ice ; a thick fog soon came on, and we again hauled to the westward. Var. 103° 00′ W." Lat. 77° 55′, long. 76° 15′ W.—(*Appendix*, xcvii.) *Voyage of the Isabella and Alexander (Ross)*, 1818, pp. 148-9. London : 1819.

[1] In his letter to M. John Wolstenholme, the old navigator further alludes to the "variation of the compasse"; to its "wonderful operation"; and to its "decreasing so suddenly and swift"; and the correctness of his representation, of the violence of the disturbance to which the compass is subject in these latitudes, is corroborated by the observations of Sir Edward Parry.

Sir Edward Parry remarks : " Since the time we first entered Sir James Lancaster's Sound, the sluggishness of the compasses, as well as the amount of their irregularity, produced by the attraction of the ship's iron, had been found very rapidly, though uniformly, to increase, as we proceeded to the westward ; so much, indeed, that for the last two days (*August* 4 *and* 5) we had been under the necessity of giving up altogether the usual observations for determining the variation of the needle on board the ships. This irregularity became more and more obvious as we now advanced to the southward. The rough magnetic bearing of the sun at noon, or at midnight, or when on the prime vertical, as compared with its true azimuth, was sufficient to render this increasing inefficiency of the compass quite apparent. For example, at noon this day (*August* 6), while we were observing the meridian altitude, the bearing of the sun was two points on the Hecla's larboard bow, and consequently her true course was about S.S.W. The binnacle and azimuth compasses, at the same time, agreed in shewing N.N.W. ½ W., making the variation to be allowed on that course, eleven points and a half westerly ; corresponding nearly with an azimuth taken the following morning, which gave 137° 12′. It was evident, therefore, a very material change had taken place in the dip, or the variation, or in both these phenomena, since we had last an opportunity of obtaining observations upon them ; which rendered it not improbable that we were now making a very near approach to the magnetic pole. This observation was further strengthened on the morning of *the* 7*th ;* when, having decreased our latitude to about 73°, we found that no alter-

and named CAREY's ISLANDS :[1] "all which sounds and ilands", Baffin observes, "the map doth truly describe"; and he therefore does not give their respective positions.

ation whatever in the absolute course on which the Hecla was steering, produced a change of more than three or four points in the direction indicated by the compass, which continued uniformly from N.N.E. to N.N.W., according as the ship's head was placed on one side or the other of the magnetic meridian. We now, therefore, witnessed, for the first time, the curious phenomenon of the directive-power of the needle becoming so weak, as to be completely overcome by the attraction of the ship; so that the needle might now be properly said to point to the north pole of the ship. It was only, however, in those compasses in which the lightness of the cards, and the great delicacy in the suspension, had been particularly attended to, that even this degree of uniformity prevailed; for, in the heavier cards, the friction upon the points of suspension was much too great to be overcome even by the ship's attraction, and they consequently remained indifferently in any position in which they happened to be placed. For the purposes of navigation, therefore, the compasses were from this time no longer consulted; and in a few days afterwards, the binnacles were removed, as useless lumber, from the deck to the carpenter's store-room, where they remained during the rest of the season, the azimuth compass alone being kept on deck, for the purpose of watching any changes which might take place in the directive-power of the needle; and the *true* courses and direction of the wind were in future noted in the log-book, as obtained to the nearest quarter point, when the sun was visible, by the azimuth of that object and the apparent time."

Being desirous of obtaining all the magnetic observations possible, at a spot which was deemed to be replete with interest in this department of science, a suitable spot for observing was selected on shore ; and it was found that " the directive-force of the horizontal needle, undisturbed as it was by the attraction of the ship, was, even here, found to be so weak, in Captain Kater's azimuth compasses, which were the most sensible, that they required constant tapping with the hand to make them traverse at all." The latitude of the place of observation was 72° 45' 15"; longitude, by chronometers, 89° 41' 22"; the dip of the needle, 88° 26' 42"; and the variation, 118° 23' 37" westerly.

Some examples will be found in the Appendix, illustrative of Parry's remarks.— *Voyage of the Hecla and Griper* (*Parry*), 1819-20, pp. 37-39. London, 1821.

1 *August* 20, 1818, longitude 75° 21¾ W., variation 102° 00 W. "We were now by our reckoning in latitude 76° 54' N., *Carey's Islands* bearing S.E......The rise and fall of the tide was only four feet, its velocity half a mile, and the flood setting to the north......I was employed in observing

The next course was to the westward, with a favourable gale
blowing stiffly, which lasted till the 10th, when it fell calm
and became foggy. This occurred near the land at the entrance of a fair sound, which was named ALDERMAN JONES'
SOUND.[1] The boat was sent on shore, but owing to foul weather, soon returned, bringing a report that there was no sign
of inhabitants, but plenty of sea-morses among the ice. Then
having an easy gale at E.N.E. they " ranne along the shoare,
which now trended much south, and began to shew like a
bay". Following this track another great sound was discovered, on the 12th, in latitude 74° 20′ N., and named SIR
JAMES LANCASTER'S SOUND.[2] " From this sound to the southward", Baffin remarks, " wee had a ledge of yce between the

the deviation on each point of the compass, and found it to be the same
in amount which it had been since the 4th of August, when the variation
was 90° and the dip of the needle 84° 52′ 6″. This observation is pecu-
liarly important in any theory that may be adopted respecting the deviation of the needle : since when that force had materially diminished,
the quantity and force of the deviating tendency remained unaltered".—
Voyage of the Isabella and Alexander (Ross), pp. 150-151. London: 1819.

[1] *August* 23 (latitude 76° 20′ N., longitude 78° 10′ W., variation 107°
56′ W.). " Towards evening we successively made out the north and
south points of the land across the bottom of this bay, or inlet, which
answered Baffin's description of *Jones's Sound*. At midnight, a ridge of
very high mountains were seen to extend nearly across the bottom of it,
and joining another from the south, which was not quite so high. The
bay was completely blocked with ice, in which were some very large ice-
bergs ; and from the points of land, glaciers of solid ice were extending
for many miles into the sea".— *Voyage of the Isabella and Alexander
(Ross)*. 1818, p. 157, London : 1819.

[2] *August* 30 (lat. 74° 19½′ N., long. 78° 33′ W., var. 110° W.). This
day a strait was entered, which excited much interest on board the expedition ; the general opinion, however, was, that it was only an inlet.
Captain Sabine, who produced Baffin's account, was of opinion they were
off *Lancaster Sound,* and that there were no hopes of a passage until they
should arrive off Cumberland Strait. He observed, there was " no indication of a passage", " no appearance of a current", " no driftwood", and
" no swell from the northwest". Sail was, however, made up the opening.

August 31, at 6 P.M. (lat. 74° 03′ N., long. 81° 28′ W., var. 114° 00′ W.)
Captain Ross observes: " *The north corner,* which was the last I had made

shoare and us, but cleare to the sea-ward". Along this ledge
the navigator steered till the 14th day in the afternoon, when
they were in latitude 71° 16′ N., with land clearly percepti-
ble to the southward of 70° 30′. Here the ship became so pestered with ice, that it became necessary to tack to the eastward; and a tedious navigation, through ice, was followed for
three score leagues. No opportunity was offered for approaching the land till the 24th, in about latitude 68°. Even there
a landing could not be effected; and from thence they drifted
down to latitude 65° 40′. "Then", Baffin observes, "wee
left off seeking the west shoare, because we were in the indraft of Cumberland Iles, and should know no certaintie, and
hope of passage could be none". This was on the 27th; and,
further, taking into consideration the advanced period of the
year, with the sickly and enfeebled state of the crew, it was
determined to make for the west coast of Greenland. The
baffled and overtoiled men anchored in Cockin's Sound, on
the 28th of July.

The day after the Discovery arrived in the above-named
harbour, a visit was paid to an island in the vicinity, on which
the enfeebled people were fortunate enough to find an abundance of "scurvie-grasse, with sorrill and orpen". The
former was boiled in beer, and the two latter were eaten as
sallads. By means thereof, "with the blessing of God", the
men were restored to perfect health, in which they continued
till their arrival in England.

Cocking's Sound is represented to be a very good harbour,

out, *was a deep inlet;* and as *it exactly answered to the latitude given by
Baffin of Lancaster Sound,* I have no doubt it was the same, and *I consider
it a most remarkable instance of the accuracy of that able navigator.*" Sir
John Ross, being satisfied there was no passage in that direction, gave
over the search, and proceeded to the southward. Both Baffin and Ross,
however, were deceived by appearances. A passage through the bottom
of Lancaster Sound was discovered by Sir Edward Parry in August 1819.
— *Voyage of the Isabella and Alexander (Ross),* 1818, pp. 171-5. London:
1819. *Voyage of the Hecla and Griper (Parry),* 1819, pp. 29, et seq.
London: 1821.

and easy to be known, having three high hills like pyramids
close adjoining the entrance, one in the centre being the
lowest of the three. All along the coast, indeed, it is said,
good harbours are to be found, by reason of the numerous
islands that lie from the mainland. In the sound were such
" scales" (*Baffin*) " skulls" (*Fox*) of salmon swimming to and
fro, " that it was greatly to be admired". The tide, it was
found, rose 18 feet. The natives proved to be friendly.

By three o'clock of the 6th of August, the Discovery was
free of Cocking's Sound. On the 25th the coast of Ireland
was sighted. On the 30th the Discovery was all well at
anchor in Dover-roads; and the voyage terminated.

Master BAFFIN *his Letter to the right Worshippfull Sir* JOHN
WOLSTENHOLME, *one of the chiefe Adventurers
for the discovery of a passage to
the North-west.*

WORTHY SIR, there needs no filling a Journall or short
Discourse with preamble, circumstance, or complement; and
therefore I will onely tell I am proud of my remembrance,
when I expresse your worth to my conceit; and glad of my
good fortune, when I can auoid the imputation of ingratitude,
by acknowledgeing your many favours; and seeing it is not
vnknowne to your worship in what estate the businesse concerning the North West hath beene heretofore; and how the
only hope was in searching *Fretum Davis;* which if your
selfe had not beene the more forward, the action had wel-nigh
beene left of. Now it remayneth for your worship to know
what hath beene performed this yeere; wherefore I intreat you
to admit of my custome, and pardon me if I take the plaine
highway in relating the particulars, without vsing any refined
phrases, or eloquent speeches.

Therefore briefly thus, and as it were in the fore-front, I
entend to shew the whole proceeding of the voyage in a word:
as namely, there is no passage nor hope of passage in the north
of *Davis* Straights.   We hauing coasted all, or neere all the
circumference thereof, and finde it to be no other then a great
Bay, as the voyage doth truely shew.[1] Wherefore I cannot but
much admire the worke of the Almightie, when I consider
how vaine the best and chiefest hopes of men are in thinges
vncertaine ; and to speake of no other then of the hopeful
passage to the North West. How many of the best sort of men
haue set their whole endeauoures to prooue a passage that
wayes? not onely in conference, but also in writing and pub-
lishing to the world. Yea what great summes of money haue
been spent about that action, as your worship hath costly
experience of.   Neither would the vaine-glorious *Spaniard*
haue scattered abroad so many false maps and journals, if
they had not beene confident of a passage this way ; that if it
had pleased GOD a passage had beene found, they might haue
eclipsed the worthy prayse of the adventurers and true dis-
couerers. And for my owne part I would hardly haue beleeued
the contrary vntill my eyes became witnesse of what I desired
not to haue found; still taking occasion of hope on euery
likelihood, till such time as we had coasted almost all the circumference of this great Bay. Neither was MASTER DAVIS to
be blamed in his report and great hopes, if hee had anchored
about *Hope Sanderson,* to haue taken notice of the tydes;
For to that place which is 72 degrees 12 minutes the sea is

1 The opinion expressed by Sir John Ross, against the existence of a
passage towards the North-west out of Baffin's Bay, is as decided as that
expressed by Baffin. The modern navigator observes : " I also trust, as
I believe myself, that the objects of the voyage have been, in every important point, accomplished ; that *I have proved the existence of a bay
from Disco to Cumberland Strait, and set at rest for ever the question of a
North-west passage in this direction*". (P. iii, *Introduction to the Voyage of*
1818.)   Yet, as before remarked, both were deceived.

open, and of an vnsearchable depth, and of a good colour :
onely the tydes keepe a certaine course, nor rise but a small
height, as eight or nine foote; and the flood commeth from
the southward; and in all the Bay beyond that place the
tyde is so small, and not much to be regarded. Yet by reason
of snow melting on the land, the ebb is stronger then the
floud; by meanes whereof, and the windes holding northerly
the fore part of the yeere, the great iles of ice are set to the
southward, som into *Fretum Hudson*, and other into *Newfoundland* : for in all the channell where the sea is open, are
greate quantities of them driuing vp and downe; and till this
yeere not well knowne where they were bred.

Now that the worst is knowne (concerning the passage) it
is necessarie and requisite your worship should vnderstand
what probabilitie and hope of profit might here be made hereafter, if the voyage might bee attempted by fitting men. And
first, for the killing of whales; certaine it is, that in this Bay
are great numbers of them, which the Biscayners call the
Grand Bay whales, of the same kind as are killed at *Greeneland*, and as it seemeth to me, easie to be strooke, because they
are not vsed to be chased or beaten. For we being but one
day in WHALE SOUND (so called for the number of whales we
saw there sleeping, and lying aloft on the water, not fearing
our ship, or ought else); that if we had beene fitted with men
and things necessarie, it had beene no hard matter to haue
strooke more then would have made three ships a sauing voyage; and that it is of that sort of whale, theare is no feare; I
being twise at Greeneland, tooke sufficient notice to know
them againe; besides a dead whale we found at sea, hauing
all her finnes (or rather all the rough of her mouth), of which
with much labour we got one hundred and sixtie the same
evening we found her : and if that foule wether and a storme
the next day had not followed, we had no doubt but to haue
had all, or the most part of them: but the winde and sea rising,
shee broke from vs, and we were forced to leaue her. Neither

VOYAGES OF BYLOT AND BAFFIN.

are they onely to be looked for in WHALE SOUND, but also in SMITH'S SOUND, WOLSTENHOLME'S SOUND, and others, *etca.*

For the killing of sea-morse I can give no certaintie, but onely this : that our bote being but once a shore in all the north part of this bay, which was in the entrance of ALDER-MAN JONES HIS SOUND; at their returne our men told vs they saw many morses alonge by the shore on the ice: but our ship being vnder sayle, and the winde comming faire, they presently came aboord without further search : besides, the people in-habiting about 74 degrees, tould vs by diuers signes, that to-ward the north were many of those beasts, having two long teeth ; and shewed vs diuers peeces of the same.

As for the sea-unicorne, it being a great fish, hauing a long horne or bone growing forth of his forehead or nostrils (such as SIR MARTIN FROBISHER, in his second voyage, found one), in diuers places we saw of them : which, if the horne be of any good value, no doubt but many of them may be killed.[1]

As concerning what the shore will yeeld, as beach-finnes, morse-teeth, and such like, I can say little, because we came not on shore in any of the places where hope was of findinge them.

But here som may obiect why we sought that coast no better ? To this I answere, that while we were thereabout, the wether was so exceeding foule, we could not ; for first

[1] The oil of the sea-unicorn (*monceros, narwhal*) is of a superior quality. The horn was long the subject of a kind of superstitious respect. It was considered to be efficacious in the cure of several distempers ; and was prized as being of the very highest value. The Margraves of Bareuth possessed one which cost them six hundred thousand rix-dollars; and the kings of Denmark have a throne formed of it, which is esteemed of more value than if composed of gold. The horn is of a finer texture, and takes a better polish, than the elephant's. (*Laing's Voyage to Spitzbergen, quoted by Ross*, 1818, p. 131.) The horn brought home by Sir Martin Frobisher was preserved in Queen Elizabeth's wardrobe. (*Purchas.*) These horns were eagerly sought by the *Coreans* and *Japanese :* particularly when of a black colour. (*Cock's Diary in Japan*, 1613. *E. I. Mss.*)

we anchored in WOLSTENHOLME SOUND, where presently we droue with two anchors a head; then were we forced to stand forth with a low saile. The next day, in WHALE SOUND, we lost an anchor and cable, and could fetch the place no more; then we came to anchor neere a small iland, lying between SIR THOMAS SMITH'S SOUND and WHALE SOUND: but the winde came more outward, that we were forced to weigh againe. Neuerthelesse, if we had bene in a good harbor, hauing but our ship's bote, we durst not send her farre from the ship, having so few men (as seventeen in all), and som of them very weake : but the chiefe cause we spent so little time to seeke a harbor, was our great desire to performe the discouery ; having the sea open in all that part, and still likelihood of a passage ; but when we had coasted the land so farre to the southward, that hope of passage was none, then the yeere was too farre spent, and many of our men very weake, and withall we hauing some beliefe that ships the next yeere would be sent for the killing of whales, which might doe better than we.

And seeing I have briefly set doune what hope there is of making a profitable voyage, it is not vnfit your worship should know what let or hindrance might be to the same. The chiefest and greatest cause is, that som yeere it may happen by reason of the ice lying betweene 72 and a halfe and 76 degrees, no minutes, that the ships cannot com into those places till toward the middest of July, so that want of time to stay in the countrey may be some let : yet they may well tarry till the last of August, in which space much businesse may be done, and good store of oile made. Neuerthelesse, if store of whales come in (as no feare to the contrarie) what cannot be made in oyle, may be brought home in blubber, and the finnes will arise to good profit. Another hinderance will be, because the bottome of the sounds will not be so soone cleere as would bee wished ; by meanes whereof, now and then a whale may be lost. (The same case sometimes chanceth in *Greeneland*.) Yet I am perswaded those sounds before named will all be cleere before the twentieth of July: for we, this yeere, were in Whale Sound the fourth day, amongst many whales, and might have strooke them without let of ice.

Furthermore, there is little wood to be expected either for fire, or other necessaries; therefore coales and other such thinges must be prouided at home; they will be so much the readier there.

Thus much I thought good to certifie your worship, wherein I trust you will conceiue that much time hath not beene spent in vaine, or the businesse ouer carelessly neglected; and although we haue not performed what we desired (that is, to have found the passage), yet what we have promised (as to bring certaintie and a true description), truth will make manifest that I haue not much erred.

And I dare boldly say (without boasting) that more good discouerie hath not in shorter time (to my remembrance) beene done since the action was attempted, considering how much ice we have passed, and the difficultie of sayling so neere the pole (vpon a trauerse). And above all, the variation of the compasse, whose wonderfull operation is such in this bay, increasing and decreasing so suddenly, and swift, being in some part, as in WOLSTENHOLME SOUND and in SIR THOMAS SMITH'S SOUND, varied aboue fiue points or 56 degrees, a thing almost incredible and matchlesse in all the world beside; so that without great care and good obseruations, a true description could not have beene had.[1]

In fine, whatsoeuer my labours are, or shall be, I esteeme them too little to expresse my thankfull minde for your many fauours, wherein I shall be ever studious to supply my other wants by my best endeauours, and euer rest at your worship's command,

WILLIAM BAFFIN.[2]

[1] See note, p. 140 *ante*.   [2] *Purchas*, vol. 3, pp. 843-844.

It is conceived, that "occasion of slander" against the actions and writings of this honest and able man, is for ever quelled; and that, hereafter, "neuer dyinge fame will enroule his name in Tymes Chiefest Chronicle of Eternytie, where *no enuious Momus* shall haue power to rase out the smallest tytle thereof".[1]

§ XI.

Voyage of Captain Hawkridge.

IT has been observed : "It is scarcely known under whose employ, in what ship, or even in what year, Captain Hawkridge sailed".[2]

Some light appears to be thrown on the subject by the following proceedings in the Court of Committees of the East India Fellowship. It appears from the records, that on the 20th of January 1618-19, SIR JOHN WOLSTENHOLME announced "an intended tryall to be made once againe in discou'nge the Norwest passage". As an inducement to the Court to contribute their assistance to this new attempt, he states, it is understood, "that in Botton's Bay, wch runneth in 450 leagues from the mouth, a great tyde of floode runnes, and riseth sometimes 17 or 18 feet in height, wch is supposed cannott be but by some current in the sea in some other place, wch in pbabillitie may proue the desired passage".[3] Sir John Wolstenholme further states, so satisfied is he of the feasibility of the project, that he intends "to make a good round aduenture in his own pticuler, and to pswade as many friendes as he may, whereby to raise meanes to furnishe forthe two pinnaces, wch will cost *li*.2,000". This appeal to the generosity of the worshipful body was no less successful

---

[1] See *Baffin's Letter to Sir Thomas Smith*, pp. 98-99, *ante.*

[2] *Arctic Voyages*, p. 235.

[3] See p. 89, *ante*, and note; and *Harriott's* "*Three Reasons*", p. 90.

than former applications of the same description had been. " Seeing", the record states, "that the matter is small for this Companie, and that these workes bringe forthe some good (as the whale-fishinge was found by the like occasion),[1] yf the yssue proue good, they are like to be ptakers of that good ; but yf itt should succede otherwise, yet the deed is charitable ; *They*, therefore, by erecõn of hands, did graunte an aduenture of *li*.200 towards the same."[2]

It is apparent, a voyage was contemplated in 1619; and as no other voyage but the one under notice was made between that of Bylot and Baffin in 1616, and that of Luke Fox in 1631, it may be assumed, that the expedition under Hawkridge was sent out in the course of the year 1619, and that it was promoted by Sir John Wolstenholme, aided by his friends, including the East India Fellowship.

A.D. 1619. } CAPTAIN HAWKRIDGE, notwithstanding the reputation he enjoyed as a navigator, and the experience he may be presumed to have gained while serving under Sir Thomas Button, was not more successful than his fellow-volunteer, Captain Gibbons. The only difference between the two navigators, is, that one was blocked up in a " hole ", and did nothing; while the other roved about to no good purpose. All that is known of the proceedings of Captain Hawkridge, is a very meagre account given by Fox: as much as he could gather " by manuscript or relation". It seems, the navigator passed by Resolution Island : went to the southward of Button's Islands: saw Cape Charles (or Charles' Island) : cruized about some coast, but what coast is not

---

[1] A.D. 1611, whale-fishing was commenced in *Greenland*, i. e. at *Spitzbergen ;* for the land now called *Greenland* was then denominated *Groenland, Groyneland,* and *Groanland.* In the above year a small whale was killed, which "yeelded twelve tunnes of oyle". The produce of the whale-fishery in 1622, amounted to " one thousand and three-hundred tunnes".—*Purchas,* vol. iii, pp. 465, 470.

[2] Court Minute Book.—*E. I. Mss.*

known, from the 27th of July to the 6th of August; and is
supposed to have sighted Salisbury Island at some indefinite
period.

-----

§ XII.

Voyage of Captain Luke Fox.

THE navigator, whose voyage is about to be narrated, was a
native of Yorkshire : a shrewd man, somewhat conceited and
given to pedantry, but of a generous disposition. He had
been bred to the sea, and was well versed in the use of the
globes and "other mathematicke instruments". In the course
of the voyage he proved himself to be both a good mariner
and an able seaman. On one point Fox is to be particularly
commended. He spared no pains to make himself acquainted
with the subject before he embarked in the undertaking. He
not only diligently studied the writings and opinions of his pre-
cursors, but he assiduously consulted all persons, professional
or scientific, from whom he had any expectation of obtaining
information.

In his account of the " preparations to the voyage", he informs the reader, that he " had been itching after it ever since
1606, and would have gone mate with *John Knight*"; but he
was not considered, at that time, to possess sufficient experience to entitle him to fill so responsible a berth. The "itching", however, was not allayed by this rebuff. On the contrary, he proceeded to strengthen himself, to take advantage
of any fit occasion that might present itself. In process of
time, he became associated with M. HENRY BRIGGS, whose
name has already been mentioned in connexion with Sir
Thomas Button's voyage ; and by persuasion of that learned
and zealous gentleman, the "honourable knight, SIR JOHN
BROOKE", was induced, "with diuers friends", to join in the

adventure. A petition was presented to CHARLES THE FIRST, and that monarch without hesitation gave his countenance to the action, and placed one of the ships of the royal navy at the disposal of the applicants ; but the season being far spent, it was considered expedient to defer the undertaking till the next year.

In the interval M. Briggs died. One half of the adventurers fell away ; and the project would probably have been abandoned, had not the merchants of Bristol announced an intention of sending out a vessel to prosecute the discovery. This announcement excited a spirit of emulation on the part of the London merchants ; and, fortunately, at this juncture SIR THOMAS ROE arrived in London, having despatched an embassy with which he had been charged to the King of Sweden. On being applied to, he entered heartily into the project, and, through his influence, the King's Majesty sent for SIR JOHN WOLSTENHOLME, who is justly characterized as, " the never failing friend of this voyage"; and, with Sir Thomas Roe, he was appointed to " expediate the enterprise". The MASTERS and WARDENS of the TRINITY HOUSE were, also, commanded to give their aid ; and M. JOHN WOLSTENHOLME, the younger, was made treasurer.

By the combined efforts of these parties, an outfit was provided which seems to have given perfect satisfaction to the commander of the expedition, and which he details, somewhat over elaborately indeed, in the following terms. Master Fox states : "I was victualled completely for eighteen moneths, but whether the baker, brewer, butcher, and other were mr. of their arts or professions, or no, I know not; but this I am sure of, I had excellent fat beefe, strong beere, good wheaten bread, good Iseland ling, butter and cheese of the best, admirable sacke and aqua-vitæ, pease, oat-meale, wheat-meale, oyle, spice, sugar, fruits, and rice ; with chyrurgerie, as syrups, juleps, condits, trechissis, antidotes, balsoms, gummes, unguents, implaisters, oils, potions, suppositers, and purging pils ; and if

X

I had wanted instruments my chyrurgion had enough. My carpenter was fitted from the thickest bolt to the pumpe-nayle or tacket. The gunner from the sacor to the pistoll. The boatswaine from the cable to the sayle-twine. The steward and cooke from the caldron to the spoone". Moreover, in the attention which was paid to the body, the mind was not overlooked. Fox adds : " As for bookes, if I wanted any I was to blame, being bountifully furnisht from the treasurer with money to provide me". But he intimates, that, contemplating he should have little time for study, he had taken care to prepare himself beforehand for emergencies, lest on some sudden occasion, the same mischance might happen to him that befell the *Holland skipper*, who, when it was too late, " runne to his chest, to looke vpon his waggoner booke".

A.D. 1631. } The ship selected for the service was the CHARLES, a pinnace of *seventy tons* burthen, carrying a complement of twenty men and two boys, with an armament of seven guns. The voyage was commenced from Deptford on the 3rd of May.

No event of importance occurred till the 3rd of June, when, somewhat above latitude 58° 39′, N., a storm was encountered, in regard to which the navigator observes, in his peculiar style: "This fulsome ugly morning presented the foulest childe that the whole voyage brought forth, with such variety and changes of the elements, ayre, and water, as if all had conspired to make our destiny fatall". Escaping, however, without any accident, Fox proceeded to adopt measures which give evidence of good seamanship and forethought. He states : " I lay a try in the mizen course, and caused the carpenter to make loose and strengthen the fishes and wouldings of the maine-yard, which being done, I caused the mizen to be strucke, and the helme to be put on weather, to try if the ship would weathercoyle if I had occasion, to which she obeyed presently, so as I was then put into good assurance of her quicke steerage, against I was to enter into the ice."

In latitude N. 58° 30′, the ship was conceived to be not far from Cape Farewell. The article enjoining a strict look out on the part of the watch, was again read to the company; and the very proper precaution was taken, of stationing a man in the fore-top during the night. Cape Farewell was not, however, seen, and the circumstance is attributed to the hazy state of the atmosphere to landward. This was on the 13th. On the 14th of June, the weather was close, with drizzling mists, the wind contrary, and the ship in traverse. A large shoal of grampuses "following their leader passed close by", which caused, though wherefore is not evident, the navigator to "remember *Mr. William Browne* in his *Britaines Pastorals,* where hee writes, the *Tritons* wafted *Thetis* along the *British shore*". The Tritons and Thetis were brought to the recollection of Captain Fox in latitude N. 58° 10′, the variation by Azimuth and Almicanter being 18°. In 58° 50′ the sea proved almost continually smooth; and black water, which had been previously seen, was again noticed, but not so thick as before. On the 18th, the 60th parallel was attained. Overfalls and races of tide were encountered, and land being supposed to be near, all sail was taken in, and the "ship laid to hull". In the evening, about six o'clock, just as the company had risen from prayers, they found themselves close to a mountain of ice, hard to leeward; and it was not without some difficulty that collision was avoided by "flatting the ship to the S. wards". Two days afterwards land was made on the N. side of Lumley's Inlet, or Frobisher's Straits. At that instant, eleven o'clock, the latitude by dead reckoning was 62° 17′, and by a good observation made presently afterwards 62° 25′, the difference being 8′ to the westward.

Fox takes his last departure from latitude N. 58° 30′, on the west coast of Greenland. He calculates the distance he had passed in crossing over Davis's Straits at 220 leagues, or thereabouts: and the difference between the latitude made by dead reckoning and that by observation being only 8′, he infers the current setting out of the straits, from N. to S., to have been over-rated by former navigators.[1]

The arrival of Fox in this vicinity affords him an opportunity of indulging in a pleasant piece of gossip, to the following effect : " Seeing now", he proceeds to say, " that it hath pleased God to send me thus happily to the land on the N. side of *Lumleys Inlet,* so named after the Right Honourable the *Lord Lumley,* an especial furtherer to *Davis* in his voyages, as to many other lordly designes, as that never to be forgotten act of his, in building up the peere of that poor fisher-towne and corporation of *Hartlepoole* in the bishopricke of Durham, at his owne proper cost and charge, to the value of at least 2000 pounds. At my first coming thither, I demanded at whose charge the said peere-towne was builded. An old man answered : *marrye, at my good Lord Lumley's, whose soule was in Heaven before his bones were cold".*

The following day, the entrance of Hudson's Straits was made, and the navigator's account of his progress through them will be adopted. This narrative, it may be premised, exhibits many singularities in point of style. It contains many *euphuesms* calculated to excite a smile, and to induce an involuntary ejaculation with worthy *Sir Hugh,* of : " *What phrase is this ?.... why it is affectations."* These affectations cannot, however, be considered the result of a frivolous mind. They occur only in connexion with trivial matters : otherwise, the style of Fox is sufficiently sober and earnest. They may be attributed to the out-bursting of a buoyant spirit, trammelled by the contemplation of difficulty, oppressed by anxious meditation on the means of escaping danger, and eagerly seizing the most trifling opportunity to gain even momentary relief. The proceedings of Fox, with the measures he adopted to overcome the difficulties in which he found himself, and the dangers to which he was exposed, give evidence of his

---

[1] This opinion is confirmed by the observations of Ross. (*Voyage of the Isabella and Alexander,* 1818, pp. 35-37, etc. London : 1819.)

having been a man of no ordinary mind. They are characterized by decision, sound judgment, and skill. The track followed by the old mariner has been pursued by one of the most able and most enterprising of our modern navigators; and the observations made by him during his voyage, will, it is conceived, demonstrate, that in the above estimate, the merits of Fox are not over-rated.

Y^E PASSAGE THOROW FRETUM HUDSON.

June 21. This snowie morning I stoode in againe, at clocke 7. I fell about 2 leagues more to the west off the same ile I first discovered yesterday. The bay [lat. 62 deg. 12 min.] lay still full of ice. This W.N.West wind bloweth hard by puffes. Standing from hence South W., 2 leagues over *Lumleys* inlet, wee had great store of masht yce, and were faine to beare up for one, and loose for another, but the sea was smooth; after this, for 2 leagues sailing, it was cleare. At night 10, we see land, and made it upon assurance to be Cape *Warwick*, and this cleere was in the lee thereof; for standing still the same course over, wee found more yce in the south channell, and more comming out of *Fretum Hudson* then I had before. The wind blew here bleake and unquoth.

22. This day we had boarded it up in smooth water, bearing a good saile betweene Cape *Chidlie* and Cape *Warwick*, and were entred *Fretum Hudson;* and [near by] the iland *Resolution,* so named by whom I know not. But sure I am, *Davis* was the first of us that see it, naming the east end thereof Cape *Warwick*.[1]

Having made this cape (*Chidlie*), which to doe I stood over, as neere as I could for ice, but was at least 6 leagues off, it appeared high, and 4 distinct ilands. (In number, I iudge there is more.) Being now assured that God had sent me into the passage, I stoode over to the north, with Cape

1 *Cape Warwick,* or, *Earl Warwick's Foreland.* See note, p. 40, ante: first voyage of Davis: which does not corroborate the opinion of Fox.

Warwick; the middle channell was cleare of ice, and therein
I had a good observation of 61 deg. 10 min., cleare weather,
and a constant gale, otherwise I durst not have stoode to
the southwards, remembring *Gibbons*. It blew in both topsailes, but towards night the wind lessened; and I could
perceive the ice betwixt me and the cape, to drive to seaward,
of which, neere the shoare, was great store.

The flood comming on, I caused both topsayles to bee cast
over, and wee threed it, betweene ice and ice, with a well-
bent flood inwards; so as that we had got above the ile that
tyde, if this faire day had not ended in fogge. A motion
was made before this, to looke for harbour; but that I denied, for these reasons given: that I did not know what danger might fall me if I had put into the shore, where lay
much yce (as we could see), and what yce or sunke rocks
might be in the way, I was as ignorant of; besides not knowing whether the wind would serve to bring me in a safe road,
and how the tyde might set to turne or sayle in, as occasion
might fall out; but the worst was, and that was most I
feared, the wind might souther, and then there being such
store of yce in the passage, would inforce all the harbours
full, and so might cut my cable, and put me on shore upon
the rockes, it flowing much water there, as *Baffin* reports.
With these reasons wee were all perswaded to ply it up
amongst the ice, in sea-roome, rather then to indanger our
selves in harbour, or neere the shoare, where for certaine the
broken rockes, the grounded ice, the small ilands, by re-
straining the tides, must make them reverse with counter-
sets and eddies, as may be observed by LONDON BRIDGE,[1] the

[1] The ancient superstructure has been swept away; but, differing in
this respect from the "baseless fabric of a vision", the old foundations
mostly remain : in defiance of the efforts of time, and the destructive
ingenuity of man. Instead of serving as an illustration of the perils encountered by Frobisher, Davis, and Fox, from furious races and over-falls
of water, the narratives of these intrepid navigators of the northern
seas must be consulted, to form an estimate of the dangers which be-

bases of whose arches, being set in the tides course, doth so restraine his motion, that the following streames, by heightning the waters, causeth such a current, as it were, to ingulfe by the fall thereof, as you see the water-men cannot keepe their boates even on, the counter-tyde wheeling on her of the one side, the eddie coursing her upon the other, not joyning their separations, but goeing, as it were, distracted above *Cole*-harbour, before they come to themselves againe, to passe westward; and all this hazard is to no purpose, for we are safer at sea: besides, wee are not sure of any refreshing, and if wee were, we have no neede, being but newly come from home; and if the wind come to south, and so eastwards to north-east, wee being in the sea, may proceede night or day, but in harbour wee cannot; and therefore to take harbour were vanity, unlesse to loyter, spend away, and consume time, the thought whereof is ridiculous. The fogge and night came both together; and having the last 24 houres, quitted aboundance of ice to seaward, which might serve as a baracadoe, if the wind should come from thence, and keepe us safe amongst it, as after *(blessed be God)* it proved, wee made fast to a peece of ice, filld fresh water thereupon, and went all to our beds, save the watch.[1]

set the former passage through London bridge. Over the spot, in their days fraught with hazard to the bold and the experienced, crowds of persons, neither bold nor experienced, of both sexes and of all ages, in these days not only glide in safety, but without sense of apprehension.

[1] *On the protection afforded by ice*, SIR EDWARD PARRY observes: "The effects to be apprehended from exposure to the swell of the main ocean, constitute the peculiar danger of first entering the ice about the mouth of Hudson's Straits, which is completely open to the influence of the whole Atlantic. A very inconsiderable quantity of loose ice is sufficient to shelter a ship from the sea, provided it be closely packed; but when the masses are separated by wind or tide, so as to admit the swell, the concussions soon become too violent for a ship, strengthened in the usual way, to withstand for any length of time. On this account, it is prudent not to enter the ice without a fair prospect of getting seven or eight leagues within the margin. For the same reason, also, when likely to be

23. This misty morning made the sunne clime 10 degrees in height, before he could peepe through the same, which afterwards prooved a very faire calme hot day, making both ice and pitch runne, but the ship was enclosed amongst the ice driving with ebbe and flood. About 2 leagues from the south end of *Resolution,* I had no ground at 180 fathomes, some of my men said they saw smoake on land, and after it prooved true, for Captaine *James* [the Bristol navigator] was in harbour there all that same time. My master went with boate and killed nine willicks, whereof he kindly bestowed upon every messe one. They make strong and good pottage.

I pressing hard for getting cleere, that I might proceed, was demanded why I made such haste, answered, that as every mountaine consisted of severall peeces, so did my voyage upon fathomes, which must be measured here with speed, though afterward I might take leisure, which added one to another, might in time compasse all the mountaines of the world ; and that it fared with me, as the mackarell-men at *London,* who must hasten to the market before the fish stinke.

This evening the sun set cleare, the ayre breathed gently from the east, and we lay quietly all night amongst the ice.

24. This morning the wind began to gather strength from the E.S.E., the flood came on, and the ice began to separate. I caused one peece to be made fast unto the ship with 2 grap-

beset near the sea, it is better to make a ship fast to small than to large pieces, in order to avoid the heavier concussions occasioned by the latter."

On the relative advantage of entering by the centre, or along the coast, the same authority remarks : " Early on the morning of the 9th of July, the ice closed in upon us, and we remained immoveably beset for a week...... It was, however, a matter of agreeable surprise to us to find the masses of ice so quiet among themselves, as to give us no disturbance: a circumstance that seemed to indicate a greater regularity in the set of the tides near the centre of Hudson's Strait, carrying the whole of the ice along in one body, instead of producing the violent cross-sets which we had experienced in shore. In the middle of the strait we could obtain no soundings with three hundred fathoms of line."— *Voyage of the Fury and Hecla,* 1821-23, pp. 9-11. London : 1824.

nels, to the intent to towe it at the ships sterne, mooring the ship so thereunto, that she might make way N.W. for the north shore, for that it hath been alwayes said, that the north side was cleerest from ice. Thus made fast, although the wind forst on the ship, yet her way was so easie, as she could take no harme, if she had touched upon the same, because this trayle or drag stayed her way ; but the wind blowing on, the ship broke one grapnel off by the arme of the flooke, and bended the other, so as we were loose from thence ; but meeting great store of driving ice, I caused to make fast againe for safety, where we were presently enclosed for many miles.

25. This morning, the ship broke loose from that peece, I was made fast unto ; the ship and tackling being more in the winds power than the ice (it being lower), caused her to drive faster.

I caused the spritsaile to be loosed, to binde the ship's stem to the ice, which gave alwayes way with the flood, which set westward ; so the east wind forcing it backe, made it cloze with the ebbe, returning eastwards, which put mee in good hope, that further within the straight, I should finde all cleare, or at least the ice so thinne, as I might passe betweene one and another ; and with this perswasion I drew on the Company, that the S.E. winds which had blown for six or seven dayes before we came into this freet, had kept in this ice, and those west winds, which had blowne three dayes before, and at our entry, comming (from about 140 leagues) from the bottome heere, in some places 20, in some places 30, and in some 40 leagues more or lesse broad, had packt all from thence, unto this straitened place, betwixt Cape *Chidley*, and the body of *Resolution*, and so choaked this entrance, being not above 14 leagues broad. The wind E.N.E. we drive all this time inwards with the ice.[1]

---

[1] *On the effects of the west wind.* Sir Edward Parry states : "It may be observed that, in the course of our endeavours to get to the westward, as

Quantity and Shapes of Ice.

Now this prodigious thing we call ice is of two sorts, as mountainous ice, wch is a huge peece, compact, of a great quantity, some of more, some of lesse ; but in this freet you seldome have any bigger then a great church, and the most therof lesse, being of severall formes, as some 20, some 30, some 40 yards above the superficies of the water, but farre more under : of these you may tell sometimes 7 or eight in sight, so that they are no hindrance to us.[1]

The other is smaller, and that we call masht or fleackt ice. Of this you shall there have numbers infinite, some of the quantity of a rood, some a pearch, ½ an acre, some 2 acres ; but the most is small and about a foot or 2, or more above the water, and 8 or 10 or more under the water, and those are they which doe inclose you ; so as in much wind, from the topmast head you shall hardly see any water for them, but whilst you lie amongst them, it is so smooth as you shall not feele the ship stirre. Onely if it be much wind, make the ship snogge, and at returne of the tydes, when the ice doth loozen, have all care to the rudder. At shift of wind, the ice will make way one from another; in the meane time have patience, and in trailing of ice on sterne, if the ship doe

well in this voyage as in that of 1819-20, a westerly wind, though blowing directly against us, was always found ultimately to be the most favourable to our purpose, as it brings away large bodies of ice from that quarter, and consequently leaves a considerable interval of open water. The most precious opportunity to seize, therefore, in this navigation, is at the springing up of an easterly breeze, after a gale from the opposite quarter; at which time, if a ship be fortunately unhampered, considerable progress may generally be made. Not a moment of this favourable interval must be lost, as the ice invariably closes again in a few hours after the change of wind ; which is, besides, usually attended with thick weather."—*Voyage*, etc., p. 35.

[1] On entering Hudson's Strait, the expedition of 1821-23 passed a great number of ice-bergs. Fifty-four were in sight at one time. Some were not less than two hundred feet in height. (*Voyage*, etc., p. 7). See also Baffin's first voyage, p. 108, *ante*, and note.

touch but against it with the stemme, so as the stroke so-
dainely stay her way, then have care to keep the helme in
midships, for your traile with its way, will come presently
against the backe of the rudder, and it lying on either side,
is in danger to breake, or set it on wry.

There is another way, which is to muzzell the ship with a
peece of ice close to his stem and bowes; the ice being so
swifted, the ship is to drive it with head saile; but this I doe
not cŏmend, for that the ship not having fresh way, shall not
have her steering beside the edy water the forst ice shall
make; not ccmming quicke to the rudder, it shall not command her, so as if any wind be, she shall cast a thwart with
head to the wind, and drive sterne wayes, to the great danger of her rudder, if ice be in the way.

25. This day hath been wet fog unto evening 6; then it
cleered. At 10 we see land to the N., not certaine whether
Resolution or no, for there was no remarkeable thing thereon. This evening sun kist *Thetis* in our sight; the same
greeting was 5 d. W. from the N., and at the same instant
the rainebowe was in appearance, I thinke to canopy them
a bed.

At the beginning of flood, here is wheeling streames like
edie tides, I take to be caused by the ice themselves, one
drawing more water then another, and continueth all the
time of their moving, untill they be setled, so as it may be
conjectured that it doth runne $\frac{1}{2}$ tyde under other, as in most
places elsewhere. All this time, since the wind came E. ward,
it hath not blowne above course, and bonnet gale.

26. This morning the sun rose cleare, and so continued
all this cold virgin day, for I have not seene one cloud to
interpose, yet he went peeping through a cloud to bed. And
now the frost takes care that there shall no more pitch runne
from off the sun-side of the ship; and the land towards sun-
set, doth so alter by the exhalation of vapours, that it shewes

now firme land, then a bay, now high, then low, that we
cannot say whether we make maine-land, bayes, or through-
lets; the ice with the uncertain reflex of the sun, made such
unconstant shapes.

27.   This morning the sun shewed himselfe through Fly-
land, and the south wind drave away the vapours, which
fully satisfied our mistaking of land the last evening; yet
we were not mistaken, but that we drive into the passage all
this while.   This wind with tyde, helpes to separate the ice,
(a little).   It being advantageous for the N. main, I caused
to make loose, whence we furthered ½ a mile, the wind comming W. with fog, caused us to make fast againe.   God thinke
upon our imprisonment with a *supersedeas*.   This evening sun-
dog [? *down*] I hope may bring some change to our good.

This overcast day proved faire, and a pretty W.N.W. gale,
untill towards night.   My carpenter made straight a peece,
above the backe of our rudder, which was set awry with the
ice.   I caused the lead to be cast in 320 fathomes, but the
under ebbe tide did carry it so far to the E. as wee could not
thinke wee had lesse stray then 30 fathomes.   The ground
was small blacke sand, with long crooked things the length of
a needle, and the small body of two shell fishes, like lobsters,
but no bigger then maggots.

29.   This faire hot day is now almost neere at end, we lye
amongst the ice, and I doe not know what wind to pray for
to quit us of them, they lie so thicke every way; but I thinke
we feare more danger then wee are in.   God for his mercies
sake set us at libertie.   I can perceive wee drive to the N.W.
ward, and have 210 fathomes of water under vs.   The sunne
set cleere this evening.

30.   This hot day is also at an end.   I have had an ayre of
wind.   With all sayle on board, and threading betwixt the ice,
got about 4 miles N.W. wards, and stucke fast againe.   By
the way, I came by one peece of ice, something higher then the
rest; whereupon a stone was of the contents of 5 or 6 tonne

weight,[1] with divers other smaller stones and mudde thereon. It seemeth to condescend with reason, that these peeces of ice are engendred upon the winters snow, which falling in drifts by the forcing and wheeling of the wind, condensing and compacting a great quantitiy together, over the steepe brow of some high mountaine, cleaving thereto untill dissolving time of the yeare, when the earth receives her naturall warmnesse ; then inforced by their weight to tumble into the sea, carrying with them all such trees or stones as they have formerly inclosed. God be thanked the ice begun to thinne, and separate ; this hot weather doth fast dissolve them.

This night, clock 2, came a small iland of ice, brought up with the latter flood, and by his draught being deeper in the tydes way then the flact or masht ice, had a greater motion continued by the undertyde then that which had enclosed us, of which we were fast unto one of the biggest content, to wit, 3 acres. This iland did drive right with us, and but that some few masht ice interposed, thereby diverting the course thereof, some 2 or 3 ships length, it had drove directly upon us, and had crusht us mainely, if not to peeces, it being 9 or 10 fathomes above water ; and if it had boarded us, being undermined by the waters continual working, the outside thereof by that shake might have fallen into the ship, and have sunke her. This was the greatest danger we were in since I came into *Fretum Hudson*, the fault being in the watch, who did not call, that we might have set the ship the one way or the other about the peece we were fast unto, before we were so ingaged as I could doe neither. About one houre after, the said iland tooke his recourse back againe to the east, with the ebbe faster then the other ice could doe.

July 1. This morning 8, the sunne was up, before we saw it ; the day was warme, and close, but calme, so as I could

1 " Masses of rock, not less than a hundred pounds in weight, are sometimes observed in the *middle* of a floe, measuring half a mile, or more, each way." — *Voyage*, etc., p. 32.

not stirre for want of wind.   The straight doth cleere, and
this N. land, that hath continued with us since we departed
with *Resolution* it now bearing from E. and S. to N. and by E.
The tyde doth set as the land doth lie, south-east and north-
west.

This night 7, it was an ayre, farre better then a younger
brother, the ice well thinn'd.   I caused the ship to be loosed,
and by that time the master with the boat was come from
killing of fowle, I stood to the N. about foure miles. This fayre
day being at an end, I made fast, set the watch, and went to
cabin.

2.   This morning 2, an easie gale breathed from the E. by
south, which caused mee to send to the boatswaine to call up
the company, where a chiefe one amongst us, being too suddenly awaked, speaking somewhat peevishly, I told the rest
that the matter was not great, for the children did so when
they were awaked out of their sleep.   I began now to find the
want of a shallop, which at home I did so earnestly desire, for
my cocke boat would nor rowe nor sayle to any purpose, so
as I durst hardly send her from me, for when it was any bil-
low, she was not to be rowed, and with saile to windward shee
would doe nothing, although I had caused a large lee board
to be made to helpe her.

This meridianall observation, the wind came west, and I
was in 61 d. 57 m., and stood in close to this inremarkeable
shore, & so all the land within this straight may be called,
for it is all shoring, or descending from the highest mountaine to the sea.   Whereon, the snow falling by degrees, doth
presse and burthen it selfe, making the masse more solid,
which at the spring time, when it loosneth from the earth, its
own weight doth force downward into the sea, being all composed of fresh water, it may be conceived that the most ice
we meete in this passage is thus ingendred.   In the vallies
betwixt the mountaines, is some snow undesolved.   We are
now cleare of chattered ice, yet (in sight) are some ilands,

about which wee can compasse as we please. Here lyeth many
small ilands close by the mayne, and there doth appeare to
be fayre sounds into the land. Upon the sea, this calme time
that hath beene, doth swimme a kind of corrupt slime; one
may thinke it may come by generation of great fishes, for it
feeles soft and unctious, but put it into the fire it will not
burne.

I doe thinke that all this time of our imprisonment, this
north shore hath beene free, as I could espie it at *Hiperions*
going downe: which valed with a blacke skreene of moyst
fogge, wet through our coates before we see it againe. This
fayre dayes westwind blew cold and uncouth from out the
passage. Wee are all upon kinde tearmes, drinking one to
another. God hold it.

3. This morninge the sunne lickt up the fogges dew, as
soone as hee began to rise, and made a shining day of it; I
cannot say hot, it being counter-chect by a coole top-sayle
gale, from west, north-west, which made our noses runne.
The cleare day emboldened me to stand within two leagues of
land to the deepe of 32 fathomes, the ground white sand and
gray with shels: the water was falling: the houre 11 before
noone, the sunne and moone in opposition. A good tyde set
along the shoare to the northwards. The sunne set cleare.
It was faire weather and calme. The ship drove along the
shore this night to the westward.

This morning at clocke one, I called to lanche the boate,
to send to shore, to try the tyde, and against that time that
I could send to land, I had drawne those instructions following, and given them to *Iohn Coatesworth,* whom I appointed
alway to goe in the boate, at whose return I expected an account.

These are the Instructions.

First, you shall take with you into the boate, one halfe
houre glasse, one halfe minute glasse, one logge and line,

cleane paper, one pensill of blacke leade, and one compasse,
with some peeces of iron.

Secondly, one quarter saw, two axes, three carbins guns
with powder and shot, two or three lances, two swords, two
pikeaxes, and every man his one day bread.

Thirdly, at your departure from the ship, turne the halfe
houre, and when it is neere out, set your logge to goe by the
halfe minute, that thereby you may estimate the distance betweene the ship and land, as also what the boate can rowe an
houre.

Fourthly, when you shall approach neere the shore in the
tydes way, I meane cleare of Bay, Point, or Rocke, anchor the
boate, sound the deep, and marke the tyde how it doth set,
and by your logge what it doth passe in the halfe minute.
Having rode there for halfe a glasse, weigh your anchor, and
goe to land, and duely observe, what quantity of water it doth
flow, or fall perpendiculer, in one glasse : whether the height-
ening, or lessening be equall in every glasse, while yee stay,
or noe.

Fifthly, being thus on land with your compasse, set all
lands or islands in sight, draw the form with your paper and
pensill, and estimate their distance.

Sixtly, remember I give you no libertie to goe within the
land.   Yet if for recreation : goe no further then the full sea
marke, and armed, leaving two to keepe the glasse and boat.
Looke for stones of orient colour, or of weight, seamors teeth,
vnicornes horne, or whale finne, plants, herbes, or any thing
spungy [? that may] fleet out of the sea.   If you finde scurvie grasse, orpin, or sorrill, bring them all on board to me.

Seventhly, if you will goe above the full sea marke, looke
for footing of wilde beasts ; by that, or their dung, you may
imagine what they are : if deere, doe not chase them into the
land for feare of being betrayed, for the people in those parts
are all treacherous, how faire soever they intreat you.   Remember also that the losse of you, or the boate, is the utter
overthrow of the whole voyage.

Eightly, if you finde of their tents, and they fled, doe no harme to any of their buildings, but bring with you the most things of marke, leaving in the same place, a peece of iron, bigger or lesser, as you estimate the same to be of worth unto us. And so neare as you can, chuse a beach of sandy bay to land in, for there you shall espie most likelihood of inhabitants.

Ninthly, leave one carbine, one lance, and one short sword, to defend the boat, with whose (two) keepers, you shall give charge, that if either they shall espie any token from the ship, as striking the maine topsaile, mison, and spritsaile, gunshot, or firesmoke, or be assaulted by any the inhabitants, that then they shall discharge the said carbine. To the first intent, that you repaire with speed on board ; to the second for their rescue, and your own safetie. When you come cleere in the tydes way, try it as before in the 4 article; the rest is referred to your own discretion, and so I pray God for your safe returne.

July 4. This morning at clocke 6, the wind came faire, the weather like to be thicke and raine, I beckoned them to come on board, but they saw me not. At their departing the dawning being cleare, the ayre calme, and it was within an houre of sun-rising, the sea smooth, the ship nearer the shoare then at any time before, since we came into the passage, and the whole day towards, I would not loose this opportunity to send to land the boat. After 5 houres they returned, and gave account that it was flood-tide about clocke 5, and that they thinke it flowed halfe an houre. The land lay N.N.W. In this time, with the ship, we drive by an iland of ice a ground in 50 fathome. They found where people had been of old ; their tent walls were of stones laid one upon another, and square built ; found one knife haft, three severall sorts of herbes, but my chirurgion knew not what they were ; one peece of drift wood ; they found the dung and footing of deere

z

(lately made); and if they may be beleeved, they affirme that in ¼ of an houre, it did flow above 4 foot water, and that it had above 5 fathomes upright to flow to the full sea marke, which they could easily perceive by the beach, they being forced to rowe and saile 4 miles before they could come to a place to land at. This E.S.E. wind blew on with stiffe gale and durt. At noone it fell thicke raine, and continued untill 4 next day morning, in which time wee made way neare 30 leagues in cleare sea, and then had like to have beene imbayed with ice [that] lyeth thick off *Prince Henries* Foreland,[1] the south land bearing round from W.N.W. ½ westerly to 108 degrees southwards, to cleere which wee were glad to put tackes a board, and turne it forth to the northwards, where it was cleare of ice.

5. This morning the sun was vailed with drisling raine. I stood over for the N. shoare; the master would have perswaded me to stand over for the S., saying the capes on the S. which wee had seene, were *Savage* Ilands, so named by *Bylot*, this being after wee had an observation of 62 deg. 40 min., var. 29 deg. We had some circumstance about it, but he went away well satisfied; and it proved as I tolde him, for at night wee had *Savage* Ilands N., but noe land northward in sight. This evening the sunne set with a weather gall opposite, and *Zephyrus* blewe on a pretty gale, at the same instant the lead was wet in 150 fathomes, the line having 20 fath. straie to the E., and I thought the tyde set W. The most of this day I stood away N.W., but was glad sometime to alter course to the N. for ice, for the S. land lay all full.

6. This day hath bin very hot. Before this S. wind came I did thinke the wind had blowne either right up, or right

---

[1] Sir Edward Parry was informed by the master of a Hudson's Bay ship, that little serious obstruction was encountered in Hudson's Straits, "except from a body of ice, which they usually have to penetrate near *Charles's Island*, and which from the frequency of its occurrence has obtained the name of "*Charles's Patch*".—*Voyage*, etc., p. 17.

downe the passage, viz. E. or W., as for the most part it doth.
The W. is cleare, faire, and hot sun-shine, but the aire is
cold; when it veereth about, as once in 3 dayes, and by the S.
it is either thick raine, soft sleet, or warme fog, the wind E.
or thereabout; these done, he changeth to the W. againe,
bringing the weather faire as before.   I did thinke that this
day the tide set forth : this morning we saw Cape *Charles* 12
leag. off, S.S.E.[1]

7.   The sunne did rise cleare.   At clocke 8 came on a
fogge, and continued unto one ; wee had store of ice to the
S. off us; then it cleared and we were come to the westward,
amongst much ice, and had sight of a high iland, bearing W.
about 6 or 7 leag. off.   Wee saw also the high land of the N.
maine 12 leag. off. The sun set valed, and we had no ground
at 150 fath.   It fell to raine, and I tooke in both topsailes,
and stood to and againe among the ice.

8.   This morning was cold, with some snow, and the W.
wind blew hard.   We made the ship fast to a great peece of
yce, which she plowed through the rest, by force of the gale,
although we had made her as snug as we could.   At noone
we were in 63 deg. 31 min.   Now the wind calmed, and I
made loose, and stood to the N.; and at sun-setting I had
sight of the N. maine againe; the sun set cleare this evening.

10.   This morning sun rose cleare, and I stood to the N.,
close to an iland nere the maine, which iland, at my returne,
I named Ile *Nicholas* ; from which, with a S.W. wind, I stood
over to the southward, and stood with the iland I saw the
7th day before, I hoped it would prove *Salisbury*.   This day
ended, wee made fast againe, for all this north channell was
thick with ice, upon which we filled 2 hoggsheads with fresh
water.   I loosed againe, and with a small gale came within
4 miles of *Salisburies* Iland, for it can be no other ; it is high
land, but not clifted.   I caused to make fast againe, for that
nere the land and the middle channell was all full of ice, and

---

[1] *Hudson* named all on the S. in his straite.—*Fox.*

no ground at 120 fath. ; and untill 6 the tide set westward,
and then it returned. What tide it was I could not discerne,
although I came so nere the land for that purpose. I made
loose againe presently, because the masters mate was of opinion that it was cleare to the W., or at least that was the
cleerest way ; for my parte, I had no more purpose to have
tryed betweene *Salisbury* and the N. maine, or *Mill* Ile, so
named by *Bylot*, for *Mill* Ile being a great iland lying in
the middle of the N. channell, must needs straiten all the ice
that fleets from the N.W. ; yet for the good of the voyage,
it was fit to try all conclusions ; but thus striving to the W.,
we were presently inclosed againe, where we lay vntill the
next morning, all too nere the iland, if I could have got further off. This night had a stiffe gale at west, with one showre
of raine. The sunne was obscured 2 howres before night, and
wee slept safe in our old innes.

12.   I cald at clocke 3, and by 6, with haleing, saleing,
toweing, and pulling, wee were got cleere, and thought to have
gone about the east end of the iland, but the flood faceing of
the winde, had choaked all the east end; so there being one
glade or cleere betweene the shoare and the channell ice, we
plide it up therein for 2 or 3 miles, but comming nere the W.
end it was all choaked there, so shutting betweene one and
another for the N. maine, I stood to see what better comfort,
but at halfe straite ouer I was forced backe againe, for ice and
fogge.   Well, wee stand againe for *Salisburies* ile, of which
I was now assured; and so named by my predecessour *Hudson*,
after the right honourable and not to be forgot *Robert Cicell*,
Earle of *Salisbury*, then Lord High Treasurer of *England*, an
honourable furtherer and adventurer in this designe as well
as in others, as appeareth by Sir *Walter Raleiyh* in his *Guian-
ian* discoveries.   In my standing over I espied a glade wherein
I hoped if I did returne I might recover the N. maine, wherefore I called to tackle about the ship.

The master not seeing what was on the weather bowe, bid

the helme man to put on lee, the ship obeying her helme, presently answered, so as in her winding, her way being not fully
ended, she checkt upon a peece of ice and twined off her cut
water which was before the stemme; thus constrained, I bore
up the helme, and went along to the east end of the ile, and
makeing fast to a peece of ice, the carpenter made good
againe the hurt wee had received; the first harme and all I
received. In the meane time our men went to supper. The
afternoone was more then seven houres old before this was
done. Then I called againe to make loose, for I thought that
the ice was now with winde and ebbe well cleared from the
east end of the iland, as it proved, but many discontented
and doubtfull speeches past, but to no purpose, for I must
runne to discover this losse time. When motion was made to
make fast againe, which I denyed for these reasons, that wee
could see the sea to be reasonable free and cleere at the east
end from the iland, and the south channell would be to be
dealt withall, or if not, the passage was forbidden, untill the
ice were dissolved, and to fasten nere the land I would upon
no condition listen unto, for the winde comming to blow to
land, I must upon necessity bee put thereon, the shippe alwayes pulling the ice she was fast unto faster then the other
could drive; and for anckoring there was none, if the land
had not beene steepe to, for the eddie tides, which every rocke,
bay, or poynt made, would have wheeled the shippe about in
the ice, so as it had not beene possible to have kept my rudder
from breakeing, and amongst ice there was no loosing of any
saile to have beaten it off shoare. It seemeth these reasons had
the force of perswasion, for wee willingly past about the ile to
the south, as well where we found all over laid with ice, so
that wee must make fast. Having toyled thus all day untill
night, I thought it fit to repose.

13.   This morning clocke 4, I called to make loose; wee
had much to doe to get cleere being all fast immured : it was
easie wind.   I could perceive by the bearing of the land that

we had drove about 2 miles S. wards; now we thred-needles to the east, hopeing at further distance from the ile to get cleare into the south channell; at clocke 10 the west winde brought on thick fogges, so as we could not see one hole to peepe through; the ice inclosed us and there we lay. It blew hard untill clocke 7, then it both calmed and cleared. I loosed, and plying 2 leagues to the southwards, had the south maine in sight from the south east to the S. west.

14.   All this day, untill night 7, we kept our colde lodging, and then looseing with an easie breath from N.E. we minnemd [?] betwixt ice and ice, S.Westward, untill we got cleare.

On the 15th of July, Fox was in the vicinity of the islands named respectively, Digges, Salisbury, Nottingham, Mansil, and Southampton; with Cape Pembroke and Carey's Swans' Nest on the latter island.   This circumstance affords the navigator an opportunity, of which he readily avails himself, to make honourable mention of the personages, who had been the main supports of the successive adventures to the North-west; and he concludes in the following emphatic words, no less true than just.   " *They were so named*", he says, " *as a small remembrance for the charge, countenance, and instruction given to the search of the enterprise ; and which, though smaller, neither time nor fame, ought to suffer oblivion to burie : for whensoever it shall please God to ripen those seedes and make them redie for his sickle, whom he hath appoynted to be the happie reaper of this crop, must remember to acknowledge, that those honourable and worthie personages were the first advancers.*"   This remark applies with no less force to the navigators themselves, than to the parties in whose service they were engaged.

In this locality, in latitude 63° 20', a phenomenon is also made the subject of observation.   It is noted : " that here,

and especially neere within the mouth of this strait, the compasse doth almost loose his sensitive part, not regarding his
magneticall *Azimuth* without much stirring". In endeavouring to account for this phenomenon, the navigator remarks :
" the smooth water may be some cause, the ship wanting
her active motion, but I should [? think it] strange the cold
should benum it, as it doth us : nay I should rather thinke,
that the sharpnesse of the ayre, interposed betwixt the needle
and his attractive poynt, may dull the power of his determination. Or, here may be some mountaines, of the one side or
the other, whose minerals may detaine the nimblenesse of the
needle moving to his respective poynt; but this", he adds,
" I leave to philosophie".

From the 16th to the 19th the navigation was among the
islands above noticed. On the evening of the 20th, " the
first sight of starres" was had, including, " *Charles Waine*,[1]
Aurora, Botes, and *Antonius*". The following day land was
passed, whether an island, or no, could not be ascertained :
which " lay like a ridge, or, to simily it, like to the *Retyres* in
the mouth of the river of *Seine* in *Normandy*". In this portion
of his journal, Fox remarks : " I do hold that all those peeces
of ice here, are ingendered about those low Capes and Bayes,
as *Mansils* also is, where easie tides goe. They are soon froze
over, and the snow falling thereon soon thickeneth them :
so that by degrees they increase". And this not an improbable conjecture.

Cary's Swans' Nest was made, it is presumed, on the 21st,
stretching N. both from the E. and W. ends. Some of the
crew, who had chased swans to the shore, reported there was
" earth, strange moss, quagmires, and water plashes". The

---

[1] In the diary of *M. Richard Cock,* cap'e m^rchant of the English factory at Firando in Japon, 1613-23 (*E. I. Mss.*), this star is designated
CHORLS-WAIN ; and *Ben Jonson* uses the A instead of the O. From this,
the etymology may be traced *to the Saxon* "Ceopl", or "Capl", and the
Teutonic **kerl** ; and *Charles Wain* may be considered to mean the *Churl's,*
or *Peasant's Wain.* **C. R.**

23rd (lat. 61° 37′) was a fair, clear day, with easy winds, warm air, and no ice. The 24th, the lat. was 62° 20′, var. by azimuth and almicanter, 26° 31′. The 25th, the lat. was 62° 36′. The 26th, in lat. 63° 20′, was "as hot a day as any in England, and the Pettie dancers and Henbanes", as the Aurora Borealis is termed, "flashing during the night": wherein doth Master Fox wish "joy to our *Antipodes*".

On the 27th, in lat. 64° 10′, an island was descried, which was taken to be the N.E. side of *Sir Thomas Button's Ut Ultra*. The evening on which the discovery was made, was as fair as could be imagined. No land, within ten leagues, was to be seen to the N.E., or E., or S.E.; but it was imagined a shore could be traced from N.N.E. to W. southward. An examination of this island proved it to be a place of sepulture. The corses were laid, with their heads to the westward, on the rocky bed of the island, walled about with blocks of stone, and protected, at top, from the weather with old sledges, "artificially made". Each plank was from nine to ten feet long, and four inches thick, but, "in what manner the tree they have bin made out on, was cloven or sawen, it was so smooth, that it could not be discern'd". The longest of the corses did not exceed four feet. They were wrapped in deer-skins; and arms, with other implements carved in bone, were deposited with them. The mariners took advantage of the occasion to promote their own comfort. It is observed: "we rob'd the graves to build our fires, and we brought on board a whole boate's lading of firewood".

Having given the name of *Sir Thomas Roe's Welcome* to this island, a designation which has since been extended to the straits in which it is situated, Fox discontinued his progress towards the northward, and took a southerly course. The reason he gives for this proceeding is as follows: "for I was directed by the letter of my instructions, to set the course from *Caries Swanne's Nest*, N.W. by N., so as I might fall with the west side in 63 d., and from thence southward, to search the passage diligently, all the bay about, untill I came to *Hudson's Bay*".[1] Fox obeyed his instructions, though he evidently entertained an opinion, that this was the fittest part to search for the passage; "being moved by the high flowing of the tyde and the *whales*, for all the tydes that floweth that bay, commeth [neere] from thence".

Going west about Sir Thomas Roe's Welcome, another island, white, like the one that had been left, was raised, to which the name of BROOKE COBHAM was given, in commemoration of the services of a man to whom Fox expresses himself as being greatly indebted for delivering his petition to his Majesty, and for bringing him into the Royal Presence, "there to shew the hopeful possibility of the attempt": an act as graceful on the part of the monarch, as the acknowledgment is becoming to his subject. To another group of islands in the same vicinity, the name of BRIGGES HIS MATHEMATICKES, was given.

From the 29th, the track lay along the east coast of America; and on the 2nd of August, Fox was off an island in latitude 61° 10', which he presumed to be the *Hopes Check'd* of Sir Thomas Button. On the 6th, he looked into *Hubart's Hope*, and satisfied himself it was a "vaine hope" to find the passage in that direction; and then he saw land gently descending to the sea side, "the greenest and best like", he says, he had seen since he "came out of the river of *Thames*, and as it were inclosed with thick rowes of trees betweene one meadow and another, distinct, as it were *Barne Elmes* nere *London*, and at sight thereof" he "did thinke of them". This was in lat. 59° 5'. Standing on along shore, they came to the mouth of a great river, at the south entrance of which was a cliff, represented to be "like unto *Balsea cliffe*, near *Harwich*". On the 8th, *Port Nelson* was made, and having debated the pro-

---

[1] The author of the *Arctic Voyages* imputes blame to Fox, for not having continued his northerly course. He overlooks, at least does not allude to, the instructions under which Fox acted.

priety of wintering there, it was determined merely to look in and then proceed on the voyage.

On the 10th of August, Fox entered Nelson river, and plied up about a mile with the flood. He would have gone higher, but was prevented by the shallowness of the water. He was content, however, for he was enabled to moor in a snug berth, which afforded facilities both for refitting the vessel, and for putting together a pinnace, that had been brought out in frame, and of which the navigator was in great need. These necessary proceedings were not completed till about the 19th. Both sides of the river are represented to be full of small woods ; and the north shore to be a clay cliff, like the Naze in Essex, but not so high. On shore were found : good grass, store of wood, black-berries, straw-berries, grosel-berries, vetches, and several sorts of shrubs. Various fragments of the timbers of a vessel, of casks, and of chests, were also found. A cross, which, it was conjectured, had fallen down, or had been pulled down ; and " a board broken in two, the one halfe quite gone, whereon had been the Kinges armes, and an inscription of the time of *Sir Thomas Button*, with his owne name : when and why he tooke harbour, with other expressions", were viewed with great interest. The cross was re-erected, and this inscription, on lead, nailed thereon : "*I suppose this crosse was first erected by Sir* THOMAS BUTTON, *in* 1613. *It was againe raised by* LUKE FOX, *Capt. of the Charles, in the right and possession of my dread soveraigne* CHARLES THE FIRST, *King of Great Brittaine, etc., the* 15*th of August,* 1631. THIS LAND IS CALLED NEW WALES." Fox was under sail when the piece of board was brought to him, and he carried it away with him : otherwise, he says, " I would have endeavoured to have renued the same, as the act of my noble predecessors". Fox in this proceeding exhibited a just and generous spirit, which is to be commended.

On the night of the 19th the following observations occur : " At 10 were many pettiedancers. I hope faire weather to

come, yet have wee had such as I pray our neighbours, in
England, have no worse ; and they cannot have better harvest
weather to have in their crop. And though this may be
thought nothing pertinent to the history of a sea journall ;
yet having been disswaded from this voyage, in respect of the
ice, I may thus much write for the incouragement of others,
that may happen to navigate this way, God giveing goode
successe to this enterprise, that a sea voyage of discovery (to
a place unknowne, and farre remote and in the like clime)
cannot be taken in hand with more health, ease, and pleasure.
I am sure it hath been warme ever since we came from the
ice."

The 21st, in about latitude N. 57° 10′, it is observed, that
since quitting Sir Thomas Roe's Welcome, not a single indication in favour of the desired passage had occurred. No
high land had been seen : no deep water had been found ; and
on trying the tide four times in this locality, it proved invariably to come from the eastward. Fox therefore concluded
they were " so far from their *primum mobile*", that it was
scarce worth looking for. Having chronicled these observations, the navigator adds : " The moone is in the increase, and
I thank God it doth make the nights grow lighter. The ship
is anchored, the watch is set, a mark is set on the lead-line ;
and sleepe like a theefe doth slily steale vpon me". From the
above day till the 27th, the line of the coast was followed, on
Easterly, E.S.easterly, and S.easterly courses, the hopes of
discovering the passage in that direction, diminishing daily.
It was calculated on the latter day, that they were sixty
leagues E.S.E. from Port Nelson, and in latitude 55° 50′.

Three days afterwards, *Captain James, of Bristol,* in the
Maria, and *Captain Luke Fox,* in *His Majesty's ship Charles,*
met in Hudson's Bay. At first some difficulty was experienced
in communicating, but at length the Maria's shallop with the
lieutenant, coxen, and three others on board, came alongside
the Charles. The rowers were taken between decks, enter-

tained at several messes, most carefully examined as to their proceedings, and every particular extracted from them : though, it must be confessed, Fox did not make any attempt to conceal his own proceedings, but, on the contrary, seems to have communicated them without any reserve.

The day following that on which the two ships met, the Captain of the Charles dined, by invitation, on board the Maria. Fox represents his reception to have been cordial, and his entertainment to have been as hospitable as circumstances would admit; but the visit did not impress him with a favourable opinion either of the craft, or of her commander: who was considered to prove himself by his conversation "a practitioner in the mathematicks", but "no seaman". With regard to the vessel, it seems there was not sufficient accommodation in the great cabin, so the party dined between decks, and though the ship was but in "two courses, and main bonnet", so much water was thrown in, that " sause would not have been wanted, if there had been roast mutton". This circumstance caused Fox to ponder, "whether it were better for James his company to be impounded amongst ice, where they might be kept from putrefaction by piercing ayre, or in open sea, to be kept sweet by being thus daily pickled". Having seriously observed, " they were really to be pittied", the facetious navigator resumes his jocular tone, describing the ship " taking her liquor as kindly as them selves, for her nose was no sooner out of the pitcher, but her nebe, like the duck's, was in't againe". Seventeen hours were spent in company with the Maria, which Fox declares, were the " worst spent" of any during the voyage.

Having taken leave of his rival, Fox stood southward along the land, till he came to a " knoale bearing S.W.", which was somewhat higher than the rest of the shore. This was in latitude 55° 14', and by account 95 leagues from Port Nelson. This spot, or a spot close in the vicinity, was named *Wolstenholmes Vltima Vale*. The navigator was convinced from observation of there being no passage "from 65° 30′ circularly to 55° 10′," and adopted the above name, as expressive of his opinion that Sir John would not lay out any more moneys in search of this bay; and his opinion was well founded.[1] Quitting Ultima Vale on the 3rd of September, a course was shaped, N.E. by E. Next day land was seen, in latitude N. 57° 55′, which was named ILE SLEEPE.

The 7th of September Cary's Swans' Nest was seen. The following day Cape Pembroke was made in latitude N. 62° 23′; and it is placed by Fox at two or three leagues N.E. from the Swans' Nest. Then, with the wind at S.E., they "plyde up" across a bay to a point which was named CAPE LINSEY. On doubling it, the land trended N. and then N.E. Next, on the 13th, in latitude 62°, across a second bay, another headland was discerned, with a "knowell thereon", and it was designated "POINT PEREGRINE". The following day, the S.W. side of Sea-horse Point was sighted. This headland is described as being of "an indifferent height, descending by degrees into the sea". An accumulation of ice was now fallen in with, which rendered it necessary to alter the course, and it was accordingly shaped "close hald, E.N.E." Sight was had of Mill Island on the 15th; and the passage by which the west side was made, Fox named HURIN'S THROUGH-LET, "for that he, upon the fore-yard, conducted in the ship."

The ship remained at anchor from the 15th till the 18th of September. With the morning flood he "plied vp by the N. mayne, and stopt the ebbe in sixty fathoms neere shore", and about five miles S. of a fair headland, made by the land trending E. and N. from the same, which was named KING CHARLES HIS PROMONTORY, and another cape to the N., the land lying there N. and S. 4° W., was called CAPE MARIA. The latitude of King's Cape, by account, was made to be 64° 46′, and that of

---

[1] The loss of Sir John Wolstenholme on this particular voyage, is estimated by Fox at £400; and his aggregate losses on account of the Northwest enterprise, at £1100.

Queen's Cape, 65° 13'. Near the former, to the N., were
three islands, passable round about, standing like an equi-
lateral triangle, which were called TRINITIE ISLANDS, "in remembrance of the house in Deepford Strand". A fourth,
lying outside, was named ISLE COOKE, Fox thinking of "his
good friend and countenancer, Mr. Walter Cooke, an assistant
in that corporation.

On naming the King and Queen's Capes, the healths of
their majesties and of the young princes were pledged. "This
little recreation we had at this celebration", the narrator remarks, "hath much comforted our men that were aboue,
and something cheered those that were downe, as the master,
the boate-swaine and his mate, the gunner, carpenter, ex-
poser, [Christopher] Russel, yet they seem to be the worse,
since this certaine triall of the tyde to come from S.E. with
his constant flowing and ebbing, doth make them conceiue,
that this hard labour is in vaine : yet they say nothing to mee
but this N.W. tide was mistaken : for *the Masters of the
Trinity House were very carefull that I should bee well man'd,
so that I had not aboue 5 but were capable of an accompt, and
therefore easier to be gouerned, and more helpefull to the designe.* Thus", he continues, "wee ended the euening in
feasting, and reposed vntill clocke 12 in the night, and then
we weighed anker againe; Mr. Hurin and my selfe, hoping by
this faire meanes to indure our sufferings, thereby to see the
hopes of the supposed passage this way". Passing by a headland on the 20th of September, in latitude 65° 50', to which
the name of LORD WESTON'S PORTLAND was given, Fox, on
the 22nd reached a point, in latitude 66° 47', where the land
trended to the S.E.; and this he called FOXE HIS FARTHEST.[1]

---

[1] Between Lord Weston's Portland and Fox's Farthest, the charts in-
troduce a POINT PEREGRINE. This name is not to be traced in Fox's journal, or chart, in this place. It may have been inserted on the authority of
Hurin's journal, of which a manuscript exists, but to which I have not
obtained access. 𝕮. 𝕽.

Fox represents he was sent out on the voyage in consequence of a statement made by Sir Thomas Button, that the
tide in the vicinity of Nottingham island came from the north-
west, a point, however, which was disputed, on good grounds,
but without success, by Bylot, who served in the expedition
with Sir Thomas Button. By exact observation, Fox ascertained that the tide came from the S.E. at Nottingham
island ;[1] and the same, he alleges, proved to be the case at the
point he designated "his farthest".[2] The master thought,
and Fox concurred with him, that the adventurers would be
satisfied when they found the voyage had been undertaken on
a wrong report of the tides, and that it was expedient to
turn towards England. Other circumstances contributed to
strengthen this opinion. It is observed : "The winds were
north-west, nor could I stay the change thereof, for the most
of my best men, as master, gunner, carpenter, boatswaine his
mate, and one or two of the common men, were downe ; the
rest complaining of cold paines, and no marvell, they having

[1] On the 1st of August 1821, the currents were tried in mid-channel,
between Nottingham Island and the northern land, with the following
results : at 8 A.M., E. by S., 1 mile per hour ; at 9.40, E. by S., 6-16 mile ;
at 11.15, slack (? low) water, noon, W.N.W., 1¼ mile per hour.—*Voyage
of the Fury and Hecla*, 1821-23, p. 24. London : 1824.

[2] On the *tides* about here, Sir Edward Parry observes : " The rapidity
and irregularity of the tides in this neighbourhood were particularly remarked by our early navigators; and, indeed, gave the name of Mill
Islands, "by reason of the grinding of the ice". There can be little doubt
that this irregularity is principally occasioned by a meeting of the tides
hereabouts, for there is tolerable evidence of the flood coming from the
northward down the great opening leading to Fox's Farthest, and which
I have called Fox's CHANNEL. This tide meeting the rapid stream which
sets from the eastward through Hudson's Strait, must of necessity produce such a disturbance as has here been noticed." In a note, Sir Edward
adds : " Baffin particularly insists on this being the case [the northerly set
of the tide down Fox's channel], both near Trinity Islands, and off Southampton Island; and I think, notwithstanding a contrary opinion held by
Fox and Yourin, our observations of the tides in this neighbourhood, and
subsequently at Winter Island, seem to confirm those of Baffin."—*Voyage
of the Fury and Hecla*, 1821-23, p. 30. London : 1824.

beene over-toyled in the bottome of Sir Thomas Button's Bay
(and that undiscovered, betwixt him and Hudson), with
watching and warding day and night, manning shipe, boate,
and pinnace, both in anchoring and sayling; but especially
at the leade, when in all tyme of my sayling the said Bay,
there was never one from keeping the same". It is added :
" The weather had beene for about 3 weekes before, nothing
but snowe, frost and sleet at best, our selves, ropes, and sayles
froaze, the sun seldome to be seene, or once in five dayes, the
nights 13 houres long, the moone wayning. And in conclusion, I was enforced either to seeke for harbour, or freeze to
death in the sea". Objections existed to seeking for a harbour. There was none nearer than Port Nelson; and if that
place were made, it was feared the provisions would not last
out, or, that the people would be rendered incapable of service. At least, so Fox thought, remembering the sufferings
experienced by the crews engaged in the expeditions under
Hudson and Sir Thomas Button.[1] On these considerations,
on the 21st of September, sail was made towards England.

The 22nd, standing along the coast, Fox named a headland
about twenty leagues below Lord Weston's Portland, CAPE
DORCHESTER, designating the north side of it POYNT BARTE,
and the south brow CARLETON.

On the 23rd Fox embodies the following extravagant idea:
" This morning *Aurora* blusht, as though she had usher'd her
master from some unchaste lodging, and the ayre so silent, as
though all those handmaides had promised secresy". Passing
by the Charles' Foreland of Bylot, a fair sound was observed,
and named THE PRINCE HIS CRADLE, with an island to the
west, which was designated THE PRINCE HIS NURSE. Distant,
E.S.E., ten leagues from Prince's Foreland, a fair headland
was named CAPE DORSET, and three leagues to the E. of that

---

[1] Answere to uncertaine rumours (or aspersions) given forth against
me, concerning my coming home from the Northwest, etc.—*N. W. Fox*,
pp. 244-249.

another cape was distinguished by the appellation of C. COOKE.
Between these capes, in a deep bay, lay an island, which was
named Isle NICOLAS.[1] In the evening they were eight leagues
from Isle Nicolas, with Salisbury Island bearing W. by S. ½
S., distance 12 leagues. The course was then directed between Savage Islands on the N. main, and Charles Cape (or
island) on the S. main. On the 25th of September, it is
observed: "this day was some snowe. God continue this
W.N.W. wind, for wee have many that already have made a
scurvie voyage of it. The mr. is up againe". Queen's Cape
was afterwards made, and in the vicinity two islands were
seen. One was named SACKFIELD, and the other CROWE, after
Sir Sackfield Crowe, late treasurer of the navy. Then, passing by the Isles of God's Mercy (about lat. 62° 40′), Resolution was sighted on the 27th. From this date, nothing
occurred of interest till the vessel arrived in England. Captain Luke Fox concludes his narrative in the following words:
"The 31, blessed be Almighty God, I came into the *Downes*,
with all my men recovered and sound, not having lost one
man nor boy, nor any manner of tackling, having beene forth
near 6 moneths. All glory be to GOD".

In relation to this voyage it has been observed: "on the
25th of September, he [Fox] begins to think they had made
but a 'scurvie voyage of it', and that in his opinion it was the
best they could do to bear up homewards".[2] Fox's observation will not bear this interpretation. It refers to the un-
healthy condition of many of the people, and not to the character of the voyage; and his determination to bear up homewards, for the reasons already detailed, was taken on the
21st. Moreover, there is very good evidence to shew that

[1] C. Linsey, C. Portland, C. Dorset, and C. Dorchester, were named after
the Lords Commissioners of the Admiralty, to whom Fox considered himself indebted for the furtherance of his undertaking. Isle Nicolas was
named after their Secretary; C. Cooke, after the Secretary of State.

[2] Arctic Voyages, p. 242.

Fox did not consider he had, by any means, " made but a
scurvie voyage of it". In his " answer to aspersions", already
quoted, he declares, he has "proceeded in these discoveries
further than any other of his predecessors, in lesse time, and
at lesse charge": that he has " cleared up all the expected
hopes upon the W. side of Button's Bay from 64½ circularly
to 55, and on the point from Swans' Nest to Sharke Point [?],
not perfectly discouered but now by him"; and that he " carried a tyde, comming from south east through Fretum Hudson, all along that east side to 66 degrees 30 minutes, or
thereabouts, things not knowne heretofore".

With this voyage, the connexion of the Worshipfull the East
India Fellowship with the North-west project, terminated.
It appears from the minutes of the Court of the Committees,
that in the years 1625 and 1631, SIR JOHN WOLSTENHOLME
applied for further assistance. Pecuniary aid was not, however, given on either occasion; but the Court consented to
forego the monopoly they held in spices, and agreed to permit the vessels which might be engaged in the enterprise, to
be laden with that commodity at Bantam : provided they
made their way through the contemplated passage. And to
the Honourable Successors of the Worshipful Fellowship, the
writer expresses his acknowledgments for permission to use
the information traced by him in their records.

§ XIII.

Voyage of Captain James.

THIS navigator, already named in connexion with the voyage
of Captain Luke Fox, having been selected by the merchants
of Bristol, to search for a passage by the North-west, was

placed in command of a vessel named the MARIA, of *seventy tons* burden, which had been expressly built for the service, victualled for eighteen months, and manned with twenty-two hands.

A.D. 1631. } Captain James sailed from the Severn in the same year, in the same month, and on the same day of the week, that Captain Luke Fox sailed from the Thames, namely, on the 3rd of May 1631.

On the 4th of June an immense quantity of ice was fallen in with off Cape Farewell. The ship was struck repeatedly and violently. Strenuous efforts were made to stave off the driving masses, but in vain. The poles used for the purpose were shivered, and the Maria became more and more enclosed until the 6th, when, fearing to be crushed astern by some "extraordinary" pieces of ice, the commander ordered some sail to be "let fall"; and the ship was driven stem on against an iceberg ahead. It was thought the vessel was rent in twain; but a trial of the pumps proving the contrary, all hands went to prayers, to return thanks for their merciful deliverance. Soon afterwards the shallop was crushed, and taken on board to be repaired, the long-boat being hoisted out and towed astern; but the long-boat got adrift, and was not recovered without great difficulty, being "much bruised", and two men in her being "much hurt". At length, on the 17th, the Island of Resolution was made. Not possessing, or not exercising, the judgment evinced by Fox, Captain James kept close in with the land. On the 17th, the navigator observes: "We had got about the southern point of the island; and the wind, at west, drove both us and the ice upon the shore. When we were driven within two leagues of the coast, we came among the strongest whirlings of the sea that can be conceived. There were great pieces of ice aground in forty fathoms of water; and the ebb, coming out of the broken grounds of the island, among those isles of ice, made such a destruction, that we were carried sometimes close by the rocks, and sometimes so close by those high pieces, that we were afraid they would fall upon us". A boat was then despatched to look out for a place of security, and was nearly lost; the ship, in the meantime, being either driven furiously, by the currents, over rocks which were visible at no great depth, or " whirled round about back again, notwithstanding the sail that was aboard". In this extremity more sail was made, and the ship proceeded with still greater rapidity over rocks covered but by a few feet of water, till at length it was deemed expedient to let fall an anchor, though with little expectation of its holding. " But", it seems, " by good fortune, the ship ran against a great piece of ice that was aground". By this *piece of good fortune* the main knee of the beak-head was broken, four of the main shrouds were carried away, together with an anchor at the bow.

In getting into a place of refuge which they discovered, the ship, notwithstanding all their endeavours, settled on a sharp rock, about a yard above the mainmast; and as the water ebbed, " she hung after her head, and held to the offing". The proceedings which were adopted on the occasion of this mischance, are thus narrated : " We made fast cables and hawsers aloft to the masts, and so to the rocks, straining them tough with our tackles ; but, as the water ebbed away, the ship was turned over, that we could not stand in her. Having now", the narrator continues, " done to the best of our understandings, but to little purpose, we went all upon a piece of ice, and fell to prayer, beseeching God to be merciful unto us". Afterwards, the ship, it is said, " was so turned over, that the portless of the forecastle was in the water, and we looked every minute when she would overset : indeed, at one time, the cables gave way, and she sank down half a foot at that slip". However, when the tide made, the vessel righted, and floated off, without sustaining any material damage. The scene of these events was named THE HARBOUR OF GOOD PROVIDENCE.

From thence, Captain James made his way into another harbour, lat. N. 61° 24', which was named PRICE's COVE. The experience of this navigator induces him to " advise no one to come near those dangerous shores, for fear he lose his ship".

Sail was made on the 24th.   On the 5th of July they were in lat. N. 63° 15', Salisbury island bearing W. by N. 7 leagues. Soon afterwards, Prince Charles's Cape, with Mill Islands, were seen; and on the 15th they were between Digges Isle and Nottingham Isle. The 16th, a course was taken towards Mansfield's Island. Plenty of ice was fallen in with, and the ship is represented to have " struck more fearful blows" than had been experienced at any previous time.

On the 29th, notwithstanding all sail was made, with a stiff gale blowing, the ship is represented to have been so firmly enclosed, that " she stirred no more than if she had been in a dry dock".   Whereon, the whole party went boldly on the ice, to sport and recreate themselves, letting the ship stand still under all her sails.   The 1st of August, Hubbard's Hope was fallen in with, and during the following night the Maria struck heavily on a rock ; but " it pleased God", Captain James informs the reader, " to send two or three good swelling seas, which heaved them over the rocks into three fathom". The 16th, sight was had of Port Nelson ; and no mischance occurred till the 21st, when, perceiving the ship to be driving, an attempt was made to weigh the anchor. By the chopping of a sea, and through a small rope having got foul of the cable, the crew at the capstan were overthrown. By this accident the master was bruised ; the two mates were hurt, one in the head, and the other in the arm ; one of the lustiest men was struck on the breast by a bar, " that he lay sprawling for life"; another had " his head betwixt the cable, and hardly escaped"; and the leg of the gunner was so much lacerated, that it was found necessary to amputate the limb. Pursuing a south-easterly course, a cape was made on the 2nd of September, in lat. N. 55° 5', to which the name of HENRIETTA MARIA was given.   On the 6th, Captain James and his crew found themselves in the predicament of "Jonas in the whale's belly, the sea did so continually overrack them": an event which Luke Fox did not contemplate, though he anticipated their being thoroughly pickled. The 7th, an island was seen, in lat. N. 53° 5', and named LORD WESTON'S ISLAND.

On the 12th, through the alleged carelessness, or perverseness, of the watch, the ship again struck on a rock. The first blow was struck when Captain James was in a deep sleep; and he thought, when he was first wakened, it was to provide himself for another world. A scene of confusion ensued. First, all the sails were hauled back, but that did no good; on the contrary, the vessel beat harder. Then all the sails were struck amain, and furled up close. Next, the stern was torn down, to bring a cable to the capstan from an anchor laid out astern. Afterwards, all the water in the hold was started, and some set to the pumps, to pump it out. The beer, after some consideration, escaped a similar fate; but the coals were thrown overboard most readily. This done, all hands rushed to the capstan, and hove with such good will, that the cable parted; but with all speed another was provided. All this time the vessel kept striking so furiously, that some of the sheathing was seen to swim. Whether the ship leaked, or not, could not be ascertained, on account of the water that had been started in the hold; but it was feared a death-wound had been received, and a variety of articles were thrown into the long-boat. At length, after five hours' buffeting, "it pleased God she beat over all the rocks"; and the state of the vessel having been ascertained to be sufficiently bad, the crew all went to prayers, and returned thanks matters were no worse. In connexion with the cause of this transaction, Captain James evinces an extraordinary spirit. He observes: "I controuled a little passion, and checked some bad counsel that was given me, to revenge myself upon them that had committed the error".

After the above escape, an island in the vicinity of Lord Weston's Island was named THE EARL OF BRISTOL'S ISLAND; and two others on the 22nd, in lat. N. 52° 10', SIR THOMAS ROE'S ISLAND, and EARL DANBY'S ISLAND.

Having found a suitable harbour in an island, subsequently named CHARLTON ISLAND, Captain James determined to winter there. How he fared will appear from the following narrative.

THE WINTERING IN CHARLTON ISLAND.

On the 3rd [of October 1631], about noon, the wind dulled, and we had up the anchor, standing farther into the bay in four fathom and an half water; here we came again to an anchor with our second anchor, for many of our men are sick, and the rest so weakened that we can hardly weigh our sheet-anchor. I took the boat and went presently on shore to see what comfort I could find: this was the first time that I put foot on this island, which was the same that we afterwards wintered upon; I found the tracks of deer, and saw some fowl; but that which rejoiced me most was, that I saw an opening into the land, as if it had been a river. To it we made with all speed, but found it to be barred, and not a foot water at full sea, on the bay, and yet within a most excellent fine harbour, having five fathom water. In the evening I returned aboard, bringing little comfort for our sick men, more than hopes.

On the 4th it snowed very hard, yet I got ashore and appointed the boat to go to another place (which made like a river) and to sound it; in the mean time I went with four more some four or five miles up into the country, but could find no relief for my sick, but a few berries only. After we had well wearied ourselves, I returned to the place I had appointed them to tarry for me; where at my coming I still found her, she having not been where I ordered her, for it had blown such a severe gale of wind that she could not

row to windward; thus we returned aboard with no good
news.   It continued foul weather with snow and hail, and
extremely cold till the sixth, when with a favourable wind I
stood in nearer to the shore and moored the ship.   On the
7th it snowed all day, so that we were fain to clear it off the
decks with shovels, and it blew a very hard storm withal; it
continued snowing and very cold weather, and it froze so
that all the bows of the ship with her beak-head were all
ice; about the cables also was ice as thick as a man's middle;
the bows of the boat were likewise frozen half a foot thick,
so that we were fain to beat it off.   The sun shined very
clear, and we bore the top-sails out of the tops which were
hard frozen in them into a lump, so that there they hung a
sunning all day in a very lump, the sun not having power
to thaw one drop of them.   After the boat was fitted we
rowed towards the shore, but could not come near the place
where we were used to land, for it was all thick water with
the snow that had fell upon the sands that are dry at low
water; this made it so difficult to row that we could not get
through it with four oars; yet something higher to the
westward we got ashore.   Seeing now the winter to come
thus extremely on upon us, and that we had very little wood,
I made them fill the boat and went aboard, and sent the
carpenter to cut wood, others to carry it to the water-side
whilst the boat brought it on board; for I doubted that we
should not be able to go to and again with the boat.   It
was miserable cold already aboard the ship, every thing
froze in the hold and by the fireside; seeing therefore we
could no longer make use of our sails, it raised many doubts
in our minds that we must stay and winter.   After we had
brought as much wood on board as we could conveniently
stow, and enough, as I thought, to have lasted two or three
months, the sick men desired that some little house or hovel
might be built on shore, whereby they might be the better
sheltered to recover their healths: I took the carpenter and

others whom I thought fit for such a purpose, and chusing out a place, they went immediately to work upon it; in the mean time, I, accompanied with some others, wandered up and down the woods to see if we could discover any signs of savages, that we might the better provide for our safeties against them; we found no appearance that there were any upon this island nor near it. The snow by this time was half leg high, and through it we returned comfortless to our companions, who had all this time wrought upon our house; they on board our ship took down our top-sails the mean while; and made great fires upon the hearth in the hatchway: so that having well thawed them, they folded them up and put them betwixt decks, that if we had an occasion they might bring them again to yard.

From the 19th to the 20th it snowed and blowed so hard that the boat could hardly venture on shore, and but seldom land, unless the men waded in the thick congealed water, carrying one another; we sensibly perceived withal, how we daily sunk into more miseries. The land was all deep covered with snow, the cold strengthened and the thick snow-water encreased, and what would become of us, our most merciful God and Preserver knew only. The 29th I observed an eclipse of the moon with what care possible I could, both in the trial of the exactness of our instruments, as also in the observation. This month of October ended with snow and bitter cold weather.

On the 4th of November they found a place to get on shore, and so once in two or three days till the 9th, bringing beer to our men on shore in a barrel, which would freeze firmly in the house in one night; other provisions they had store. The ice beer being thawed in a kettle was not good, and they broke the ice of the ponds to come at water to drink. This pond water had a most loathsome smell with it; so that doubting least it might be infectious, I caused a well to be sunk near the house; there we had very good water,

C C

which tasted, as we flattered ourselves, like milk. The 10th, having enough boards for such a purpose, I set the carpenter to work to make a boat which we might carry over the ice, and make use of her wherever there was water. At noon I took the latitude of this island by two quadrants; which I found to be 52 degrees. I urged the men to make traps to catch foxes; for we daily saw many; some of them were pied black and white, whereby I gathered that there were some black foxes, whose skins I told them were of great value, and I promised that whoever could take one of them should have the skin for his reward; hereupon they made divers traps, and waded in the snow, which was very deep, to place them in the woods.

The 12th our house took fire, but we soon quenched it; we were obliged to keep an extraordinary fire night and day, and this accident made me order a watch to look to it continually, since if our house and cloathing should be burnt we should be in a woeful condition; I lay ashore till the 17th, all which time our miseries increased. It snowed and froze extremely, at which time we looking from the shore towards the ship, she appeared a piece of ice in the fashion of a ship, or a ship resembling a piece of ice; the snow was all frozen about her, and all her fore-part firm ice, and so she was on both sides, also our cables frozen in the hawse. I got me aboard, where the long nights I spent with tormenting cogitations, and in the day-time I could not see any hopes of saving the ship. This I was assured of, that it was impossible to endure those extremities long; every day the men must beat the ice off the cables, while some within, with the carpenter's long calking iron, digged the ice out of the hawsers: in which work the water would freeze on their cloaths and hands, and would so benumb them that they could hardly get into the ship without being heaved in with a rope.

The 19th, our gunner, who, as you may remember, had his

leg cut off, languished irrecoverably, and now grew very weak, desiring that for the little time he had to live, he might drink sack altogether, which I ordered he should.   The 22d in the morning he died, an honest and a strong hearted man.   He had a close boarded cabin in the gun-room, which was very close indeed, and as many cloaths on him as was convenient, and a pan of coals and a fire continually in his cabin; notwithstanding which warmth, his plaisters would freeze at his wound, and his bottle of sack at his head; we committed him, at a good distance from the ship, unto the sea.

On the 23d, in the morning by break of day I sent for our men aboard, who shut up the house and arrived by ten, being forced to wade through the congealed water, so that they received the boat with difficulty.   There drove by the ship many pieces of ice, though not so large as the former, but much thicker: one piece came foul of the cable and made the ship drive.   As soon as we were clear of it we joined our strength together, and had up our eastermost anchor; and now I resolved to bring the ship aground.   The wind was now south, which blew in upon the shore, and made the lowest tides.   We brought the ship into twelve feet water, and laid out one anchor in the offing, and another in sholewater, to draw her on land at command: our hope also was, that some stones that were to the westward of us would send off some of the ice; we then being about a mile from the shore.   About ten o'clock in the dark night the ice came driving upon us, and our anchors came home.   She drove some two cables-length, and the wind blowing on the shore, by two o'clock she came aground and stopt much ice, yet she lay well all night, and we took some rest.

The 25th the wind shifted easterly, and put abundance of ice on us.   When the flood came we encouraged one another, and drew home our anchor by main force, under great pieces of ice; our endeavour being to put the ship to the shore: but to our great discomfort, when the half-tide was

made, the ship drove among the ice to the eastward, do
what we could, and so she would on the shole of rocks.
These two days had been, and this day was, very warm weather, and it rained, which it had not yet but once done since
we came hither, otherwise it had been impossible we could
have wrought. Withal the wind shifted also to the south,
and at the very instant blew a hard puff, which so continued half-an-hour. I caused the two top-sails to be had up
from betwixt decks, and we hoisted them up with two ropes
in all haste, and we found the ship ashore when she had
not half a cable's length to drive on the rocky sholes. By
reason of this wind it flowed very much water, and we drew
her up so high that it was doubtful if ever we got her off
again. She continued thus beating till two o'clock the next
morning, and then she settled again, whereupon we went
to sleep, seeing the next tide we expected again to be tormented.

The 26th in the morning tide our ship did not float.
After prayers I called a consultation of the master, my lieutenant, the mate's carpenter and boatswain, to whom I proposed, that now we were put to our last shifts, and therefore
they should tell me what they thought of it, viz.: Whether
it were not best to carry all our provisions on shore; and
when the wind should come northerly, to draw her further
off and sink her? After many reasonings, they allowed of
my purpose, and so I communicated it to the company, who
all willingly agreed to it; and so we fell to getting up of
our provisions.

The 27th, I also made the carpenter fit a place against all
sudden extremities, for that with the north-west or northerly
wind I meant to effect our last project. In the run of her
on the starboard side he cut away the cieling and the plank
to the sheathing some four or five inches square, some four
feet high from the keel of her, that so it might be bored out

in an instant. We brought our bread which was remaining
in the bread-room up into the great cabin, and likewise all
our powder, setting much of our light dry things betwixt
decks.

The 29th at five in the morning the wind came up at
west-north-west, and began to blow very hard. It was ordinary for the wind to shift from the west by the north round
about : so first I ordered the cooper to go down into the
hold, and look to all our casks ; those that were full to mell
in the bungs of them, and those that were empty to get up,
or if they could not be gotten up to stave them ; then to
coil all our cables upon our lower tire, and to lay on our
spare anchors, and any thing that was weighty, to keep it
down from rising. By seven o'clock it blew a storm at
north-west. The ship was already bedded some two feet in
the sand ; and whilst that was a-flowing she must beat.
This I before had in my consideration, for I thought she
was so far driven up that we should never get her off. Yet
we had been so ferreted by her last beating that I resolved
to sink her right down, rather than run that hazard. By
nine she began to roll in her deck with a most extraordinary great sea. And this was the fatal hour that put us to
our wits-end : wherefore I went down into the hold with
the carpenter, and took his auger and bored a hole in the
ship and let in the water. Thus with all speed we began to
cut out other places to bore through ; but every place was
full of nails. By ten, the lower tire was covered with water,
for all which she began so to beat in her deck more and
more, that we could not work nor stand to do any thing
in her, nor would she sink so fast as we would have her,
but continued beating double blows, first abaft and then
before, that it was wonderful how she could endure a quarter
of an hour with it. By twelve her lower tire rose, and that
did so counterbeat on the inside, that it bored the bulk-

heads of the bread-room, powder-room, and fore-piece, all
to pieces. And when it came betwixt decks, the chests
fled about, and the water did flash and fly wonderfully, so
that now we expected every minute when the ship would
open and break to pieces. At one she beat off her rudder,
and that was gone we knew not which way. Thus she continued beating till three, and then the sea came upon the
upper deck, and soon after she began to settle. In her we
were fain to sink the most part of our bedding and cloaths,
and the chirurgeon's chest. Our men that were on shore
stood looking upon us, almost dead with cold and sorrow to
see our miseries and their own; we looked upon them again,
and both upon each other with woeful hearts. Dark night
drew on, and I ordered the boat to be hawled up, and commanded my loving companions to go all into her, who expressed their faithful affection to me, as loth to part from
me. I told them that my meaning was to go ashore with
them, and thus lastly I forsook the ship. We were fourteen
poor souls now in the boat, and we imagined that we were
leaped out of the frying-pan into the fire. The ebb was
made, and the water extraordinary thick with snow, so that
we thought assuredly it would carry us away into the sea.
We therefore double-manned four oars, appointing four
more to sit ready with oars; and so with the help of God we
got to the shore, hawling up the boat after. After we had
hawled up the boat on the 29th of November, we went along
the beach-side in the dark towards our house, where we
made a good fire, and with it and bread and water we comforted ourselves, beginning after that to reason one with
another concerning our ship. I required that every one
should speak his mind freely. The carpenter especially was
of opinion, that she was foundered, and would never be serviceable; but I comforted them the best I could to this effect.
" *My masters and faithful companions, be not dismayed for
any of these disasters, but let us put our whole trust in God.*

It is he that giveth, and he that taketh away ; he throweth down with one hand, and raiseth up with another. His will be done. If it be our fortune to end our days here, we are as near Heaven as in England ; and we are much bound to God Almighty for giving us so large a time of repentance ; who, as it were, daily calls upon us to prepare our souls for a better life in Heaven. I make no doubt but he will be merciful unto us both here on earth, and in his blessed kingdom. He doth not, in the mean time, deny that we may use all honest means to save and prolong our natural lives ; and, in my judgment, we are not so far past hope of returning into our native country, but that I see a fair way by which we may effect it. Admit the ship be foundered (which God forbid. I hope for the best), yet have those of our own nation and others, when they have been put to those extremities, even out of the wreck of their lost ship, built a pinnace, and returned to their friends again. If it be objected, that they have happened in better climates, both for temperateness of the air, and for pacific and open seas, and provided withal of abundance of fresh victuals ; yet there is nothing too hard for courageous minds, which hitherto you have shewn, and, I doubt not, will still do to the uttermost of your power." They all protested to work to the utmost of their strength, and that they would refuse nothing that I should order them to do to the utmost hazard of their lives. I thanked them all. And so for this night we settled ourselves close about the fire, and took some rest till day-light.

The 30th, betimes in the morning, I caused the chirurgeon to cut off my hair short, and to shave away all the hair of my face, for it was become intolerable, and because it would be frozen so great with isicles. The like did all the rest ; and we fitted ourselves to work. The first thing we were to do, was to get our cloaths and provisions ashore, and therefore I divided the company. The master, and a convenient company with him, were to go aboard, and get things out of the hold; the cockswain, with his gang, were to go into the boat, to bring and carry things ashore; myself, with the rest, to carry them half a mile through the snow, unto the place where we intended to build a store-house. As for the heavier things, we proposed to lay them on the beach. In the afternoon the wind was at south-south-west, and the water veered so low an ebb, that we thought we might get something out of the hold. We launched out our boat, therefore, and with oars got through the thick, congealed water. It froze extreme hard, and I stood on the shore with a troubled mind, thinking verily, that with the ebb, the boat would be carried into the sea, and then we were all lost men; but, by God's assistance, they got all safe to the ship, and made a fire there, to signify their arrival on board. They fell presently to work, and got something out of the hold upon the decks; but night coming on, they durst not venture to come on shore, but lay on the bed in the great cabin, being almost starved.

The 1st of *December* was so cold, that I went the same way over the ice, to the ship, where the boat had gone yesterday. This day we carried upon our backs, in bundles, five hundred of our fish, and much of our bedding and cloaths, which we were fain to dig out of the ice. The 2d was mild weather, and some of the men going over the ice, fell in, and very hardly recovered; so that this day we could land nothing, neither by boat nor back. I put them, therefore, to make us a store-house on shore. In the evening the wind came up at west, and the ice broke and drove out of the bay. It was very deep and large ice, that we were afraid it would have spoiled the ship. The 3d day there were divers great pieces of ice that came athwart the ship, and she stopt them, yet not so as we could go over them. We found a way for the boat; but when she was laden, she drew four feet water, and could not come within a flight shot of the shore; the men, therefore, must wade through the congealed water, and carry things out of the boat upon their backs. Every time they waded in the ice, it was most lamentable to behold. In this extreme cold evening, they cut away as much ice from about the boat as they could, and picked it with handspikes out of her, and endeavoured to hoist her into the ship; there being small hopes that she could go to and again any more. But use what means they could, she was so heavy that they could not hoist her in, but were forced to leave her in the tackles, by the ship-side.

The 4th, being *Sunday*, we rested, and performed the sabbath duties of Christians. The 5th and 6th were extreme cold, and we made bags of our store-shirts, and in them we carried our loose bread, over the ice, on shore upon our backs. We also digged our cloaths and new sails, with handspikes of iron, out of the ice, and carried them ashore, which we dried by a great fire. The 7th day was so exceeding cold, that our noses, cheeks, and hands, did freeze as white as paper. The 8th and 9th it was extremely cold, and it snowed much; yet we continued our labour in carrying and rolling things on shore. In the evening the water raised the ice very high, and it broke two thawghts of our boat, and broke in the side of her; but for that time we could not help it.

The 10th. All our sack, vinegar, oil, and every thing else that was liquid, was now frozen as hard as a piece of wood, and we cut it with a hatchet. Our house was all frozen on the inside; and it froze hard within a yard of the fire-side. When I landed first upon this island, I found a spring under a hill's-side, which I then observing, I caused some trees to be cut, for marks to know the place again by. It was about three-fourths of a mile from our house. I sent three of our men which had been with me thither. Upon the 24th these wandering through the snow, at last found the place, and shoveling away the snow they made way to the very head of it. They found it spring very strongly, and brought me a can of it, for which I was right joyful. This spring continued all the year, and did not freeze, but that we could break the

D D

ice and come to it. We laboured very hard these three or four days to get wood to the house, which we found to be very troublesome, through the deep snow. We then settled our bedding and provisions, providing to keep *Christmas-day* holy, which we solemnized in the joyfullest manner we could. So likewise did we *St. John's-day,* upon which we named the wood we did winter in, in memory of that honourable knight, Sir John Winter, *Winter's Forest.* And now, instead of a Christmas tale, I will describe the house that we did live in, with those adjoining. When I first resolved to build a house, I chose the warmest and convenientest place, and the nearest the ship withal. It was among a tuft of thick trees, under a south bank, about a flight shot from the sea-side. True it is, that at that time we could not dig into the ground to make us a hole or cave in the earth, which had been the best way, because we found water digging within two feet, and therefore that project failed. It was a white light sand, so that we could by no means make up a mud-wall. As for stones there were none near us; besides we were all now covered with the snow. We had no boards for such a purpose, and therefore we must do the best we could with such materials as we had about us. The house was square, about twenty feet every way, as much namely as our main course could well cover. First we drove long stakes into the earth, round about which we wattled with boughs, as thick as might be, beating them down very close. This, our first work, was six feet high on both sides, but at the ends was almost up to the very top. There we left two holes for the light to come in at, and the same way the smoak did vent out also. Moreover I caused, at both ends, three rows of bush trees to be stuck up, as close together as possible. Then, at a distance from the house, we cut down trees, proportioning them into lengths of six feet, with which we made a pile on both sides, six feet thick, and six feet high; but at both ends ten feet high, and six feet thick.

We left a little low door to creep into, and a portal before that, made with piles of wood, that the wind might not blow into it. We next fastened a rough tree aloft, over all, upon which we laid our rafters, and our main course over them again; which lying thwartways over all, reached down to the very ground on either side; and this was the fabric of the outside of it. On the inside we made fast our bonnet sails round about; then we drove in stakes, and made us bedstead frames, about three sides of the house, which bedsteads we doubled one under another, the lowermost being a foot from the ground. These we first filled with boughs, then we laid our spare sails on that, and then our bedding and cloaths. We made a hearth in the middle of the house, and on it made our fire; some boards we laid round our hearth to stand upon, that the cold damp should not strike up into us. With our waste cloaths we made us canopies and curtains, others did the like with our small sails. Our second house was not more than twenty feet distance from this, and made, for the wattling, much after the same manner, but it was less, and covered with our fore course. It had no piles on the south-side, but, in lieu of that, we piled up all our chests on the inside; and, indeed, the reflex of the heat of the fire against them did make it warmer than the mansion-house. In this house we dressed our victuals, and the subordinate crew did refresh themselves all day in it. A third house, which was our storehouse, was twenty-nine paces off from this, for fear of firing. This house was only a rough tree fastened aloft, with rafters laid from it to the ground, and covered over with our new suit of sails. On the inside we had laid small trees, and covered them over with boughs, and so stored up our bread and fish in it, about two feet from the ground, the better to preserve them; the other things lay more carelessly. Long before Christmas our mansion-house was covered thick over with snow, almost to the very roof of it; and so likewise was our second house, but our store-house all over, by reason we made no fire in it. Thus we seemed to live in a heap and a wilderness of snow; for out of our doors we could not go, but upon the snow, in which we made us paths middle deep in some places, and in one special case the length of ten steps. To do this, we must shovel away the snow first, and then, by treading, make it something hard under foot. The snow, in this path, was a full yard thick under us. And this was our best gallery for our sick men, and for my own ordinary walking; and both houses and walks we daily accommodated more and more, and made fitter for our uses. On the 27th we got our boat ashore, and fetched up some of our provisions from the beach-side, into the store-house, and so by degrees did we with the rest of our provisions, with extremity of cold and labour, making way with shovels through the thick snow, even from the sea-side to our store-house; and thus concluded we the old year 1631.

The first of *January*, 1632, and for the most part all the month, was extreme cold. The 6th I observed the latitude with what exactness I could, it being clear sunshiny weather, which I found to be 51 degrees 52 minutes; this difference is by reason that there is a great refraction. On the 21st I observed the sun to rise like an oval along the horizon; I called three or four to see it, the better to confirm my judgment; and we all agreed that it was twice as long as it was broad. We plainly perceived withal, that by degrees, as it got up higher, it also recovered its roundness. The 30th and 31st there appeared, in the beginning of the night, more stars in the firmament than ever I had before seen, by two-thirds; I could see the clouds in Cancer full of small stars. About ten o'clock the moon rose, and then a quarter of them were not to be seen. The wind, for the most part of this month, hath been northerly, and very cold. The warmest of which time we employed ourselves in fetching wood, working upon our pinnace, and other things. In the begin-

ning of this month the sea was all firmly frozen over, so that
we could see no water any where. Our men found it more
mortifying cold to wade through the water in the beginning
of *June*, when the sea was full of ice, than in *December*, when
it was increasing; our well, out of which we had water in
December, dried up in *July;* the ground, at ten feet deep,
was frozen. The quantity of ice may very easily be made to
appear by mathematical demonstration; and yet I am not of
the opinion that the bay freezes all over. For the 21st the
wind blowing a storm at north, we could perceive the ice to
rise something in the bay.

February. The cold was as extreme this month, as at any
time we had felt it this year, and many of our men complained of infirmities: some of sore mouths, all the teeth in
their heads being loose, their gums swoln with black rotten
flesh, which every day was to be cut away; the pain was so
great that they could not eat their ordinary meat. Others
complained of pains in their heads and their breasts; some,
of weakness in their backs; others, of aches in their thighs
and knees; and others, of swellings in their legs. Thus were
two-thirds of the company under the chirurgeon's hands;
and yet, nevertheless, they were forced to work daily, and go
abroad to fetch wood and timber, notwithstanding most of
them had no shoes to put on. Their shoes, upon their coming to the fire out of the snow, were burnt and scorched upon
their feet; and our store-shoes were all sunk in the ship. In
this necessity, they made this shift, to bind clouts about their
feet; and endeavoured, by that poor help, the best they
could, to perform their duties. Our carpenter likewise, by
this time, fell sick, to our great discomfort. I practised some
observations by the rising and setting of the sun, calculating
the time of his rising and setting by very true running glasses.
As for our clock and watch, notwithstanding we still kept
them by the fireside, in a chest, wrapped in cloths, yet were
they so frozen that they could not go. My observations by

these glasses, I compared with the stars coming to the meridian. By this means we found the sun to rise twenty minutes before it should; and in the evening, to remain twenty minutes, or thereabouts, longer than it should: all this, by reason of the refraction. Since now I have spoken so much of the cold, I hope it will not be taken ill, if I, in a few words, make it some way appear to our readers. We made three differences of the cold, all according to the places: in our house, in the woods, and in the open air in our going to the ship. For the last, it would be sometimes so extreme, that it was almost unindurable; no cloaths were proof against it, no motion could resist it; it would so freeze the hair on the eyelids, that we could not see; and I verily believe that it would have stifled a man in a very few hours. We daily found, by experience, that the cold in the woods would freeze our faces, or any part of our flesh that was bare; but it was not so mortifying as the other. Our house, on the outside, was covered two-third parts with snow; and on the inside, frozen and hung with isicles. The cloaths on our beds would be covered with hoar-frost; which, in this habitation, was not far from the fire. The cook's tubs, wherein he watered his meat, standing about a yard from the fire, and which he all day long plied with snow water; yet, in the night season, whilst he sleeped but on watch, they would be firm frozen to the very bottom. And therefore he was forced to water his meat in a brass kettle, close adjoining to the fire. And I have many times both seen and felt, by putting my hand into it, that side which was next the fire very warm, and the other side an inch frozen. The chirurgeon, who had hung his bottles of sirrups, and other liquid things, as conveniently as he could, to preserve them, had them all frozen. Our vinegar, oil, and sack, which we had in small casks in the house, were all firm frozen. It may further, in general, be conceived, that in the beginning of June the sea was not broken up, and the ground was yet frozen; and this we found by experience, in the burying of our men, in setting up the King's standard, towards the latter end of June, and by our well; in coming away in the beginning of July, at which time, upon the land, for some other reasons, it was very hot weather.

March. The first of this month, being *St. David's-day,* we kept holiday, and solemnized it in the manner of the ancient Britons, praying for the happiness of his Royal Highness Charles Prince of Wales, afterwards Charles II.

The 26th. This evening the moon rose in a very long oval along the horizon. By the last of this month, the carpenter had set up seventeen ground timbers, and thirty-four staddles; and, poor man, he proceeded the best he could, though forced to be led to his labour. In short, all this month it was very cold, the wind about the north-west, the snow as deep as it was all this winter. But to answer an objection that might be made. You were in a wood (some men may say unto us), and therefore you might make fire enough to keep you from the cold. It is true we were in a wood, and under a south bank too, or otherwise we had all starved. But I must tell you, withal, how difficult it was to have wood in a wood. And first I will make a muster of the tools we had. The carpenter, in his chest, had two axes, indeed; but one of them was spoiled in cutting down wood to pile about our house before Christmas. When we first landed we had but two whole hatchets, which, in a few days, broke two inches below the sockets. I called for three of the cooper's hatchets. The carpenter's ax, and the cooper's best hatchet, I caused to be locked up; the other two hatchets to be new helved; and the blades of the two broken hatchets to be put into a cleft piece of wood, and then to be bound about with rope yarn, as fast as might be, which was to be repaired every day; and these were all the cutting tools we had. Besides, the 6th of February, the carpenter had out his best ax about something, and one of the company, in his absence, by his indiscreet handling of it, broke that two inches below the socket. We were, henceforward, forced to use these pieces of tools the best we could. Wherefore I gave orders that the carpenter should have one of the cooper's hatchets; they that looked for timber in the woods, to have the other; and they that cut down wood to burn, were to have the two pieces; and this was before Christmas. The three that were appointed to look for crooked timber, stalked and waded, sometimes on all fours, through the snow; and where they saw a tree likely to fit the mould, they heaved away the snow, and then saw if it would fit the mould; and then they must make a fire to it, to thaw it, otherwise it could not be cut; then they cut it down, and fit it to the mould; and then, with other help, get it home, a mile, through the snow. Now, for our firing, we could not burn green wood, it would smoke so intolerably; nay, the men would rather starve without, in the cold, than sit by it. As for the dry wood, that also was bad enough; for it was full of turpentine, and would send forth such a thick smoak, that would make abundance of soot, which would make us all look as if we had been free of the company of chimney-sweepers. Our cloaths were quite burnt to pieces about us; and, for the most part, we were without shoes. But to our fuelers again. They must first, as the former, go up and down in the snow, till they saw a tree standing, for the snow covered those that were down-fallen; then they must hack it down with their pieces of hatchets, and then others must carry it home through the snow. The boys, with cutlasses, must cut boughs for the carpenter; for every piece of timber that he worked, must first be thawed in the fire; and he must have a fire by him, or he could not work. And this was our continual labour throughout the forementioned cold; besides our tending upon the sick, and other necessary employments.

April. The first of this month being *Easter-day,* we solemnized it as religiously as God gave us grace to do. Both this day and the two following holidays were extreme cold; and now sitting all about the fire, we reasoned and considered together about our estate; we had five men, whereof the carpenter was one, not able to do any thing; the boatswain and many more were very infirm, and of all the rest we had but five that could eat of their ordinary allowance.

The 6th was the deepest snow we had had all this year, which filled up all our paths and ways by which we were used to go to the woods; this snow was something moister and greater than any we had had this year, for formerly it was as dry as dust and as small as sand, and would drive like dust with the wind: the weather continued with this extremity till the 15th, at which time the spring was harder frozen than it had been all the year before. I had often observed the difference betwixt clear weather and misty refracting weather, in this manner, from a little hill which was near adjoining our house; in the clear weather when the sun shone with all the purity of air, that I could not see a little island which bore off us south-south-east four leagues, but if the weather was misty as aforesaid, then we could often see it from the lowest place. This little island I had seen the last year when I was on *Danby Island*. The 13th I took the height of it by an instrument, standing near the sea-side, which island I take to be 34 minutes, the sun being 28 degrees high; this shews how great a refraction here is; yet this may be noted by the way, that I have seen the land elevated by reason of the reflected air, and nevertheless the sun hath risen perfect round. The 16th was the most comfortable sunshiny day that came this year, and I put some to clear off the snow in the under decks of the ship, and to clean and dry the great cabin, by making fire in it, others I put to dig down through the ice to come by our anchor that was in shole-water; which the 17th in the afternoon we got up and carried aboard. The 18th I put them to dig through the ice near the place where we thought our rudder might

E E

be; they digged down and came to water, but no hopes of
finding it. We had many doubts that it might be sanded,
or that the ice might have carried it away already the last
year. Or if we could not recover it by digging before the
ice broke up and drove, there were little hopes of it. The
19th we continued minding our work aboard the ship, and
returned in the evening to supper ashore. This day the
master and two others desired they might lie aboard, which
I agreed to; for, indeed, they had lain very discommodiously
all the winter, and with sick bed-fellows, as I myself had
done, every one in that kind taking their fortunes. By lying
aboard, they avoided the hearing the miserable groanings
and lamentations of the sick men, all night long, enduring,
poor souls, miserable torments. By the 24th we had laboured
so hard, that we came to the sight of a cask, and could likewise perceive that there was some water in the hold. This
we knew could not be thawed water, because it froze very
hard night and day aboard the ship, and on the land also.
By the 23d in the evening we came to pierce the fore-men-
tioned cask, and found it full of very good beer, which much
rejoiced us all, especially the sick men, notwithstanding it
tasted a little of the bulged water. By this we thought that
the holes we had cut to sink the ship were frozen, and that
this water had stood in the ship all the winter.

The 24th we went betimes in the morning to work, but
we found that the water was risen above the ice where we
had left work, above two foot, for the wind had blown very
hard at north the night before. In the morning the wind
came about south, and blew hard, and, although we had little
reason for it, we yet expected a lower veer of water. I thereupon put them to work on the outside of the ship, that we
might come to the lower hole, which we had cut in the stern-
sheets; with much labour, by night, we digged down through
the ice to it, and found it unfrozen, as it had been all the
winter; and, to our great comforts, we found that on the in-

side the water was ebbed within the hole, and that on the outside it was ebbed a foot lower. Whereupon I caused a shot-board to be nailed upon it, and to be made as tight as might be, to try if the water came in any other way; to the other two holes we had digged on the inside, and found them frozen. Now I did this betimes, that if we found the ship foundered, we might resolve on some course to save or prolong our lives, by getting to the main before the ice was broken up; as for our boat it was too little, and bulged besides that. Our carpenter was by this time past hopes, and therefore little hope had we of our pinnace. But which was worst of all, we had not four men able to travel through the snow over the ice, and in this miserable state were we at this present. The 25th we satisfied our longing, for the wind now coming about northerly, the water rose by the ship's-side, where we had digged down a foot and more above the hold, and yet did not rise within board. This so encouraged us, that we fell lustily to digging, and to heave the ice out of the ship. I put the cook, and some others, to thaw the pumps, who, by continual pouring of hot water into them, by the 27th in the morning had cleared one of them, which we proving, found it delivered water very sufficiently. Thus we fell to pumping, and having cleared two feet water, we left the other to a second trial, continuing our work thus in digging the ice. By the 28th we had cleared our other pump, which we also found to deliver water very well. We found likewise that the water did not rise any thing in the hold.

The 29th it rained all day long: a sure sign to us that winter was broken up. The 30th we were, betimes, aboard at work; which day, and the 31st, were very cold, with snow and hail, which pinched our sick men more than any time this year. This evening, being May eve, we returned late from our work to our house, and made a good fire, and chose ladies, and ceremoniously wore their names in our caps, endeavouring to revive ourselves by any means. At our coming from England, we were stored with all sorts of sea provisions, as beef, pork, etc.; but now, as we had little hopes of recruiting, our cook ordered it in this manner: the beef which was to serve on Sunday night to supper, he boiled on Saturday night, in a kettle full of water, with a quart of oatmeal, about an hour; then, taking the beef out, he boiled the rest to half the quantity; and this we called *pottage*, which we eat with bread, as hot as we could; and after this, we had our ordinary of fish.   Sunday, for dinner, we had pork and pease; and at night, the former boiled beef made more pottage.   In this manner our Tuesday's beef was boiled on the Monday nights, and the Thursdays upon Wednesdays; and thus all the week, except Friday night, we had something warm in our bellies every supper; and surely this did us a great deal of good.   But soon after Christmas many of us fell sick, and had sore mouths, and could neither eat beef, pork, fish, nor pottage.   Their diet was only this: they would pound bread, in a mortar, to meal, then fry it in a frying-pan with a little oil, and so eat it.   Some would boil pease to a soft paste, and feed, as well as they could, upon that.   For the most part of the winter, water was our drink.   In the whole winter, we took not above a dozen foxes, many of which would be dead in the traps two or three days oftentimes; and then, when the blood was settled, they would be unwholesome.   But if we took one alive, and he had not been long in the trap, him we boiled, and made broth for the weakest sick men; the flesh of them, being soft boiled, they eat also.   Some white partridges we killed, but not worth mentioning.   We had three sorts of sick men: those that could not move, nor turn themselves in their beds, who must be tended like infants; others were, as it were, crippled with aches; and others, that were something better.   Most had sore mouths.   You may now ask me, how these infirm men could work?   I will tell you.   Our surgeon, who was a diligent and sweet-conditioned man as ever I saw, would be up betimes in the morning, and whilst he picked their teeth, and cut away the pieces of flesh from their gums, they would bathe their thighs, knees, and legs. The manner of it was thus : there was no tree, bud, or herb, but we made trial of it; and this being first boiled in a kettle, and then put in a small tub and basons, they put it under them, and covered them with cloths upon it. This so molified the grieved parts, that though, when they rose out of their beds, they would be so crippled that they could scarce stand, yet, after this was done half an hour, they would be able to go (and go they must) to wade through the snow to the ship, and about other business. By night they would be as bad again, and then they must be bathed, anointed, and their mouths dressed again, before they went to bed : and in this diet, and in this manner, we went through our miseries. I was always afraid that we should be weakest in the spring, and therefore I reserved a tun of Alicant wine unto this time. Of this, by putting seven parts of water to one of wine, we made some weak beverage; which, by reason that the wine had been froze, and lost its virtue, was little better than water. The sicker sort had a pint of Alicant a day, by itself; and of such poor *aqua vitæ*, too, as we had, they had a dram allowed them next their hearts every morning. And thus we made the best use of what we had, according to the seasons.

May. The 1st, we went aboard by times, to heave out the ice; the 2nd, it did snow and blow, and was so cold, that we were forced to keep house all day. This unexpected cold, at this time of the year, did so vex our sick men, that they grew worse and worse; we could not now take them out of their beds, but they would swoon, and we had much ado to keep life in them. The 6th, *John Wardon*, the master of my ship's chief mate, died; whom we buried in the evening, in the most Christian-like manner, on the top of a bare hill of land, which we called *Brandon-hill*.

The 15th I manured a little patch of ground that was bare of snow, and sowed it with pease, hoping to have some shortly

to eat; for as yet we could see no green thing to comfort us.
The 18th our carpenter, *William Cole*, died; a man beloved
of us all, as much for his innate goodness, as for the present
necessity we had of a man of his quality : he had endured a
long sickness with patience, and made a very godly end. In
the evening we buried him by Mr. Wardon, accompanied
with as many as could go, for three more of our principal
men lay then expecting a good hour. And now were we in
the most miserable state that we were in all the voyage. Before this extreme weakness, he had brought the pinnace to
that pass, that she was ready to be bolted, etc., and to be
joined to receive the planks; so that we were not so discouraged by his death, but that we hoped, ourselves, to finish
her, if the ship proved unserviceable. This pinnace was
twenty-seven feet by the keel; she had seventeen ground-
timbers, thirty-four principal staddles, and eight short staddles : he had contrived her with a round stern, to save labour,
and indeed she was a well-proportioned vessel; her burden
was twelve or fourteen tons. In the evening the master of
our ship, after the burial, returned aboard, and, looking about
him, discovered some part of our gunner under the gun-room
ports. This man we had committed to the sea at a good
distance from the ship, and in deep water, near six months
before. The 19th, in the morning, I sent men to dig him
out. He was fast in the ice, his head downwards, and his
heels upwards, for he had but one leg; and the plaister was
yet at the wound. In the afternoon they had digged him
clear out, and he was as free from noisomness, as when we
first committed him to the sea. This alteration had the ice,
and water, and time only wrought on him, that his flesh
would slip up and down, upon his bones, like a glove on a
man's hand. In the evening we buried him by the others.
This day one *George Ugganes*, who could handle a tool best
of us all, had pretty well repaired our boat, and so ended this
mournful week. The snow was by this time pretty well

wasted in the wood; and we having a high tree on the highest place of the island, which was called our watch-tree, from the top of it might see into the sea, but found no appearance of breaking up yet. And now by day sometimes we have such hot glooms that we cannot endure the sun, and yet in the night it freezes very hard. This unnaturalness of the season tormented our men that they grew worse and worse daily.

The 23rd, our boatswain, a careful man, having been long sick, which he had heartily resisted, was taken with such a pain in one of his thighs, that we thought he would have died presently. He kept his bed in great extremity; and it was a maxim among us, that if any one kept his bed, he could rise no more. This made every man to strive to keep up for life.

The 24th was very warm sunshine, and the ice consumed by the shore-side, and cracked all over the bay with dreadful noise. About three in the afternoon, we could perceive the ice, with the ebb, to drive by the ship, whereupon I sent two, with all speed, to the master, with order to beat out the hole, and to sink the ship, as likewise to look for the rudder betwixt the ice. This he presently performed; and a happy fellow, one *David Hammon*, pecking betwixt the ice, struck upon it, and it came up with his launce; who, crying that he had found it, the rest came and got it upon the ice, and so into the ship. In the mean time, the little drift which the ice had, began to rise and mount into high heaps against the shole shores and rocks, and likewise against the heap of ice which we had put for a barracado to our ship, but with little harm to us; yet we were forced to cut away twenty fathom of cable which was frozen in the ice. After an hour, the ice settled again, not having any vent outwards. This was a joyful day to us all; and we gave God thanks for the hopes we had of it.

The 25th was a fine warm day; and, with the ebb, the ice drove against the ship, and struck her soundly. The 26th, I took the chirurgeon with me, and went again to the wood,

and to that bay where, last year, we had lost our man, John
Barton ; but we could find no sign of him.   The 28th, it was
pretty clear betwixt the ship and the shore, and I hoped the
ice would no more oppress us ; wherefore I caused the lower
holes to be firmly stopped, the water then remaining three
feet above the ballast. The 29th, being Prince Charles's birth-
day, we kept holiday, and displayed His Majesty's colours
both on land and aboard, and named our habitation, *Charles
Town*, by contraction, *Charlton*, and the island, *Charlton
Island.*

The 30th we launched our boat, and had intercourse sometimes between the ship and the shore by boat, which was
new to us. The last day of this month we found some
vetches to appear out of the ground, which I made our men
pick up and boil for our sick.   This day we made an end of
fitting all our rigging and sails, and it being a very hot day
we dried our fish in the sun, and aired all our other provisions.
There was not a man of us at present able to eat of our salt
provisions but myself and the master. It may be remembered that all this winter we had not been troubled with any
rheums nor phlegmatic diseases. All this month the wind
was variable, but for the most part northerly.

June. The first four days snowed and hailed, and blew
very hard, and it was so cold that the ponds of water froze
over, and the water in our cans was frozen even in the very
house. Our cloaths also that had been washed and hung out
to dry did not thaw. All day the 5th it continued blowing
very hard on the broad side of the ship, which made her
swag and wallow in her dock, notwithstanding she was sunk,
which shook her very much. The ice withal drove against
her, and gave her many fearful blows. I resolved to endeavour to hang the rudder, and when God sent us water, notwithstanding the abundance of ice that was yet about us, to
heave her further off. In the afternoon we under-run our
small cable to our anchor, which lay a-stern in deep water,

and so with some difficulty got up our anchor. This cable
had lain slack under foot, and under the ice all winter, and
we could never have a clear slatch from ice to have it up
before now. We found it not a jot the worse. I put some
to make coal-rakes, that they might go into the water and
rake a hole in the sand to let down our rudder. The 6th we
went about to hang it; and our young lustiest men took it
by turns to go into the water and to rake away the sand, but
they were not able to endure the cold half a quarter of an
hour, it was so mortifying; and use what comforts we could,
it would make them swoon and die away. We brought it to
the stern-post, but then we were forced to give it over, being
able to work at it no longer. Then we plugged the upper
holes aboard, and fell to pumping the water out of her again.

The 7th we wrought about our rudder, but were again
forced to give over, and so put out our cables overboard with
messengers unto them, the anchor lying to that pass that we
might keep her right in the dock when we had brought her
light. By the 8th at night we had pumped all the water
out of her, so that at high water she would float in her dock,
though she were still docked in the sand almost four feet.
This made us consider what was to be done. I resolved to
heave out all the ballast; for the bottom of her being so
soaked all the winter, I hoped was so heavy that it would
bear her. If we could not get her off that way, I then thought
to cut her down to the lower deck, and take out her masts,
and so with our casks to buoy her off. The 9th betimes in
the morning we fell to work, we hoisted out our beer and
cyder, and made a raft of it, fastening it to our shore-anchor.
The beer and cyder sunk presently to the ground, which was
nothing strange to us, for any wood or pipe-staves that had
laid under the ice all the winter would also sink down as
soon as ever it was hove over board.

This day we heaved out ten ton of ballast; and here I am
to remember God's goodness towards us, in sending those

F F

forementioned green vetches; for now our feeble sick men, that could not for their lives stir these two or three months, could endure the air, and walk about the house. Our other sick men gathered strength also: and it was wonderful to see how soon they were recovered. We use them in this manner twice a day; we went to gather the herb or leaf of those vetches as they first appeared out of the ground, and then we washed and boiled them, and so with oil and vinegar that had been frozen we eat them. It was an excellent sustenance and refreshing; the most part of us eat nothing else. We likewise bruised them, and took the juice of them and mixed it with our drink: we also eat them raw with our bread.

The 11th was very warm weather, and we hung our rudder. The 13th I resolved to know the latitude of this place; so having examined the instruments and practised about it this fortnight, I found it to be 52 degrees 3 minutes. The 14th we had heaved out all the ballast, and carried all our yards and every thing else on shore, so that we now had the ship as light as possible it could be.

The 15th we did little but exercise ourselves. By this time our men that were most feeble grew strong and run about, the flesh of their gums being settled again, and their teeth fastened so that they eat beef with their vetches: This day I went to our watch-tree, but the sea, for any thing I could perceive, was still firm frozen, and the bay full of ice, having no way to vent it.

The 16th was wondrous hot, with some thunder and lightning, so that our men went into the ponds ashore to swim and cool themselves, yet the water was very cool still.

The 17th, the wind came northerly, and we, expecting a high tide, in the morning betimes, put out our small cable astern, out at the gun-room port; but the morning tide, we had not water by a foot. In the evening, I had laid marks by stones, etc., and thought that the water flowed apace. Making signs, therefore, for the boat to come ashore, I took

all that were able to do any thing with me aboard : and at
high water, although she wanted something to rise clear out
of the dock, yet we heaved with such good-will, that we heaved
her through the sand into a foot and an half deeper water ;
and further we durst not bring her, for the ice was all thick
about us.   After we had moved her, we all went to prayers,
and gave God thanks that he had given us our ship again.
The 18th, we were up betimes ; the cooper, and some with
him, to bring fresh water, myself, with others, to gather stones
at low water ; which, we piling up at low water, the cockswain
and his gang fetched them aboard, where the master, with
the rest, stowed them to the offing, by which means we could
the better come and stop the two upper holes firmly ; after
which, we fitted other convenient places to make others, to
sink her if occasion were.

The 19th, we were all up betimes to work, as afore specified.   These two days our ship did not float, and it was a very
happy hour which we got her off, for we never had such a
high tide all the time we were here.   In the evening we went
up to our watch-tree ; and this was the first time I could see
open water any way, except that little by the shore-side where
we were.   This put us in some comfort, that the sea would
shortly break up, which, we knew, must be so to the northward, seeing, that way, we were certain there were about two
hundred leagues of sea.   The 20th, we laboured as formerly,
the wind at north-north-west.   The tide rose so high, that
our ship floated, and we drew her off into a foot and half
deeper water.   Thus we did it by little and little, for the ice
was still wonderfully thick round about us.

The 22nd, there drove much ice about us and within us,
and brought home our stern-anchor at high water.   Notwithstanding all the ice, we heaved our ship further off, that so
she might lye afloat at low water.   The next low water, we
sounded all about the ship, and found it very sound ground.
We discovered stones three feet high above the ground, and

two of them within a ship's breadth of the ship, whereby did more manifestly appear God's mercy to us; for if, when we found her on shore, she had struck one blow against those stones, it had bulged her. Many such dangers were there in this bay, which we now first perceived. In the evening we towed off the ship into the place where she rode the last year, and there moored her, steering the ship night and day, flood and ebb, among the dispersed ice that came athwart us.

The 23rd, we laboured in fetching the provisions on board, which to do, we were forced to wade, to carry it to the boat, a full bow-shot; and all by reason the wind was southerly. This morning I took an observation of the moon's coming to the south, by a meridian line of a hundred and twenty yards long, which I had rectified many weeks beforehand.

The 24th, I took another observation of the moon's coming to the meridian. I had formerly cut down a very high tree, and made a cross of it. To it I now fastened, uppermost, the King and Queen's pictures, drawn to the life, and doubly wrapped in lead, and so close, that no weather could hurt them. Betwixt both these, I affixed His Majesty's royal title, viz., *Charles the First, King of England, Scotland, France, and Ireland,* as also of *Newfoundland,* and of these territories, and to the westward as far as *Nova Albion,* and to the northward, to the latitude of 80 degrees, etc. On the outside of the lead, I fastened a shilling and a sixpence of His Majesty's coin; under that, we fastened the King's arms, fairly cut in lead; and under that, the arms of the city of Bristol. And this being Midsummer-day, we raised it on the top of the Bar-hill, where we had buried our dead fellows; by this ceremony, taking possession of these territories for His Majesty's use. The wind continuing southerly, and blowing hard, put all the ice upon us, so that the ship now rode among it in such apparent danger, that I thought verily we should have lost her.

The 25th in the morning the boatswain with a convenient

crew began to rig the ship, the rest fetching our provision on
board. About ten o'clock, when it was something dark, I
took a launce in my hand, and one with me with a musket,
and went to our watch-tree to make a fire on the most eminent place of the island, to see if it would be answered.
Such fires I have formerly made, to have knowledge if there
were any savages on the main or the islands about us. Had
there been any, my purpose was to have gone to them, to
get intelligence of Christians, or some ocean seas thereabouts.
When I was come to the tree I laid down my launce, and so
did my consort his musket, whilst I climbed up to the top
of the tree. I ordered him to put fire to some low tree
thereabouts. He unadvisedly put fire to some trees that
were to windward, so that they and all the rest too, by reason
it had been very hot weather, being dry, took fire like flax
and hemp; and the wind blowing towards me, I made haste
down the tree; but before I was half-way down the fire took
on the bottom of it, and blazed so fiercely upward that I was
forced to leap off the tree and down a steep hill, and in short
with much ado escaped burning. The moss on the ground
was as dry as flax, and it run most strangely, like a train
along the earth. The musket and launce were both burnt.
My consort at last came to me, and was joyful to see me,
for he thought verily I had been burnt: and thus we went
homeward together, leaving the fire encreasing and burning
most furiously. I slept but little all night after, and at
break of day ordered all our powder and beef to be carried
aboard this day. I went to the hills to look to the fire, where
I saw it still burn both to westward and northward. Leaving
one upon the hills to watch it, I came home immediately,
and made them take down our new suit of sails, and carry
them to the sea-side, ready to be cast in if occasion were,
and to make haste to take down our houses. About noon
the wind shifted northward, and our centinel came running
home, bringing us word that the fire followed him at his

heels, like a train of powder. There was no occasion to bid
us pull down, and carry all to the sea-side. The fire came
towards us with a most terrible rattling noise, bearing a full
mile in breadth; and by that time we had uncovered our
houses, and going to carry away our last things, the fire was
come to our town, and seized it, and, in a trice, burnt it
down to the ground. We lost nothing of any value, for we
had brought all into a place of security. Our dogs, in this
condition, would sit down on their tails, and howl, and then
run into the sea, and there stay. The wind shifted easterly,
and the fire ranged to the westward, seeking what it might
devour. This night we lay together aboard the ship, and
gave God thanks, who had been thus merciful unto us.

The 27th, 28th, and 29th, we wrought hard in fetching our
things aboard, as likewise our water, which we towed off with
the ebb, and sent it to the ship with the flood. We were
forced to go about the eastern point for drift-wood; for the
tools were all so spent, that we could cut none. Therefore
about three days before, I had caused our pinnace to be sawed
to pieces, and with that we stowed our cask, intending to burn
it at low water; and such other times as we could not work
in carrying things aboard, I employed in fetching stones;
and we built three tombs over our three dead companions,
filling them with sand, in a decent and handsome manner.
The least tomb had two tons of stones about it. The 30th,
we earnestly continued our labour, and brought our sails to
yard; and by eleven o'clock at night had made a pretty ship,
meaning to have finished our business with the week and
month, that we might the better solemnize the Sabbath ashore,
and so take leave of our wintering island.

July. The 1st of this month we were up betimes, and I
caused our ship to be adorned the best we could: our flag in
the poop, and the King's colours in the main-top. I had
provided a short account of all the passages of our voyage to
this day. I likewise wrote in what state we were in at pre-

sent, and how I intended to prosecute this discovery, both to
the westward, and to the southward, about this island.   This
brief discourse I had concluded with a request to any noble-
minded traveller that should take it down, or come to the
notice of it, that, if we should perish in the action, then to
make our endeavours known to our Sovereign Lord the King.
And thus, with our arms, drums, and colours, cook and kettle,
we went ashore ; and first we marched up to our eminent
cross, adjoining to which we had buried our dead fellows.
There we read morning prayers, and then walked up and
down till dinner-time.   After dinner we walked up to the
highest hills, to see which way the fire had wasted ; we descried that it had consumed to the westward sixteen miles at
least, and the whole breadth of the island.   Near our cross
and dead it could not come, by reason it was a bare sand.
After evening prayer I happened to walk along the beach-
side, where I found an herb resembling scurvy-grass ; I had
some gathered, which we boiled with our meat for supper.
It was most excellent good, and far better than our vetches.
After supper we went to seek for more of it, which we carried
off to the quantity of two bushels, which did afterwards much
refresh us.   And now the sun was set, and the boat came
ashore for us ; whereupon we assembled ourselves together,
and went up to take the last view of our dead, and to look
to their tombs, and other things.   So fastening my brief,
which was securely wrapped up in lead, to the cross, we presently took boat and departed, and never put foot more on
that island.

Thus terminates the unaffected, but not unaffecting, narrative given by Captain James of the crosses he experienced,
with his Company, on Charlton Island.   Subjected to sufferings of no ordinary description, this officer exhibited un-
daunted courage, patient endurance, unceasing energy, and
indomitable perseverance ; while his benevolent disposition,

amounting almost to a failing at sea, shone ashore, amidst the dark scenes in which he was involved, with the lustre of a good deed. The Company of the Maria, too, proved themselves obedient, faithful, and stout-hearted fellows. With their commander, they are entitled to be held in honourable remembrance, with all others who have distinguished themselves by the zealous and honest performance of their duty.

The Maria sailed from Charlton Island on the 2nd of July; and after encountering a succession of minor perils, but without making any discoveries, Captain James arrived in the road of Bristol on the 22nd of October 1632.

Conclusion.

THE following testimony to the merits of those who may be deemed the pioneers in North-polar navigation, is borne by one competent to offer an authoritative opinion on the subject; having pursued the same tracks, and having achieved renown in the same service. The spirit of justice which pervades these remarks; the cordiality with which praise is awarded to the distinguished ancients; and the modest estimate which is formed of the efforts of the moderns, by one conspicuous among them for his talents and success, are circumstances that will be duly appreciated, and must be viewed as conferring honour on the writer.

CAPTAIN SIR EDWARD PARRY remarks :[1] " In revisiting many of the spots discovered by our early British navigators in the Polar regions, and in traversing the same tracks which they

---

[1] Journal of the Third Voyage for the Discovery of a North-west Passage, etc.; performed in the years 1824-25, in His Majesty's ships Hecla and Fury. London : 1826.

CONCLUSION. 225

originally pursued, I have now and then, in the course of my
Narratives, had occasion to speak of the faithfulness of their
accounts, and the accuracy of their hydrographical information. I should, however, be doing but imperfect justice to
the memory of these extraordinary men, as well as to my own
sense of their merits, if I permitted the present opportunity
to pass without offering a still more explicit and decided testimony to the value of their labours. The accounts of Hudson,
Baffin, and Davis are the productions of men of no common
stamp. They evidently relate things just as they saw them,
dwelling on such nautical and hydrographical notices as,
even at this day, are valuable to any seaman going over the
same ground; and describing every appearance of nature,
whether on the land, the sea, or the ice, with a degree of
faithfulness which can alone perhaps be duly appreciated by
those who succeed them in the same regions, and under similar circumstances........It is, indeed, impossible for any one,
personally acquainted with the phenomena of the icy seas, to
peruse the plain and unpretending narratives of these navigators, without recognizing, in almost every event they relate,
some circumstance familiar to his own recollection and experience, and meeting with numberless remarks which bear
most unequivocally about them the impress of truth.

"While thus doing justice to the faithfulness and accuracy
with which they recorded their discoveries, one cannot less
admire the intrepidity, perseverance, and skill, with which,
inadequately furnished as they were, those discoveries were
effected, and every difficulty and danger braved. That any
man, in a single frail vessel of five-and-twenty tons, ill-found
in most respects, and wholly unprovided for wintering, having
to contend with a thousand real difficulties, as well as with
numberless imaginary ones, which the superstitions then ex-
isting among sailors would not fail to conjure up,—that any
man, under such circumstances, should, two hundred years
ago, have persevered in accomplishing what our old navigators

G G

did accomplish, is, I confess, sufficient to create in my mind a feeling of the highest pride on the one hand, and almost approaching to humiliation on the other : of pride, in remembering that it was *our* countrymen who performed these exploits ; of humiliation, when I consider how little, with all our advantages, *we* have succeeded in going beyond them.

" Indeed, the longer our experience has been in the navigation of the icy seas, and the more intimate our acquaintance with all its difficulties and all its precariousness, the higher have our admiration and respect been raised for those who went before us in those enterprises. Persevering in difficulty, unappalled by danger, and patient under distress, they scarcely ever use the language of complaint, much less that of despair ; and sometimes, when all human hope seems at its lowest ebb, they furnish the most beautiful examples of that firm reliance on a merciful and superintending Providence, which is the only rational source of true fortitude in man. Often, with their narratives impressed upon my mind, and surrounded by the very difficulties which they in their frail and inefficient barks undauntedly encountered and overcame, have I been tempted to exclaim, with all the enthusiasm of Purchas :

' HOW SHALL I ADMIRE YOUR HEROICKE COURAGE,
        YE MARINE WORTHIES, BEYOND NAMES
                OF WORTHINESS'.

APPENDIX

OF

SUPPLEMENTARY NOTES.

Appendix.

SHIPS, OFFICERS, ETC.

IN all expeditions that consisted of more than two vessels, one
was appointed to lead, with the denomination of *Admiral ;*
and another was appointed to keep a look-out astern, with
the denomination of *Vice-admiral.* By day, the Admiral carried a proper signal, and by night shewed a distinguishing
light. These vessels were of medium size, between three and
four hundred tons, strongly built, to carry a heavy armament,
and were required to sail well. They carried soldiers as well
as mariners.

The officer in command of the entire fleet, was named the
General, and he sailed in the Admiral. The second in command, was denominated the *Lieutenant-general,* and he sailed
in the Vice-admiral. Both these officers were invested, by
patent from the Sovereign, with power to exercise martial
law ; and several of these documents, granted by Elizabeth
and James I, to the early commanders employed by the Worshipful Fellowship of the Merchants of London trading into
the East Indies, are to be found among the East India Mss.

On board each ship there was also : a *Captain,* who "ruled
in matters of controversy, and in sea-fights"; a *Master,* who,
under sureties, was held responsible for the goods brought
into the ship ; a *Purser,* who was held accountable, also under
sureties, for the goods on board, and who superintended their
delivery from the ship ; a *Romager,* who regulated the stow-
age : a *Counter-master,* or master's mate, who kept the keys

of the hatches; and a *Pilot*, "to direct only in gouerning and leading" the ship from port to port.

DISCIPLINE.

From the commencement of the East India Traffic, the Commanders of vessels were instructed to pay the strictest attention to the following points, viz.: I. To the performance of Divine Worship twice every day. II. To the repression of blasphemous expressions, prophane swearing, lewd conversation, dicing, and every other description of gaming, which is described as being a fruitful cause of quarrels, frequently leading to murder, and an especial object of God's indignation. III. To the careful removal of every kind of "filthyness" from within board; cleanliness being emphatically declared to be "a notable preseruation of health"; and want of cleanliness, to be the "cause of breeding sickness". IV. In their intercourse with strangers, particularly with uncivilized people, the crews are directed to avoid any kind of violence: to conduct themselves with civility and kindness, the same tending to promote the "honour of the countrie". v. That the crews, after having been long confined to sea-fare, may not injure themselves, either by eating immoderately of proper food, or by partaking of improper food, the Commander is instructed to select the discreetest of the company for the purpose of purchasing what may be required: which is to be brought on board, and then divided according to the wants of the respective messes. VI. The sick are objects of solicitude. It is ordered that care be taken not to allow waste of the fresh meat that may be procured on the passage; and that "the comfortable thinges wherewth euery shippe is furnished be not spent in ryatt and banquetting, and soe the sicke pishe [perish] for want of thinges needful". And it is added: "Espetiall care must be had that when those that are the most weak psonns come to fresh victualls after long abstinence att sea, they be not suffered in any wise to eat of those fresh meates which shall be gotten on shore, but that yo^u cause such fresh victualls as yo^u can prouide to be boyled in pottage, till yt be sodden in peeces, and the cheefe substance lefte in the broth, and giue them of that broth onelie to feede vpon moderatelie for twoe or three daies *till their stomackes be somewhatt setled and their bodies comforted*".[1] If in some recent cases, some judicious measure of this kind had been adopted, it is probable many lives would have been saved.

Opposed to gaming, the drama appears to have been considered a beneficial source of recreation; and the following curious and interesting entries connected with the subject, occur in the journal of the *Dragon* (Captain Keeling), bound with the *Hector* (Captain Hawkins) and the *Consent* towards the East Indies.[2]

1607.

September 4. [At Serra Leona.] Towards night, the kinges interpter came, and brought me a letter from the Portingall,[3] wher in (like the faction) he offered me all kindly services. The bearer is a man of maruailous redie witt, and speakes in eloquent Portugues. He layt abord me.

       5. I sent the interpreter, according to his desier, abord the Hector, whear he brooke fast, and after came abord mee, wher *we gaue the tragedie of Hamlett*.

    30. Captain Hawkins dined with me, wher *my companions acted Kinge Richard the Second*.

    31. I envited Captain Hawkins to a ffishe dinner, and *had Hamlet acted* abord me: *wch I p'mitt to keepe my people from idlenes and vnlawfull games, or sleepe.*

[1] Court Miscellany Book. (*E. I. Mss.*)

[2] *E. I. Mss.* This journal is printed in Purchas, but with many omissions; of which the above extracts form a part.

[3] A small Portuguese craft, at anchor in the road of Sierra Leone.

A generall pportion of victuallinge made for the *Dragon,* of 600 tunns, 150 marchants and mariners. Februarie, 1606-7.

Breade	ffor 21 mo. att 24*li*. a man p. mo., 30 dais to a mo., is	675 C. wight.
Meale	ffor 3 mo. att 24*li*. p. mo. for a man ...	096½ C. —
Ship beare ...	ffor 3 mo. att a pottle a man p. diem ...	028¼ tunns.
	ffor leakadge and lees	004½ tunns.
Beare, stronge,	ffor one moneth	009½ tunns.
	ffor leekinge and lees	001½ tunns.
Sider	ffor 12 mo. at a quarte a man p. diem ...	040 tunns.
	ffor leakedg, after tenn in the 100 ...	005½ tunns.
Wyne	ffor 8 mos. 1 pinte a man p. diem	041 pipes.
Beafe drisalted	ffor 2 mo. att 1*li*. a man p. diem ...	020½ C.wight.
Beafe pickled	ffor 4 monneth, 1½*li*. a man p. diem ...	241 C. wight.
Porck pickled	ffor 10 monneths, at 4*li*. for 5 men p. diem	322 C. wight.
Pease	ffor 9 mo. att halfe a pint	210 bushells.
Beanes... ...	a man, p. diem, ⅔ pease, and ⅓ beanes ...	105 bushells.
Backalew ...	ffor 3 mo., att a fish a man p. diem ...	112 C. at 120 yᵉ C.
Stockfish ...	ffor 1 mo. at ½ a fish a man p. diem ...	19 C. at 120 yᵉ C.
Lynge	ffor a monneth, at 4 mease to a fish, 5 men to a mess	003 C. ¾ fish.
Oatmeale ...	ffor 4 mo. at ½ a pint a man p. diem ...	141 bushells.
Steal wheate[1]	ffor 4 monneths att ½ a pint	144 bushells.

To which is added what is termed,

Victualling Extraordinarie, viz. :

Cheese, 005 weyes ; butter, 021 firkins ; sweete oyle, 600 gallons ; vinegar, 006 tunns ; aquavite, 150 gallons ; honny, 003 barrells ; mustard seed,[2] 006 bushells ; rice, 002 C. wight ; salt, 006 h.h., bay, and white ; rape oyle for lampes, 0033 h.h. ; wax candles, 100 pounde ; tallow candles, 150 pounde ; water caske, 040 tunns ; barricos[3] (breakers), 040 tunns.

[1] ? *French grain.* A few years afterwards, the Company's purveyor reported, that *English grain sufficiently hard to be ground,* could be procured ; and that a further importation of French grain was unnecessary.

[2] " 1 mustard *querne*" [mill] is included in the inventory of the "Great Susan", 1600.—*Court Book,* p. 5.

[3] The term "barrico" was used so late as Best's Narrative of the Mutiny of the Bounty.

Great attention was paid to the quality of the meat. The beasts were purchased alive, inspected by duly qualified officers on the part of the Company, driven to the Company's slaughter-house at Blackwall, and there killed and cured. In the contracts for meat, it is stipulated for: "The oxen to be fatt, and large groweth flesh, and euery one to waighe upwards of 5 cwt. waight. The hogge to be large and goode; among all which, none to be soaken sows,[1] or measlee, and to containe one hundred waight p̱. hogg, and none to be under three-quarters; to be waighed without head or feet, and to have the lying side of the suett both to the oxen and hogge; and further, to have the tongues of the said oxen without the roote waighed into the beefe".[2]

ARMAMENT.

In the inventories of stores in vessels belonging to the East India Company, the following arms are enumerated, viz.:

I. *Ordnance.* Consisting of *demi-canon,* of 60 cwt. each; *culverins,* of 42, 36, and 29, cwt. each; *demi-culverins*; *sakers,* 20 cwt. 2 qrs. each.[3] Also *fowlers* and *murthering-pieces,* the

[1] *i.e.* "not in pig".

[2] A book of "Contracts and Bargains made for Prouis'ons", etc. (*E.I. Mss.*)

[3] The following *table* of particulars connected with ancient ordnance, may not be unacceptable.

	Length, feet.	Weight, cwt.	Diam. of bore, ins.	Diam. of shot, ins.	Weight of shot, lbs.	Charge lbs.
Cannon "Royal", or "of Eight"	12	80	—	—	—	—
Demi-cannon:						
1 extraordinary	13	60	$6\frac{3}{4}$	$6\frac{1}{8}$	36	18
2 ordinary	12	56	$6\frac{1}{2}$	6 1-6	32	$17\frac{1}{2}$
3 least	10 to 11	54	$6\frac{1}{4}$	6	30	14
Culverines:						
1 extraordinary	13	abt. 80	$5\frac{1}{2}$	$5\frac{1}{4}$	20	$12\frac{1}{2}$
2 ordinary	—	50	$5\frac{1}{4}$	5	17 5oz.	$11\frac{1}{2}$
3 least	—	40	5	$4\frac{3}{4}$	14	10
Demi-culverines:						
1 extraordinary	$10\frac{3}{4}$	30	$4\frac{3}{4}$	$4\frac{1}{2}$	12 11oz.	$8\frac{1}{2}$
2 ordinary	10	27	$4\frac{1}{2}$	$4\frac{1}{4}$	10 11oz.	7 4oz.
3 least	9 to 10	—	$4\frac{1}{4}$	4	9	$6\frac{1}{4}$

Continued.

latter being furnished with two chambers each.[1] The *shot* consisted of round, grape, case, and langrell.

II. *Small-arms.* Consisting of *musketts ;* and *hargabushes* of *croke,* i.e., arquebuses which, in firing, were placed on a crook or rest, and were both longer and heavier than the musket. *Callivers* are also named. For these arms, *priming-flasks, bandoleers,* and *matches,* were provided in proper proportions. The bandoleers were wooden cases, covered with leather, each containing a charge. Of these, a musketeer usually carried twelve, attached to a belt slung across the left shoulder, and resting on the right side.

III. *Miscellaneous :* including *swords* and *steel targets,* or bucklers; *bills ;* long and short *pikes ; fier-pikes,* with and without staves ; *boare-spears ; muskett-arrows ; slurbows,* with benders; and *fier-workes* generally.

On these weapons some observations may be offered. Bishop Wilkins states,[2] a whole cannon required at least ninety men or sixteen horses for its draught; a culverin fifty men, or, eight horses; and a demi-culverin thirty-six men, or seven horses. He expresses a doubt of the superiority of cannon to the catapulta. He considers that the advantages of the catapulta consist : first, in its being more easy of transport;

	Length, feet.	Weight, cwt.	Diam. of bore,ins.	Diam. of shot,ins.	Weight of shot, .bs.	Charge lbs.
Sakers :						
1 extraordinary ..	10	... — ...	4	... 3¾ ...	7	... 5
2 ordinary... ...	9	... — ...	3¾	... 3½ ...	6	... 4
3 least	8	... — ...	3½	... 3 ...	4¾	... 3½
Minions :						
1 largest	8	... 10 ...	3½	... 3 ...	3 12oz.	3¼
2 ordinary... ...	7	... 8 ...	3	... 2⅛ ...	3 2oz.	2½
Falcon	6	... — ...	2¼	... 2⅛ ...	1 5oz.	1¼
Falconet	—	... — ...	2	... — ...	—	... —

[1] The *gingall* of China is similar in its construction ; and there is reason to believe the arm was introduced into that empire by the Portuguese : though gun-powder was previously known and used.

[2] " Mathematical Magick ; or the Wonders that may be performed by Mechanical Geometry ". London : 1680.

second, in the facility with which, being made of wood, it may
be constructed at all times and in all places ; third, in its
comparative smallness of cost ; and fourth, on account of the
great saving in regard to "ammunition". "But", he observes,
" this enquiry cannot be fully determined without particular
experience of both". The fowlers and murthering pieces were
usually mounted on the forecastle. Sir John Hawkins[1] considers "their execution and speedie charging and discharging to
be of great moment", and as calculated to render most efficient
service, both at close quarters, and in boarding. The musket-
arrows were short, and put into the barrel after a " tampkin"
[tompion] had been driven. In a great fight between Sir John
Hawkins and the Spaniards, in May 1594, their efficacy was
proved. After the fight, " the enemy confessed they were of
singular use and execution, for they passed with facility through
both sides of the upper works of the shipp, which were musket
proof, and wrought extraordinary disasters". The slurbows
appear to have been a species of catapult, or a powerful bow
worked with a " rack and bender".[2] From them were thrown
missiles resembling the modern carcase, viz., " brasse balles
of artificial fire, of very great account, either by sea or land".
Slurbows were also used to propel " fier-arrows". One of
these projectiles, during a naval engagement in 1588, " was
shott into the beake head of the *Swallow*, of her maiestie,
which was not seen till it had burned a hole in the nose as big
as a man's head". The " fierworks" were not mere inoffen-
sive displays of the pyrotechnic art. They were of a highly
destructive character, and calculated to clear a deck in a very
short space of time.

[1] *Observations*, etc. Edition of the Hakluyt Society, 1847.
[2] An engine of this description, from an antique marble, is delineated
in a work entitled "*Discorso sopra la castrametatione et disciplina mili-
tare de Romani.*" *A Lione* : 1556. There is also a rude figure in Bishop
Wilkins' work before noticed.

NOTE B. DUTCH VOYAGE.

The fleet sailed from the *Texel* on the 23rd, or 24th, of June, 1598. It consisted of five ships, measuring in the aggregate 745 tons, and carrying 491 men, viz.:

I.	*The Hope,* Admiral,	of tons 250	:	men	130.
II.	*The Charity,* Vice-Admiral,	„	160	: „	110.
III.	*The Faith,*	„	160	: „	109.
IV.	*The Fidelity,*	„	100	: „	86.
V.	*The Good News,*	„	75	: „	56.

Of the above, *The Fidelity* and *The Faith* alone returned to Holland. These two vessels, with the rest of the fleet, entered the *Straits of Magellan* on the 6th of April, 1599. On the 18th, they anchored in latitude 54°, wintered there, and lost one hundred men. This is not surprising, if it be true, as stated, that, " alway the storm found them worke ; and miserable was their toyle without any furtherance to their intended voyage. Raine, winde, snowe, hayle, hunger, losses of anchors, spoyles of ship, and tackling, sickness, death, sauages, want of store, and store of wants, conspired a fulness of miseries. But specially the colde encreased their appetites, and this decreased their prouision". On the 3rd of September the fleet weighed. For four days the ships kept together ; but on the fifth, *The Faith* and *The Charity* were compelled to put back. It is represented, " they were left behind in much miserie, tempest, hunger, leakes, etc." To their greater discomfort, also, one of the masters died. For a period of two months, it is said, " they had not one fayre day to drie their sayles : while the devil added mutinie in this miserable companie, and theeverie". After enduring " a world of straights in the straights", they departed homewards on the 22nd of January 1600, and arrived in the *Maes* on the 14th of July following.

It was not only in the Straits of Magellan, that the crews

of this ill-fated expedition suffered from want of provisions. Three months previous to their arrival there, they were put on an allowance of a quarter of a pound of bread per diem, per man; with a proportionate allowance of wine and water. On this occasion, according to one of the sufferers, the men, in the sore extremity of hunger, were fain to " eate the calve skinses" wherewith the ropes were served.

The rest of the ships encountered different fates, invariably disastrous. *The Hope* continued in company with the ship in which William Adams was embarked, till the 24th of February 1600. On that day, during a tremendous storm, they parted company. *The Hope* was " no more seen"; and was never afterwards heard of. *The Charity* and *The Good News* remain to be noticed. One of these ships, but which is not known, was captured by the Spaniards on the coast of Chili. The other, with Adams on board, was driven on the coast of Bungo, a province in the island of Kiusiu, appertaining to the empire of Japan; from whence the vessel never returned. This occurred in April 1601. When the ship anchored in Bungo, the " companie" on board was reduced by sickness and famine to twenty-four; and of these only " foure were able to goe." Shortly afterwards the complement was further reduced by six deaths.

Of the officers, *Sir Jacques Mahu*, or *Mahay*, general of the fleet, died in September 1593, in 3° S. of the line. He was succeeded in the command by *Simon de Cordes*, vice-admiral, who was slain through the treachery of the Spaniards, at the island of Mocha, in latitude 38° to the westward of South America. *Binningham, Bockholt*, and *Sebalt de Wert*, were captains. The last, with a companion, made good his return to Holland, on board *The Fidelity* and *The Faith*. One captain was slain on the voyage, in a skirmish with savages : one reached Japan, where he was detained five years. Being permitted to depart, at the earnest intercession of Adams, he proceeded to Johore, and there joined, as master, a Dutch fleet of nine sail. Off *Malacca*, a battle was fought with " an armada of Portugals", in which he was " shot, and presently died." One of the pilots was *Timothy Shotten*, which had been "with *Mr. Thomas Candish* in his voyage about the world".[1]

———

NOTE C. WAYMOUTH'S EXPEDITION.

MUSTER-ROLL, ETC., OF THE OFFICERS AND CREWS.

NO.	NAME.	NATIVE PLACE.	RATING.	PAY.
I	George Waymouth	Devonshire	Captain ...	Condl.
II	Wm. Cobreath ...	Ratcliff	,,	£6:0:0
III	Ino. Cartwright ...	London	Preacher	£3:0:0
IV	Bartw. Adams[2] ...	,, ...	Surgeon...	33s. 4d.
V	John Drew	—	Master ...	50s.
VI	John Lane	Penton, Devon ...	,,	50s.
VII	Thos. Yerworth ...	—	Purser ...	40s.
VIII	Ed. Pullison ...	—	,,	40s.
IX	Wm. Bateman ...	Ipswich	Trumpeter	30s.
X	Wm. Bully	Penton, Devon ...	Gunner ...	40s.
XI	Ino. Blackmoor ...	—	Mr.his mate	40s.
XII	Cornels. Mecum ...	—	Boatswn.	30s.
XIII	Ed. Andrewes ...	Chatham, Kent ...	Shipwright	34s.
XIV	Thos. Boren	London	Steward...	26s. 8d.
XV	Ricd. Membrey ...	Penton, Devon ...	Cooper ...	28s.
XVI	Heny. Trend ...	,, ,, ...	Mariner...	28s.
XVII	Timy. Powler ...	Topsham, ,, ...	,,	28s.
XVIII	Thos. Ward	Penton, ,, ...	,,	30s.
XIX	Nichs. Downe ...	,, ,, ...	,,	28s.
XX	Richd. Scott ...	Wapping	,,	30s.
XXI	Richd. Haddock ...	Topsham, Devon	,,	26s.
XXII	Ths. Brownscombe	Bankfull, Devon	,,	30s.
XXIII	Ths. Browne ...	Weymouth, Dorset	,,	30s.
XXIV	Ed. Watson	Southampton, Hts.	,,	28s.
XXV	Anty. Walker* ...	—	,,	34s.

———

[1] Fourth Circumnavigation of the Globe : by Oliver Noort.—Voyage of Sebalt de Wert (*Purchas*, vol. i, lib. ii, pp. 71-79 ; and pp. 125-132).—Adams' Narrative.

[2] Also: "There is geuen him, for the p'vision of his chest, wth sufficient salues and instruments fitt for his vocation to srue. for a surgeon, the sum of viii*li*......Ed. Wood, " surgeon, cittizen of London, dwelling wthin Aldgate", enters into this agreement on behalf of his " s'ruant".

William Cobreath

II. By me john Chartwright.

VI.

XI. John Clarkmore

XIII. Edward

XIV. By me Gerrard Gowen

IX.

X.

XXI.

XVI. Henry Grono

XVII.

XVIII.

XIX.

XX.

XXIV.

XXIII.

XXII.

XXXII.

XXXIIII.

XXVIII.

xxvi	John Ware*... ...	—	Mariner	28s.
xxvii	Thos. White* ...	—	,,	28s.
xxviii	Saml. Queensbery*	—	,,	30s.
xxix	John Queensbery*	—	,,	30s.
xxx	Wm. Chapell* ...	—	,,	30s.
xxxi	Robt. White* ...	—	,,	30s.
xxxii	Thos. Wilson* ...	—	,,	30s.
xxxiii	Thos. Stud	Penton, Devon ...	,,	28s.

NOTE D. PRICES.

MEMORANDA relative to the PRICES of APPAREL, MANUFACTURES, PROVISIONS, and SUNDRIES, at the Commencement of the Seventeenth Century.

I. PARTICULARS of the APPAREL *supplied to the expedition proceeding to the North West, under Captain Waymouth,* Anno 1602.

	s.	d.	li.	s.	d.
For a *pair of breeches* there goeth a hide, wch doth cost	9	0			
11 lambskins and ½ to fur them, at 6d the skin is	5	9			
For making of the same is	2	6			
For laying the fur of the same is . .	1	3			
Som y^t a paire of breeches doth cost is .			0	18	6
For a *cassocke* there goeth a hide, wch doth cost	9	0			
11 lamb skins and ½ to fur the same, at 6d the piece	5	9			
For laying in the fur of the skins is . .	1	3			
For making the same is . . · .	3	0			
Som that a cassocke doth cost amots vnto .			0	19	0
For a *hood* the lether cost, besyde the peece left is	0	10			
3 lamb skins to fur the same, at 6d is . .	1	6			
For making and furring of it . . .	0	11			
So each cap doth cost the som of .			0	3	3

* The engagements on behalf of these parties were made by Capt. Waymouth.

	s.	d.	li.	s.	d.
For a *gowne* there goeth a hide and a half, wch cost	13	6			
For the lining, 6 yards of frize at 13d the yard is	6	9			
For making the same is	2	6			
Som that a gowne doth cost amõts vnto .			1	2	9
For a paire of *mytins,* the same is made wth peec. cloth	0	0			
To fur the same, 2 skins is	1	0			
For making the same is	0	6			
Som y^t a paire of mytins doth cost .			0	1	6
For every paire of *socks* there goeth ⅓ of a yard, wch at 12d the yard is . . .	0	4			
For making of each paire is . . .	0	1			
Som y^t a paire of socks doth cost .			0	0	5
To a *shirt* there goeth 2 ells ¾ and ½ white Hamburgh (lynen), at 10d the ell is .	2	5			
For the making is	0	2			
Som y^t a shirt doth cost is .			0	2	7
For every *waistcoat* there goeth 2 yardes ¼ and ½ a q^r of (Welch) cotton or plane, wch at 18d the yarde is	3	2			
For the making is	0	4			
Som y^t a waist coat doth cost is .			0	3	6

II. (A.D. 1606.) A Computacõn of the Chardge for setting forth to Sea upon a Third Voyage to Bantam and the Moluccos upon a new accompte, and for discou^{ry} of furder trade and other places, wth the Dragon, Hector, and a Pynnace, as ffolloweth, viz.—

THE DRAGON. (600 Tons.)

Dragon. The price of the Dragon by appraysem^t

amounted to £2400	16	00
Her repaire and chardges in setting forth will coste 4770	00	00
Her victualls 2195	00	00
Imprest to men 0784	00	00
10849	16	00

THE HECTOR. (500 Tons.)

Hector. her price by appraysem^t . . . 1416	00	00
her repaire and chardges of setting forth 3000	00	00
her victualls 1726	00	00
Imprest to men 322	00	00
6464	00	00

THE PYNNACE.

Pynnace. A pynnace of 120 tunns, and all her chardges of setting forth, wth victuals and ymprest . . . 2600	00	00
Soma totalis . 19913	16	00

The MARCHANDIZE the be bought and sent in theis ships :

Leade.	Leade for 150 ffother at 10li. p ffother £1500	00	00
Iron.	Iron for 140 tonns, Eng. and Span. at 12li. p tunn 1800	00	00
Tynn.	Tynn in small bars,5 tunns at 72li. p tun. 0360	00	00

CLOTHES.

Clothes.	30 Venice redds at 12li. . . 360	00	00
	20 Stametts at . . 20li. . . 400	00	00
	10 popingey greenes at 12li. . . 128	00	00
	5 yellowes at . . 11li. . . 055	00	00
	5 flame coullo^{rs} äls. gallants at 15li. 075	00	00

Clothes.	2	blacks at	.	.	20*li*.	.	£040	00	00
	5	violetth grayne at	.		18*li*.	.	. 090	00	00
	5	murreys grayne at			18*li*.	.	. 090	00	00
	5	blewes at	.	.	15*li*.	.	. 075	00	00
	5	plunketts at	.	.	12*li*.	.	. 060	00	00
	5	French greenes at			12*li*.	.	. 060	00	00
	5	grass greenes at	.		12*li*.	.	. 060	00	00
	5	azars at	.	.	12*li*.	.	. 060	00	00

107 clothes . . 1545 00 00

DEVONSHIRE KERSIES.

Devonshire	20	Stametts at 4*li*.	.	.	.	80	00	00
kersies.	10	violleth graine at 4*li*.	.	.		40	00	00

	30 Venice redds		
	10 popingey greenes	att 50*s*.	. 150 00 00
	10 flame coullo^{rs}		
	10 grasse greenes		
	10 gallants		
	10 yallows	att 50*s*.	. 75 00 00
	4 blacks		
	6 blewes		

120 kersies . . 0345 00 00

KEIGHLEY'S NARROW LISTES OF THE BEST SORTES.

		li. *s*. *d*.
15 Venice redds		
10 popingey greenes		
15 flame colors	70 peecs at 53¼ ᵱ peece	0183 06 08
10 grasse greenes		
10 yellowes		
10 watchetts		

North: dozons.	Northern doozens redds att 4*li*. 5*s*. ᵱ peece . . .	0042 10 00
Hams: Kersies.	{ 10 blewes 10 watchetts } 20 peeces at 3*li*. 12*s*. .	0074 00 00

Sayes.	20 peecs sayes of dyvers colors at 52s. . . .	£0052 00 00
Iron work.	Head pecs, white, grauen and gilded wth som few shirts of male	0100 16 08

Somma totalis of all the m^rchndize   6001 16 08

Stocke remayning in the East Indies . .	3000 00 00
The Dragon, setting forth	10849 16 00
The Hector, setting forth	6464 00 00
The Pinnace, setting forth	2600 00 00
Soma totalis .	22913 16 00
Marchandize outwardes will coste . . .	6001 16 08
The some of the whole chardge outwards .	28915 12 08

Dragons ladinge. For the Dragon, ouer and aboue 6500 sackes of pepp, and 460 bahars of cloues, wch is esteemed the goods in that countrie will puide 4000 sacks of pepp at 6r. p sack . . . . . . 24000r.

Hectore. For the Hectore, to be laden at the Moluccos wth pepp, nutts, and mace, will coste 40000r.

Pynnace. The ladinge of the Pinnace att the Moluccos with pepp, nutts, cloues, and mace . . . . 12000r.

The ladinge of theis 3 shipps, ouer and aboue the goods in the countrie, will cost in royalls of 8, rated at $4\frac{1}{2}$ss. p royall . 76000r.

	li.	*s.*	*d.*
W^{ch} is, starlinge . . .	17100	00	00
The totall some of the chardge outwards, and of the ladinge homewards	28915	12	08

	li.	*s.*	*d.*
Somma totalis outwards & homewards	46015	12	08

Beside men's wages att the retourne of theis shipps . . 10000 00 00

The total reduced to £40000 by abatem't of some particulers.   *The w*^{ch} *computac'on being reuiewed, is reduced from* 46000*li.* 12*s.* 8*d. to aboute*   40000 00 00

" Miscellaneous Court Book".

III. SUNDRIES.

I. *Shipping materials.* In 1615 and 1616, *anchors* of from 100 to 1000 weight, cost £1 10s. per cwt.; those from 1000 to 2000 weight, £1 13s. per cwt.; those of 2000 weight and upwards, £1 15s. per cwt. " *Murthering-pieces*, standing a tryall", 5d. per lb. In 1621, *tar* was £110 per last.[1] *Cables* and *cordage*, in 1622, 28s. 6d., and 28s. per cwt.;[2] 1623, 24s.; 1624, 24s. 6d.[3]; 1625, 29s.; 1626, 26s. 6d., and 27s. 6d.; 1627, 25s. 6d.; 1630, 30s.; 1631, 34s.; 1635, 37s. 6d.; 1637, 25s. 6d., and 28s.

II. *Apparel.* In 1621, a *canvas shirt* cost 3s. 4d.; a *woollen shirt*, 15s.; and *irish hoese*, 2s. 3d. per paire.

III. *Provisions.* In 1581, wheat was £1 per quarter (p. 33, *Narratives*). In 1615, *strong beer* was worth £3 3s. the tun; *great oatmeal*, 30s. per quarter; *good old pease*, 24s. per qr.; *new pease*, 28s. per qr.; and " *Newland fish* ", 9s. per 100.

---

[1] Contract with George Hall, Deptford Stroud.—*Court Miscellaneous Book. E. I. Mss.*

[2] The higher price was paid for " *rus-band* ", the lower for " *rhyn-band* ", or " *rus-band and rhyn-band, mixed* ".

[3] During a portion of this year, the retail prices of some provisions were as follow : *roasting beef*, 3 stone, 2 lbs. for 5s. 4d. ; *half a mutton*, from 6s. to 7s.; *half a lamb*, 3s.; *chickens*, three for 2s.; *pullets*, three for 3s.; a pottle of *claret*, and three pints of *sack*, 2s. 10d.; a pottle of *white*, 1s. 4d.—From " The Accompte of Wm. Pingley and Giles Sheppard, Stewards for the *Exchange* at Erith, for p'vision bought for her there". 3rd to 17th July 1624. *E. I. Mss.*

IV. A TABLE OF THE PRICES OF PROVISIONS.

Year.	Beef, p. cwt.	Pork, p. cwt.	Biscuit, p. cwt.	Bolted meal, p. cwt.	Ship beer p. tun.
1621 ...	18s. ...	18s. ...	... 13s. 6d. ...	13s.	40s.
1623 ...	17s. & 18s.[1] ...	22s. & 23s. 4d.	14s. 6d. & 15s. 6d.	14s.	—
1624 ...	20s. 6d. ...	20s. 6d. ...	... 15s. ...	13s. 6d.	—
1625	22s. 6d. & 25s. 6d.	22s. ...	... 15s. ...	14s.	—
1626 ...	21s. & 22s. ...	21s. & 22s. ...	... 13s. ...	13s.	—
1627 ...	— ...	— ...	... 12s. 3d. ...	11s.	—
1628 ...	20s. ...	20s. ...	... 12s. ...	11s.	—
1629 ...	20s. ...	22s. ...	... — ...	—	—
1630 ...	20s. ...	22s. ...	... — ...	—	—
1631 ...	19s. ...	23s. 4d. ...	... — ...	—	—
1633 ...	20s. ...	24s. ...	... — ...	—	—
1634 ...	24s. ...	25s. ...	... — ...	—	—
1636 ...	19s. ...	19s. ...	... — ...	—	—
1637 ...	20s. 6d. ...	28s. ...	... — ...	—	—
1638 ...	27s. & 24s. ...	29s. & 32s. ...	... — ...	—	42s.

NOTE E. BUTTON'S EXPEDITION.

SOME ANSWERS TO DEMANDS MADE IN WRITING, BY SIR THOMAS BUTTON, WHILE AT ANCHOR IN NELSON'S RIVER.

Laus Deo, 1612. *December the* 22.

The course and distances from place to place, from Cape Cleare to this river in New Wales :

VARIATN.		LEAGUES
24.	*Imprimis,* from Cape *Cleare* to Cape *Desolation,* strait course by common compasse, North W. by W. ½. The latitude of 59d. 40m.	428
26½d.	From *Desolation* to the Ile of *Resolution,* course is N.W. by W. ; the latitude, 61d. ; the distance	170

[1] Where double prices are noted, two contracts were made in the course of the year : in the spring and fall. Except when otherwise stated, the prices throughout this notice have been obtained from " *A Book of Contracts* and *Bargains* for *P'visions*", etc.— *E. I. Mss.*

VARIATN.		LEAGUES.
	From *Resolution* to *Sir Dudley Diggs*	
30d.	*his ile,* lat. 62d. 40m. N.W., the distance	142
	From *Sir Dudley Diggs his ile,* to the	
22d.	*Cheeks,*[1] the course is W. ½ northerly ; the	
	distance	193
	From the *Cheeks* to *New Wales,* lat. 57,	
22d.	the course is S. by W. ; the distance .	90

The courses are all·by the common compas. Your worships and ever, or mine owne never, till death,

WILLIAM HAWKERIDGE.

My answere to the first demand, under your favour, I thinke it not amisse to search the river, if God give strength to our men, before our departure from it, to have the knowledge how farre it doth extend ; and that we may meet with some inhabitants, which may further our expectations ; but I cannot thinke of any profit to be made by it.

My answere to the 2 demand, is, to search to the northward about this westerne land, untill, if it be possible that we may finde the flood comming from the westward, and to bend our courses against the flood, following the ebbe, searching that way for the passage.[2] For this flood which we have from the eastward, I cannot be perswaded but that they are the veynes of some headland to the northwards of the *Cheeks,* and by the inlets of rivers which let the floods tides into them, which headlands being founde all, I do assure myselfe that the tyde wilbe found to come from the westward.

Herein I have showed my opinion so farre my judgement will afford, untill further reasons induceth me to the contrary. *Per me,* JOSIAS HUBART.

---

[1] ? "Hopes Check't".

[2] "Well guest, Hubbart". (Marg. n. by Fox.) "The answer given by one James Hubert, the pilot of the Resolution : How the discovery might be best prosecuted when they should be able to go to sea ? shows the sound notions entertained by this man respecting the true mode of searching for the passage."—*Arctic Voyages,* p. 199.

VARIATN.		LEAGUES.

From the *Durses* in *Ireland,* being in 52

11d. lat., to *Cape Farewell* in *Groenland,* lat. 58.56, the course is W.N.Wterly, and the distance is 460

The southernmost part of the Iland of Resolution is in lat. 60d. 34m.

29d., a From *Cape Farewell* to the Iland of *Re-*
great *solution,* the course is W. and by N., and
mistake.[1] the distance is 208

3 points. *Sir Dudley Diggs his Iland* is in lat. 62d. 40m., and is in distance from the Ile of *Resolution,* upon a W. and by N. ⅓ northerly course 180

3d. The *Cheekes* lie in 61d. 17m. lat. from *Sir Dudley Diggs his Iland;* thereto the course is W. and by S., and the distance is 190

2d. differ- *Our wintering being in lat. of 56d. 8m.*
ent. Great From the *Cheekes* to our wintering place,
in the va- the course is S. and by W. ½ westerly, and
riations. the distance is 87

The 27 of November.

I made an observation of the moone and the planet Mars, and for that I stand in doubt, for the houre to be exactly found out by any diall-block, or other instrument, to hang a planet to find where the foremost guard was right under the Pole starre, at which instant I found ♂ and ☽ to be one degree and 41 minutes asunder; by which working, I suppose or deeme it to bee as followeth: this our wintring place, III degrees, and 15 of longitude [?] from our meridian of the citie of *London.*

Per me, Josias Hubart.

[1] These marginal notes by *Fox* are not altogether intelligible; which may, in some degree, be attributed to errors of the press.

In the name of God. Amen.

Of the courses from the *Mission Head* in *Ireland*, being bound towards the Northwest passage, Captain *Thomas Button*, gentleman, being our generall, in the good ship called the *Resolution : John Ingram* captaine and master of the pinace called the *Discovrie.* 1612.

VARIATN.		LEAGUES.
	Imprimis, from the *Mission Head* in Ireland, to *Cape Discord* in Groenland, latitude 6d. [? 60°] 30min., the course is N.W. by N. northerly, and the distance is .	360
	From the *Mission Head* to *Cape Discord* in Groynland, the course is N.W. 67 W. northerly, by the compasse, the lat. 59d. 20m., and the distance is . . .	380
	From the *Mission Head* to *Cape Desolation,* the course lyeth W.N.W., and the distance	490
	From the foreside of *Cape Discord* to *Cape Farwel,* the course lyeth S.W. southerly by compasse. Distance . . .	58
	From *Cape Farwell* to the westerne part of this headland, by *Cape Desolation,* the course is W.N.W. halfe northerly, 100 leagues distant, and from this headland to *Desolation,* is 10 leagues distant : in all, from *Farewell* to *Desolation* the distance is	100
23d. as he judged.	N.N.E. by compasse, betweene *Cape Farewell* and the foresaid headland, there set a very great current to the westward	
29.	From *Cape Desolation* to the *Ile of Resolution,* the course lyeth W.N.W. westerly, altitude 62d. 30m., and the distance .	120

VAR.	From *Resolution* to *Salisbury Ile*, W. by N., altitude 63d. 15m., and from the iland to *Wostenholme's Cape*, the course lyeth W.S.W. southerly	LEAG. 12
	And from this cape to *Diggs his Ilands*	3
34.	From *Resolution* to *Wostenholme's Cape*, the course lyeth W. by N. westerly, and the distance is	153
	From *Resolution* to *Diggs his Ilands*, the course is W. by N. northerly, and the distance (altitude 63d.)	156
	From *Sir Dudley Diggs his Ilands* to *Nottingham's Iland*, N. by compasse, and the distance is	7 or 8
	From *Sir Dudley Diggs* to *Swann's Iland*, W. by S.	40
	From *Diggs his Iland* to *Hopes Checkt*, the course is W.S.W. a little westerly, and the distance is	200

The altitude is 60d. 40m.

	From *Hopes Checkt* to the *Broken Land*, where our admirall received a great storme, the course lyeth S.W. 49 leagues, altitude, 59	40
	From this *Broken Land* to the head *Northerland*, the course lyeth W., and the distance is	8

The Headland is the entring into this Bay called NEW WALES.

	From *this Head Land* unto *the Roade* of the harbour, the course lyeth S. 42 leagues, and from *Hopes Checkt* to *this Roade*, the course lyeth N.E. and by N. . . .	86

Hitherto, the Lord, of his mercy, hath blessed, preserved, and kept us from all dangers whatsoever, which wee beseech him to blesse us of his mercy, and send us well forth againe. *Amen.* *Per me,* EDWARD GLANVILE.[1]

[1] North-west Foxe, or, Foxe from the North-west Passage. Pp. 119-123.

NOTE F. FIRST E. I. SUBSCRIPTION LIST.

The subscription-list for the first India voyage is dated the 22nd of September 1599. The amount subscribed was £30,133 : 6 : 8, divided into one hundred and one shares. The largest amount subscribed was £3,000 : by Richard Cockain and Co. The smallest was £100. Amongst the subscribers were : Sir Stephen Soame, lord-mayor of London, with eight aldermen, and thirty-six livery-men of the principal city companies. The committees, or managers, of the first voyage, were :

Mr. Aldn. Godderd,

Mr. Aldn. Moore,	Mr. Tho. Symondes,
Mr. Rich. Staper,	Mr. Nich. Style,
Mr. Tho. Cordell,	Mr. Nich. Lyng,
Mr. Wm. Garway,	Mr. Rich. Wyche,
Mr. Tho. Middleton,	Mr. Roger Howe,
Mr. Tho. Campbell,	Mr. Wm. Cockin,
Mr. Rich. Wiseman,	Mr. Nich. Leet.

" Court Book "

NOTE G. VARIATION OF THE COMPASS.

1. *Of* the *manner to obserue the variation of the compasse,* or of *the wires* of the same, by the sonnes rising or setting.[1]

There are two sorts of compasses ordayned for obseruing the variation of the wires : one hath a moueable fly, the other hath none. The flouer de luce, or north part of the fly, standeth directly with the wires in both. And the vtmost circle of both is divided into poynts and degrees, there being 11 degrees and a quarter betwixt poynt and poynt. This being remembered of your compasses, then for your obseruation you are to do as followeth :

[1] *Mathematical papers* of *Thomas Harriott.* Mss. Brit. Mus., Pluto C, xxiv F., vol. viii, 6789.

In the morninge, or the eueninge, when you may see the
sonne rise or set (your compasse standing fit), you are to
marke how many degrees the sonne riseth frō the east poynt
of the fly, or setteth from the west, and note whether to the
southward or northward. This obseruation, and as many as
you can make, enter into your booke; noting of the day and
place where you make it.

Then for the finding of the variation, I have calculated a
special table for the purpose, whose title is, " A table of the
Sonnes rising frō the true East and West", which you are to
use in this manner : first, consider what declination the sonne
hath that present day, which you may know by your *regiment;*[1]
also, what is the eleuation of the pole at that place, which
you are to know vpon reckoning frō your last obseruation.

Then in the sayd table of the sonnes rising and setting,
loke in the head of the table the degrees of the sonnes declination ; and on the left side loke the degree of eleuation, and
right agaynst the same vnder the declination you before
noted; (in the comō angle) you shall find how much the
sonne riseth or setteth frō the true east and west, in degrees
and minutes, which is always to the northwards if the sonne
hath north declination, or southward if the declination be
south. And this number of degrees and minuts, so found
for breuity and distinction sake, hereafter to be vsed, is called
the sonnes *amplitude.*

Now to conclude how much your compasse doth vary, the

[1] In 1611, a small quarto volume was published, with the following
title : " A REGIMENT FOR THE SEA. Containing very necessarie matters
for all sorts of men and trauillers, whervnto is added an *Hydrographicall
discovrse touching the fiue seuerall passages into Cathay.* Written by
WILLIAM BORNE, corrected and amended by THOMAS HOOD, D. in Phisicke,
who hath added *a new Regiment, and a table of declination,* with the Ma-
ryner's guide; and a perfect sea card thervnto belonging". This volume
is illustrated with numerous cuts, amongst which is a delineation of " the
Bella Stella, or Crosse Staffe, to take the height of the sunne or starre";
and of a " Sea Astorolob, or ring". *Master Harriott's "Regiment"* has
not been traced.

breefest and most intelligible way is this: note vpon the same
fly you made your obseruation by, or vpon any other in any
boke that hath degrees in the vtmost circle, the degree that
the sonne rose, or set vpon : then frõ that marke reckon, or
nomber, the degrees of the sonnes amplitude northward, if
the same hath south declination; or reckon southward, if the
sonne hath north declination; and where the degrees end,
there is the true east, or west; which being had, it is then
manifest how much your compasse doth vary, and which way.

One example will make this playne. Suppose you be to
the southwestward of the Lyzard, and in the hight of 48 degrees, the 10 of February next, this yeare 1595 ; and that
you find the sonne to rise 7 degrees to the southward of the
east by such a compasse as hath the wires due north.

Then loke in the sonnes regiment, and you shall find the
declination of the sonne for that 10th day at noone, 1595, to
be 10° 58′ southerly. You may see that the day before it
was more by 21′, and therefore that morning it ought to be
more by almost a quarter of 21′, which is 5′; and therefore
the declination of the sonne at that present time, is 11° 3′ :
but a few minutes in this reckoning need not be regarded ;
but you may take the declination as you find it at noone
that day, which you may account 11 degrees, because it
cometh nerest therevnto.

Then in the table of the sonnes rising and setting, right
agaynst the hight of 48 degrees, and vnder the declination of
11 deg., you shall find 16 degrees and 33 minuts, which is
the amplitude of the sonnes rising frõ the true east, and to
be southwards of the east so much, because the sonne hath
south declination.

Now marke vpon the compasse vpon what degree the sonne
rose ; then reckon frõ it northward, according to your rule,
because the sonne hath south declination, the nomber of 16
degrees and 33 minuts, or 16 degrees and a half; and you
shall find them to end 9 degrees and a half to the northwardes

of the east of the compasse. And so much doth the true east
vary, or differre, frō that of your compasse, and so, per consequence, all the poynts else from the truth. That is to say,
the east of your compasse doth vary 9 degrees and a half to
the southwards frō the truth ; and therefore the north of your
compasse so much to the eastward, the south poynt to the
westward, and your west poynt to the northward. But of
what poynt soever you rectifie in your booke the variation,
you must specially note the variation of the north poynt, because it is the cheefest poynt in name, and all the rest wilbe
ordered by it.

And because the nauigation and steeradge is made com̃only
by the com̃on compasse, whose wires stand half a poynt to
the eastward of the north of the fly, it is necessary that you
also know the variation of this compasse, otherwise, sayling
by such a compasse, you can make no true reckoning of your
course, nor appoynt what steeradge ought to be made.

I will therefore giue this general rule : hauing noticed the
variation of the wires, or north poynt of one of the former
compasses, you shall find the variation of the north poynt of
the com̃on compasse thus : ffirst, in that compasse that hath
the moueable fly, moue it in such sort, that his north poynt
stand to the westward of the wires half a poynt ; then must
the wires be to the eastwards so much, and so that fly repre-
senteth the com̃on compasse.

After, reckon the degrees of your former variation from the
wires, contrary to the denomination, that is to say, if the
variation were east, reckon it westward ; or if west, reckon
eastward ; and where the degrees end, there is the true north
of the world, which being marked, you may then see both
how much, and which way, the north of the inner fly, or
com̃on compasse doth vary.

You may also do the same by that compasse which hath
no moueable fly, or by anny other drawne in any boke, so it
be divided into degrees, and that you make, or prick, or note,

half a poynt to the westwards of the north, to represent the north of your comon compasse.

But whether your compasse haue degrees, or no degrees, you may help your self by addition and subtraction, remembring that 11 degrees and a quarter make a poynt, and 5 degrees and a half, and half a quarter, do make half a poynt.

The example of this need be but short. The wires in the former obseruation varied to the eastward 9 degrees and a half: halfe a poynt to the westward is the north of the comon compasse; therefore abate it out of $9\frac{1}{2}$, there will remaine 4 degrees norwest. And so much doth your comon compasse vary in that place, being less than halfe a poynt, and to the eastward, as before, because the half poynt was lesse then the variation of the wires.

But if half a poynt had been greater, then it had varied the contrary way by the difference.

If the former rules be well vnderstode, there cannot happen any case concerning this variation; but you may very well know when to adde, or subtracte, and what is done by them, if you will vse that meane. You have your choyse; so that I need not be more tedious.

This manner of observing the variation, of all others is generall, most ready, easy, and certayne : the way that they vse by obseruation of the north starre vpon a northeast [......], is not true but only in the latitude of 40 and 50 degrees, because then only he is in the meridian or [......], which is to all seamen a paradox; and to obserue the starre by the [......], when he is hije, it is very vncertayne; but when he is low, it is a good meanes to attayne to the variation nere [......]; nether do I wish it then to be refused, being vnder the hight of 20 degrees, and at a N.E. and S.W. g[......]. So likewise it is to be preferred before any single obseruation that is made also of the sonne or starre when they are many degrees hye, or any doble of the forenoone and afternoone; which are only good at land when the horizon can not be seen [......], have written, especially *Mr. Borrowes* in his boke of the variation añexed to *Norman's new Attractiue.*[1]

Besides the benefit that it hath in shewing you your true course, it will hereafter be a meanes to obserue the longitude sufficiently exacte, and therefore I wish it the more to be regarded.

By the table, also, of the sonnes amplitude, with the rules before, may be found the variation of the compasse by the moone, or any starre, whose declination may be found in the table.

II. MASTER RUDSTON'S LETTER.

To his very good frend, *Mr. Haryott*, in Black Fryars, be these đđ.

SIR,

As, by experience, I hau found yor singular humanitie by o[r] late conferences, to make good the great fame of yor great learninge; so hath it emboldened me, by this lre., to request that you would send me word, by this bearer, what the variacõn of the needle is about Mosco; for at this present I haue such an ympediment fallen into my toes, that I cannot walke abroad, otherwise I had been the presenter of this my request vnto you myselfe; wch if it might have been, I should then haue moved some other questions, viz., whether it is probable that the variacõn can be, in any place of the world, 180 degrees; or the north point of the needle stand directly towards the south? Allso, whether a shippe sayling right east, or west, by the compasse, keepes vpon a parallel, as the comon received opinion amongst maryners is; wch I thinke not, because the east and west of the compasse is a [......] tangent to the parallel; but how little soever it so continues in sail-

---

[1] " *The inclination*, or *dipping* of the *needle*......was *first discovered by Robert Norman*, an Englishman, A.D. 1576".—*Falconer's Mar. Dict.*, 1815.

ing, it is a porcŏn, or arch, of the great circle of the east and west, and therefore (I conceive) cannot but decline from the parallel.

But, ceasing to trouble you with these manner of questions, I crave pardon for this boldness, resting, at yor comand,

Jo. RUDSTON.

9 Janny 1615.

III.

EXAMPLES *of the* VARIATION *of the* COMPASS, *observed during* CAPTAIN PARRY'S EXPEDITION *of* 1819, *etc.*

1819.		LAT. ° ′		LONG. ° ′		VAR. ° ′ ″
June 19	...	59 : 49 N. ...		48 : 09 W.		48 : 38 : 21 w.
26	...	63 : 58	...	61 : 50	...	61 : 11 : 31
July 15	...	70 : 29	...	59 : 12	...	74 : 39 : 00
17	...	72 : 00	...	59 : 56	...	80 : 55 : 27
23	...	73 : 03	...	60 : 12½	...	82 : 37 : 30
24	...	73 : 00	...	60 : 09	...	81 : 34 : 00
31	...	73 : 31	...	77 : 22½	...	108 : 46 : 35
Augst. 3	...	74 : 25	...	80 : 08	...	106 : 58 : 05
7	...	72 : 45	...	89 : 41	...	118 : 16 : 27
13	...	73 : 11	...	89 : 22½	...	114 : 16 : 43
15	...	73 : 33	...	88 : 18	...	115 : 37 : 12
22	...	74 : 40	...	91 : 47	...	128 : 58 : 07
28	...	75 : 09	...	103 : 44½	...	165 : 50 : 09 E.
Septr. 1	...	75 : 03	...	105 : 54½	...	158 : 04 : 13
2	...	74 : 58	...	107 : 03	...	151 : 30 : 03
6	...	74 : 47	...	110 . 34	...	126 : 17 : 18
15	...	74 : 28	...	111 : 42	...	117 : 52 : 22

From October 25, 1819, to July 27, 1820, at *Winter Harbour, in Melville Island,* lat. 74° 47′ 13″ N., long. 110° 49′ 00″ W., nearly three hundred observations were made of "the difference between the true and magnetic bearing of a meridian mark. The result was a mean of 127° 47′ 50″ east."[1]

---

[1] *Appendix to the Voyage of the Hecla and Griper,* pp. cxi-cxiii, and cxv.

IV. MAGNETIC DECLINATION AND DIP AT LONDON.

The following TABLE, which I am permitted, by the author, to insert,[1] was framed for the earlier periods, from the *Encyclopædia Britannica :* for the recent periods, from the *Greenwich Observations.*

DECLINATION.

		o	′	″		
1580	...	11 :	5 :	0	...	E.
1622	...	6 :	0 :	0	...	„
1657	...	—	—	—	...	Due N.
1692	...	6 :	0 :	0	...	W.
1722	...	14 :	2 :	0	...	„
1747	...	17 :	40 :	0	...	„
1780	...	22 :	41 :	0	...	„
1811	...	24 :	14 :	2	...	„
1832	...	24 :	17 :	0	...	„ (August)
1840	...	23 :	3 :	10	...	„ (December)
1841	...	23 :	16 :	8	...	„ (Mean of year)
1842	...	23 :	14 :	29	...	„ (Mean of year)
		24 :	9 :	1	...	„ (Max., July 2)
		22 :	31 :	36	...	„ (Min., July 3)
1843	...	23 :	11 :	43	...	„ (Mean of year)
		23 :	29 :	0	...	„ (Max., Jan. 7)
		22 :	49 :	6	...	„ (Min., April 20)
1844	...	23 :	15 :	19	...	„ (Mean of year)
		23 :	41 :	53	...	„ (Max., April 17)
		22 :	44 :	58	...	„ (Min., Sept. 26)

MEAN MAGNETIC DIP.

1843	...	69 : 0 : 30.01
1844	...	69 : 0 : 18.1.

A few notes are added respecting the assumed periods of the discovery of the magnetic declination.

Falconer, in his "Marine Dictionary", notices the existence, in the University of Leyden, of a manuscript tract in Latin, written "by one *Peter Adsiger*", in which the fact is

---

[1] See the *Engineers' and Contractors' Pocket-Book for* 1847-8, edited and published by John Weale, 59 High Holborn.

particularly mentioned; and he refers to Cavallo's supplement to his treatise on magnetism, where the chief part of the tract is printed, with a translation. The manuscript is dated the 8th of August, 1269. Ferdinand, the son of *Columbus*, claims the discovery for his father, in 1492. By some, it is attributed to *Sebastian Cabota*, in 1500. Each of these parties may be entitled to the claim of originality. The discovery was consistent with the pursuits of the man of science; and the profession of the navigators was calculated to lead to similar observations, independently of each other, without either being necessarily acquainted with the enquiries of the philosopher.

The discovery of the variation of the magnetic needle from a particular meridian from time to time, or the "*variation of the variation*", as the phenomenon was originally designated, is stated by Sir Hans Sloane, in the Philosophical Transactions, to have been made, in 1635, by *Gellibrand*, Gresham Professor of Astronomy. Ward, the author of the "Lives of the Professors of Gresham College" (London, 1740, p. 80), assigns the discovery, in 1625, to *Gunter*, also Professor of Astronomy in the same institution, the inventor of the scale still bearing his name, and co-operator with Napier of Merchistoun in his labours connected with logarithms. The fact appears, however, to have been observed before the earliest of of these dates; but Ward may have been misinformed as to the exact year in which Gunter made the discovery.

It has already been stated, that an Englishman, named *Norman*, discovered the inclination, or dip, of the needle, in 1576.

NOTE H.   DRAFT OF NORTH-POLAR DISCOVERIES,
1496 TO 1682.

The scale of the chart being restricted by the size of the volume, the intention, originally entertained, of inserting all the discoveries made from 1496 to 1632, could not be carried into effect. But, in the narratives, pains have been taken to fix the localities of the discoveries, by giving the longitude and latitude whenever stated. Where the latitude and longitude could not be ascertained, the position of the discovery may generally be determined by its noted proximity to some known point, or points.

The " Isles of God's Mercy" occupy, in this draft, a different position from that assigned to them in the Admiralty and other charts, which is near lat. 64°. The change has been made on the authority of the discoverer, *Henry Hudson* (see *Narratives*, p. 77); which has been followed by M. Briggs in the map furnished by him to Purchas, and by Luke Fox in the chart prefixed to his voyage. (See also *Narratives*, p. 185.)

The arms in the left corner of the draft, are those originally granted to the " Worshipfull Fellowship of the Merchants of London trading into the East Indies".

In conclusion, it may be noted that *Master Captain Best*, in the original edition of his account of Frobisher's voyages, gives a rude sketch of " Meta Incognita", conformably with his idea of its being an archipelago of islands. Also: in a work which evinces the extent of Frobisher's fame, in his own day, entitled "*De Martini Forbisseri Angli Navigatione in Regiones Occidentis et Septentrionis, Narratio Historica, ex Gallico Sermone in Latinum translata per D. Joan. Tho. Freigeium,* CIƆ, IƆ, XXC, *Noribergæ*", and which is a summary of the second voyage, there is a spirited cut thus described; " Pictvra vel Delineatio Hominum nvper ex Anglia advectorum, una cum eorum armis, tentoriis et naviculis".

FINIS.

POST-SCRIPTUM.

W<small>HILST</small> the last sheet was at press, I availed myself of an opportunity, that unexpectedly presented itself, to refer to a second copy of the *North-west Foxe,* containing a list of *errata.* In one of the answers given by Master Hubbart to the demands of Sir Thomas Button, in the *text* of Fox's work, the following passage occurs : " <small>TO HANG A PLANET</small>"; and it is so reprinted in the Appendix to the Narratives (lines seven and eight from the bottom of p. 247). The reading of the *errata* is : " I <small>HUNG A PLUMMET ON</small>". Combined with Baffin's method of ascertaining the longitude, the passage is thus rendered intelligible. **T. R.**

RICHARDS, PRINTER, 100, ST. MARTIN'S LANE.

For EU product safety concerns, contact us at Calle de José Abascal, 56–1°,
28003 Madrid, Spain or eugpsr@cambridge.org.